THE DIVIDEND CONNECTION

HOW DIVIDENDS CREATE VALUE ·IN THE· $TOCK MARKET

GERALDINE WEISS & GREGORY WEISS

$

Dearborn
Financial Publishing, Inc.

While a great deal of care has been taken to provide accurate and current information, the ideas, suggestions, general principles and conclusions presented in this text are subject to local, state and federal laws and regulations, court cases and any revisions of same. The reader is thus urged to consult legal counsel regarding any points of law—this publication should not be used as a substitute for competent legal advice.

Senior Associate Editor: Karen A. Christensen
Managing Editor: Jack Kiburz
Editorial Assistant: Stephanie C. Schmidt
Cover Design: The Complete Art Works
Interior Design: Elizandro Carrington
Graphic Artist: Katherine Weiss Taylor

Library of Congress Cataloging-in-Publication Data

Weiss, Geraldine, 1926-
    The dividend connection: how dividends create value in the stock market / Geraldine Weiss and Gregory Weiss.
        p.   cm.
    Includes index.
    ISBN 0-7931-1022-X
        1. Investment analysis.   2. Corporations—Valuation.   3. Stocks-
    -Prices.   4. Dividends.   I. Weiss, Gregory L.   II. Title.
    HG4529.W455   1995
    332.63'22—dc20   95-2645
                                                              CIP

DEDICATION

This book is dedicated to the memory of my father, Alvin, and my mother, Sylvia, who taught me the importance of values in determining choices in life.

And to my sister, Pally, whose love and friendship is neither undervalued nor overvalued but greatly valued.

Geraldine Weiss

To Jodie, Nathaniel and Jacob . . . my blue chip family, with whom I am blessed to share life's greatest total return.

Gregory Linus Weiss

ACKNOWLEDGMENTS

This book would not be complete without acknowledging the immeasurable contribution of Richard A. Weiss (1924–1994)—husband, father and friend. His sharp intellect, emotional support, creative input and boundless love will forever be remembered and honored by our work.

Katherine Weiss Taylor has been the right arm of *Investment Quality Trends,* serving as production manager and graphic artist for nearly two decades. Her skillful handiwork can be seen and appreciated in the illustrative charts within this book.

We also wish to thank John P. Taylor, our computer systems analyst, and Chris Oosterlinck, our data processor, for their important roles in compiling *The Dividend Connection.*

Contents

Preface   **ix**

Chapter 1   Finding Blue Chip Quality in the Stock Market   **1**
How Is Quality Determined in the Stock Market?   **1**
  Coca-Cola Company • Pfizer Inc.   *2*
What Is a Blue Chip Stock?   **8**
  Abbott Laboratories • American Home Products Corp.   *9*
Which Stocks Are the Bluest of the Blue Chips?   **18**
  Genuine Parts Company • Merck & Company   *19*
What Is a Faded Blue Chip?   **24**
  Ametek, Inc. • Borden, Inc.   *25*
When Should I Sell a Faded Blue Chip?   **31**
  National Medial Enterprises • Sears, Roebuck & Company   *32*

Chapter 2   Understanding Value in the Stock Market   **38**
How Is Value Measured in the Stock Market?   **38**
  American Brands, Inc. • Heinz (H.J.) Company   *42*
What Is a Dividend?   **47**
  Block (H&R), Inc. • Flowers Industries   *48*
Why Do Companies Pay Dividends?   **53**
  Harland (John H.) Company • Johnson & Johnson   *54*
Why Are Dividends Important?   **58**
  Kmart Corp. • Teleflex Inc.   *59*

Chapter 3   Comparing the Stock Price to Value   **65**
What Is an Undervalued Stock?   **65**
  Knight-Ridder Inc. • Upjohn Company   *66*
When Should I Sell an Extremely Undervalued Stock?   **71**
  Bruno's Inc. • Syntex Corp.   *72*
What Is an Overvalued Stock?   **77**
  American Greetings (Class A) • Johnson Controls, Inc.   *78*
Why Should I Sell My Overvalued Stock When It Keeps
Going Up?   **83**

AAR Corp. • *Disney (Walt) Company*   85
Do Interest Rates Affect Yields at Undervalue and
Overvalue?   **91**
   IPALCO Enterprises • *Millipore Corp.*   92

Chapter 4   The Dividend Connection   **97**
How Do Dividends Connect with Stock Prices?   **97**
   Avery Dennison Corp. • *Handleman Company*   98
What Is the Dividend Yield–Total Return Approach?   **103**
   Bristol-Myers Squibb Company • *Longs Drug Stores Corp.*   105
When Is a Dividend Safe and Sound?   **110**
   Carolina Power & Light Company • *SCEcorp.*   112
What is the Significance of Dividend Growth?   **116**
   Masco Corp. • *Quaker Chemical*   119

Chapter 5   Building Your Dividend-Rich Stock Portfolio   **124**
How Much Money Should I Have To Start?   **124**
   Bergen Brunswig Corp. (Class A) • *Zero Corp.*   125
How Should I Allocate My Investment Capital?   **131**
Should I Favor Dollar Cost Averaging?   **133**
   EG&G, Inc. • *Kimberly-Clark Corp.*   134
How Should I Construct My Stock Portfolio?   **138**
   Allegheny Power System, Inc. • *General Mills, Inc.*   140

Chapter 6   Developing Your Successful Stock Strategy   **146**
Should I Aim for Income or Growth?   **146**
   FlightSafety International, Inc. • *Florida Progress Corp.*   150
Is It Smart to Buy Stocks in a Rising Trend?   **154**
   Ennis Business Forms, Inc. • *Harcourt General, Inc.*   156
When Should I Find Stocks in a Declining Trend
Attractive?   **160**
   AFLAC Inc. • *Melville Corp.*   162
Is Market Timing Important?   **168**
   Anheuser-Busch Companies, Inc. • *Brown-Forman Corp.*
   (Class B)   168
Do Institutional Investors Influence Stock Prices?   **173**
   Air Products & Chemicals, Inc. • *AMP Inc.*   174
As a Small Investor, Do I Stand a Chance?   **181**
   AT&T Corp. • *Du Pont (E.I.) DeNemours & Company*   181

Chapter 7   Choosing the Best Stocks for Your Portfolio   **187**
Which Companies Are Relatively Debt-Free?   **187**
   Dun & Bradstreet Corp. • Luby's Cafeterias, Inc.   188
Should I Buy Foreign Stocks?   **195**
   Boeing Company • International Flavors & Fragrances, Inc.   196
Why Should I Invest Only in Blue Chip Stocks?   **201**
   Bankers Trust New York Corp. • Lilly (Eli) & Company   203
What Happens When a Blue Chip Cuts Its Dividend?   **207**
   *Cross (A.T.) Company (Class A) • International Business Machines
   Corp.   209*
How Do I Evaluate Growth Stocks?   **213**
   Hewlett-Packard Company • Pall Corp.   215

Chapter 8   Uncovering Hidden Value in Stock Industry Groups   **221**
Are Utilities Plugged into Investment Growth?   **221**
   *Consolidated Edison Company of New York • Wisconsin Energy
   Corp.   223*
How Should I Select Utilities Stocks?   **228**
   *American Electric Power Company • Detroit Edison
   Company   231*
How Safe Are the Dividends for Electric Utilities?   **236**
   Dominion Resources, Inc. • Texas Utilities Company   237
Are Pharmaceutical Stocks a Drug on the Market?   **243**
   Baxter International Inc. • Marion Merrell Dow, Inc.   246

Chapter 9   Using the Dow Jones Averages To Spot Value   **251**
What Is the Importance of the Dow Jones Industrial
Average?   **251**
   General Electric Company • Philip Morris Companies   253
Are All Dow Industrial Stocks Blue Chips?   **257**
What Is the Profile of Value for the Dow Jones Industrial
Average?   **258**
Is There a Profile of Value for the Dow Jones Utilities
Average?   **262**
Does the Dow Jones Transportation Average Have a Profile of
Value?   **263**
What Is the Average Dividend Growth Rate?   **265**
Is There a Connection Between Blue Chips and Major Market
Trends   **269**

Chapter 10   Hedging in the Stock Market   **273**
Are Stocks a Good Hedge Against Inflation?   **273**
Do Stock Market Trends Mirror the Economy?   **274**
What Stocks Are Best To Buy in a Recession?   **278**
What About Gold?   **279**

Chapter 11   Getting Started?   **281**

Index   **283**

Preface

The connection of dividends to stock market values is a verifiable bond that has governed stock prices for more than one hundred years. That bond has been strengthened over the past several decades by books and articles chronicling the validity of dividend yield as an important investment tool. It now is an acknowledged fact that dividends create value in the stock market.

How the Dividend Yield–Total Return Approach Will Help You Maximize Your Investments The Dividend Connection explores a unique investment strategy best described as the *dividend yield–total return approach*. This concept has been the road map for our top-performing stock market newsletter, *Investment Quality Trends*, which has been published since April 1966. The approach has stood the test of time, proving its merit through various social and economic cycles, including periods of high interest rates, low interest rates, inflation, deflation, recession and political transmutations. It has navigated investors safely through virtually every market condition with maximum gain and minimum risk.

As you can imagine, during three decades of publishing history, including numerous seminars and speaking engagements, we have heard and answered hundreds of questions about the stock market in general and about our dividend yield approach in particular. *The Dividend Connection* addresses the best, the most relevant, of those questions. It also explains why and how dividends create value in the stock market and how dividend yields signal historically valid buying and selling areas.

In each chapter you will find "the dividend connection"—stock charts that not only illustrate the subject under discussion, but also provide parameters of investment value, showing historically established buying and selling areas based on extremes of dividend yield. Along with each chart we have provided general information about the company the chart represents—its products and services, a bit of its history and some interpretive investment analysis to explain the dividend connection.

How Will Blue Chips Help You?   The objects of our investment affection are 350 select blue chip stocks. The number is arbitrary. The quality is mandatory. Research has shown that good quality companies with strong dividend histories offer as much, if not more, investment growth potential than poor quality companies; and they do so with far less risk. These are the companies that reward their shareholders most frequently and most generously. In good times they outperform both the economy and their lesser competitors. In bad times they resist adversity best.

Why 350 blue chips? We chose a number large enough to include a wide variety of stock industry groups, but not so large as to be an unmanageable universe to follow. These companies have the capital to attract the best managers and to invest in the research and development of new products and services, from which additional sales and earnings grow. Their products are the best known and most widely used. Their services are the most trustworthy.

Blue chip companies take great pride in their reputations for dependability. They are reluctant to lower a dividend, even in periods of cyclical stress. Such stress normally reduces the price of the stock and creates a good buying opportunity. Well-established blue chip companies offer the best potentials for increasing shareholder value through dividend growth and capital gains. History has shown that there is no profitable substitute for quality.

Finding the Key to Success—Value Investing   But there is more to achieving investment success than the pursuit and purchase of good quality stocks. We must also address the matter of value.

The concept on which our investment approach is based states: *When all other factors that rate analytical consideration have been digested, the underlying value of dividends that determines yield will in the long run also determine price.* Value, therefore, lies in yield as reflected by the dividend trend.

The Dividend Connection will help you find the key to successful investing—knowing when to buy and when to sell, and being able to identify undervalue and overvalue. The book also will define many other basic ideas of value investing. We will provide graphs, tables and charts that illustrate parameters of value for individual stocks.

In addition, we will examine technical portraits of fundamental value for the popular Dow Jones Industrial Average and the Dow Jones Utilities Average.

The Quest for the Dividend Connection *The Dividend Connection* is constructed as a dialogue between the authors and the investment community. Although our approach to value investing in the stock market is unique, we owe much of our inspiration to the work of Charles Dow, the creator of the popular Dow Jones averages and cofounder of *The Wall Street Journal*. At the turn of the century he wrote, "Values when applied to stocks are determined in the end by the return to the investor, and nothing is more certain than that the investor establishes the price of stocks. To know values is to know the meaning of the market. Value has little to do with daily fluctuations of stock prices, but it is the determining factor in the long run." *The Dividend Connection* puts Dow's theory about values into practical, modern terms and applies it to individual stocks.

Through our many years of experience, we have learned that the stock market will reward investors who recognize and appreciate good value—who have the courage to buy stocks when they are undervalued, the patience to hold them until the price moves upward and the wisdom to sell when the stocks become overvalued. To those investors, the stock market is a friend, a bestower of financial security, a giver of independence and dignity.

But the stock market is not a friend to investors who ignore the time-tested, fundamental indicators of sound stock selection. The two greatest assets an investor can have are the wisdom to understand quality and the ability to recognize value. *The Dividend Connection* will help you develop these two important skills.

What constantly intrigues us in our quest to understand value in the stock market is the profusion of factors that affect stock prices each day. More information comes into play than can ever be totally considered. Thus, stock market analysis is a creative science that demands flexibility and the skill to interpret abstract data as well as fundamental facts and figures to form solid investment decisions.

It's not easy, nor are we always correct. Still, our record of success is proof that we are on the right track. To us, nothing is more fascinating or more challenging than the search for value in the stock market. This quest is the touchstone for *The Dividend Connection*. We hope that the pages that follow will equip you with the necessary tools to build a solid, safe and profitable financial future.

—Geraldine Weiss and Gregory Weiss

Finding Blue Chip Quality in the Stock Market

How Is Quality Determined in the Stock Market?

Understanding quality and recognizing value are the two tickets to successful investing in the stock market. The first stop on the road to lifelong financial growth is to purchase stocks that have proven to be reliable investment vehicles over time. The highest-quality stocks have survived numerous economic cycles without lowering or canceling a dividend. Their sales, earnings and dividends grow continuously throughout virtually all economic conditions.

Quality is reflected in management's ability to guide a company through the inevitable rocks and shoals of a competitive business environment. An investor need not have personal knowledge of a company's management. A profile of excellence will be reflected through its financial performance and consequently in the performance of its stock.

In the real estate market, quality is determined by three measures: location, location, location. Three measures also can be applied to quality in the stock market: performance, performance, performance.

1. *Financial performance is the first measure of quality.* This includes the company's record of earnings, dividends, debt-to-equity ratio, dividend payout ratio, book value and cash flow.

2. *Production performance is the second measure.* We look for a company that manufactures useful products or services and actively

1

pursues research and development of new products or services. The company also must have demonstrated an ability to market its products or services successfully.

3. *Investment performance, as reflected in long-term capital gains and dividend growth, is the third measure.* The most important objective of an investor is a rewarding total return. A well-managed company with a strong financial performance will generate a total return that will outperform any other investment vehicle.

These three measures of quality do not stand alone. They are intertwined in the fabric of the company and its shareholders' goals. All of our research has shown that there is as much or more profit potential in high-quality stocks than there is in stocks of inferior or unproven quality—and with far less risk.

Our method of investing in the stock market focuses exclusively on blue chip stock selection. It involves limiting investment selections to blue chip stocks and purchasing or selling those stocks based on their individual profiles of undervalue or overvalue. The sweetness of low price is soon forgotten; the bitterness of poor quality is long remembered.

The Dividend Connection

Coca-Cola Company
Pfizer Inc.

The hallmark of each chapter is "The Dividend Connection." This section profiles two companies and their stock charts to illustrate the essential point made in the preceding discussion. Each profile includes the stock's ticker symbol and the exchange on which it trades.

You will find frequent references to undervalued and overvalued yield ares, which Chapter 3 explains in detail. Briefly, *undervalue* describes a condition in which a stock is priced low with a historically high dividend yield. *Overvalue* describes a condition in which a stock is priced high with a historically low dividend yield. Stocks typically fluctuate between extremes of high and low dividend yield. Therefore, when a stock is undervalued, it is recommended for purchase. When a stock is overvalued, a sale should be considered.

Coca-Cola Company and Pfizer Inc. exhibit the key measures of quality in the stock market—financial performance, production performance and investment performance.

Coca-Cola Company (NYSE:KO)

Founded in 1891, Coca-Cola is the world's leading soft drink company, producing more than 44% of all soft drinks consumed worldwide. Sold through some 2,000 bottlers in roughly 200 nations, soft drinks account for 75% of sales and 85% of profits. Coca-Cola is the company's leading product. Other major brand names include Diet Coke, Fanta, Fresca and Sprite. Coca-Cola's food division is the nation's largest citrus producer. Minute Maid frozen orange juice is the largest-selling item of its kind in America, accounting for one of every four glasses of fruit juice consumed each day.

With four of the world's top five carbonated soft drinks, Coca-Cola is the colossus of the industry. The world's most recognizable trademark and the best-selling soft drink is Coca-Cola, with nearly 7 billion unit cases sold in 1994. Sold in 120 markets, worldwide, the number one low-calorie soft drink and third-best-selling carbonated soft drink of any kind is Diet Coke. The world's fourth-best-selling carbonated soft drink, Fanta, is sold in 170 countries, making it the only true global brand in the orange soda segment. Sprite is the world's best-selling lemon-lime soft drink, sold in 168 nations. It is the world's fifth-best-selling carbonated soft drink of any kind.

The secret of Coca-Cola's success lies in competitive pricing and total global marketing. The company invests aggressively in the long-term growth of its business. It builds additional value into its enterprise by seeking new operations in high-potential markets like China, India and eastern Europe while simultaneously fueling growth in established markets.

Other Interesting Qualities

- Revenue mix is 31% U.S., 24% Latin America, 23% Europe/Middle East, 17% Canada/Pacific, 5% Africa.

FIGURE 1.1   The Dividend Connection Chart

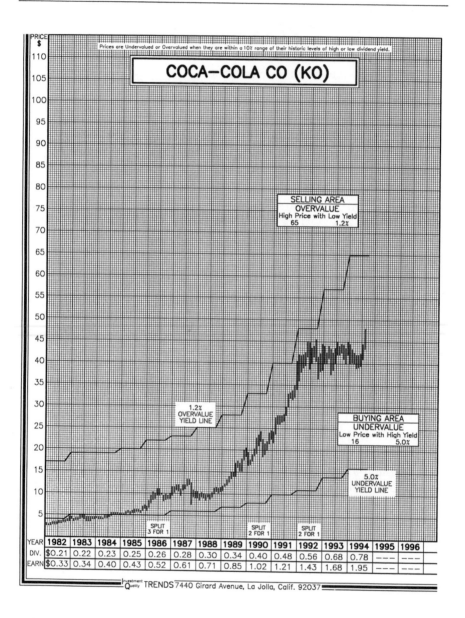

YEAR	1982	1983	1984	1985	1986	1987	1988	1989	1990	1991	1992	1993	1994	1995	1996
DIV.	$0.21	0.22	0.23	0.25	0.26	0.28	0.30	0.34	0.40	0.48	0.56	0.68	0.78	---	---
EARN	$0.33	0.34	0.40	0.43	0.52	0.61	0.71	0.85	1.02	1.21	1.43	1.68	1.95	---	---

- Coca-Cola is ranked among the five most admired companies in the nation by *Fortune* magazine.

- The company is second only to Wal-Mart in creating wealth for its shareholders.

- Dividends paid since 1893 have been increased in each of the past 32 years.

The chart of KO illustrates its yield profile at undervalue and overvalue. When this stock is priced to yield 5%, as it was from 1981 through 1984, it is undervalued and a purchase is recommended. However, when the price rises and the yield falls to 1.2%, as it did in 1992, it is overvalued and a sale should be considered.

From undervalue in 1982, KO consolidated its gains in the 5% yield area and then launched a highly carbonated rising trend. KO has scored knockout value for its shareholders over the past ten years with a 26% average annual rate of growth, earning its fine reputation for quality in the stock market.

Pfizer Inc. (NYSE:PFE)

With a mission to discover and develop innovative products that improve the quality of life for populations worldwide, Pfizer is among the top global pharmaceutical companies. Founded in 1849, the company has four business segments: health care, consumer health care, food science and animal health. With manufacturing facilities in 31 countries, Pfizer's products are available on all seven continents. Some of its major products include Cefobid, Diabinese, Feldene, Minipress, Procardia and Terramycin. Popular brand name over-the-counter products included Ben-Gay, Coty cosmetics and Visine.

Pfizer has one of the largest new product pipelines in the industry, with two major drugs that have gained wide market acceptance. Procardia XL, which the company markets only domestically, remains the nation's number one cardiovascular drug. Zoloft is among the most advanced of a new class of antidepressants that treat the biological causes of depression without many of the traditional unpleasant and sometimes toxic side effects.

As competition increases in health care, Pfizer continues to strengthen the efficiency of its global operations. Since 1988, the company has divested 14 underperforming businesses. Its restructuring initiatives continued in 1994 and resulted in an annual savings of about $130 million. Nineteen ninety-four was Pfizer's 45th consecutive year of sales growth, and both Moody's and Standard & Poor's reconfirmed the company's AAA credit rating for the eighth consecutive year.

Other Interesting Qualities

- Pfizer spends approximately 13% of annual sales on research and development.

- The company's angioplasty catheter is the leading device of its kind in Europe.

- Revenue mix is 83% health care, 8% animal health, 5% consumer health, 4% food science.

- Geographic mix is 54% U.S.; 22% Europe; 15% Asia; 9% Canada, Latin America, Africa, Middle East.

- Debt is only 13% of total capitalization.

- Dividends, paid since 1941, have been increased in each of the past 27 years.

The chart illustrates parameters of undervalue and overvalue for PFE stock. Frequent and generous dividend increases have produced a brilliant pattern of growth, lifting undervalue and overvalue yield lines and supporting rising price trends. Whenever PFE is priced to yield 4%, as it was in 1984, 1988 and 1990, it is undervalued and a good buying opportunity is at hand. However, when the stock is priced to yield 1.3%, as in 1971 through 1973, Pfizer is overvalued and a sale should be considered.

Much of Pfizer's lackluster performance in 1990 was attributed to controversy surrounding the reported inadequacies of its Shiley heart valve. Following the stock's temporary fibrillation, PFE began a monumental rise. The dividend has risen 370% over the past dozen years. A purchase at undervalue in 1982 returned more than 20% in 1994 from the cash dividend alone, while the price of the stock gained 450%. At undervalue, Pfizer's strong products, fine management and good shareholder value will add up to an attractive investment prescription.

FIGURE 1.2   The Dividend Connection Chart

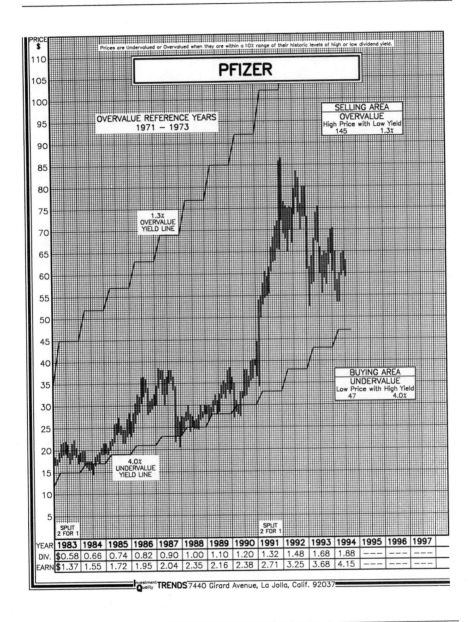

Investment Quality TRENDS 7440 Girard Avenue, La Jolla, Calif. 92037

What Is a Blue Chip Stock?

Like beauty, blue chip quality is often in the eye of the beholder. Most investors believe that whatever stocks they own are blue chips. However, that's not necessarily so.

Blue chip stocks get their name from the highest denomination of betting chips in a poker game. So it stands to reason that blue chips are the highest-quality stocks. But how does one objectively determine blue chip quality?

In our newsletter, *I.Q. Trends*, we pinpoint six simple criteria by which we measure the quality of a stock to determine if it merits the distinguished rank of a blue chip.

1. *The dividend must have been raised at least five times in the past 12 years.* Dividend growth is a hallmark of blue chip quality. A company that is making profitable progress should be able to boost its dividend at least five times in a 12-year period.

2. *The stock should carry a Standard & Poor's quality rank in the A+, A or A– category.* A+ is the highest rung on the ladder of long-term dividend and earnings performance. A identifies a stock with an excellent record of earnings and dividend growth. A– signifies above-average investment quality. In all cases, growth and stability of earnings are key elements in establishing the quality ranks.

3. *There should be at least 5,000,000 shares outstanding.* This is to ensure that there is liquidity in the market to allow institutional investors—including banks, mutual funds, insurance companies, pension funds and money managers—to purchase the stock. Institutions now account for nearly 90% of all stock market activity. Unless there are enough outstanding common shares so that institutions can buy or sell large blocks of stock without materially affecting the price, the stock will not be attractive to institutional investors and the price will languish. Money moves the market, and institutions have enough money to lift the price of a stock and make an investment profitable. A thinly traded stock can be attractive in every other regard, but unless it is attractive to institutional investors it is unlikely to make much headway.

4. *At least 80 institutions must hold the stock.* Eighty is not a huge number, but it does indicate institutional interest in the stock, which is important for the aforementioned reasons.

5. *There should have been at least 25 years of uninterrupted dividends.* Consistent dividend payments over a long period of time indicate a profitable, well-managed company that is willing to share its good fortune with its stockholders. An extensive dividend history also enables us to construct valid profiles of dividend yield at critical peaks and valleys in the investment cycle of a stock, thereby establishing undervalued and overvalued price-yield objectives.

6. *Corporate earnings should have improved in at least 7 of the past 12 years.* Here again, we look for an indication of sales and earnings progress, with profit margins sufficiently under control. Earnings do not necessarily have to grow every year, but they should experience growth in at least 7 out of 12 years.

If a stock meets all six criteria, it is a true blue chip and merits investment consideration. There are many fine companies that do not meet these blue chip standards, but experience has taught us to focus on this select group. In the stock market, as in life, there is no substitute for quality.

Figure 1.3 lists 245 stocks that meet all six criteria for blue chip quality.

The Dividend Connection

Abbott Laboratories
American Home Products

In this section we will profile two leading pharmaceutical companies listed in Figure 1.3—Abbott Laboratories and American Home Products.

FIGURE 1.3   Blue Chip Companies—A to Z

Abbott Laboratories (ABT)

Air Products & Chemicals, Inc. (APD)

Alberto-Culver Company (ACV)

Albertson's, Inc. (ABS)

Alexander & Baldwin (ALEX)

Allegheny Power System Inc. (AYP)

Alltel Corp. (AT)

American Brands, Inc. (AMB)

American Cyanamid Company (ACY)

American General Corp. (AGC)

American Home Products Corp. (AHP)

American International Group, Inc. (AIG)

American National Insurance (ANAT)

American Water Works Company (AWK)

Amsouth Bancorporation (ASO)

Angelica Corp. (AGL)

Anheuser-Busch Companies, Inc. (BUD)

Aon Corp. (AOC)

Archer Daniels Midland Company (ADM)

Armstrong World Industries, Inc. (ACK)

AT & T (T)

Atlantic Energy, Inc. (ATE)

Automatic Data Processing, Inc. (AUD)

Avery Dennison Corp. (AVY)

Ball Corp. (BLL)

Baltimore Gas & Electric Company (BGE)

Banc One Corp. (ONE)

Bandag, Inc.

Bankers Trust New York Corp. (BT)

Bard (C.R.), Inc. (BCR)

Barnett Banks, Inc. (BBI)

Bausch & Lomb Inc. (BOL)

BCE Inc. (BCE)

Becton, Dickinson & Company (BDX)

Bemis Company (BMS)

Betz Laboratories (BTL)

Block (H&R), Inc. (HRB)

Bob Evans Farms (BOBE)

Boeing Company (BA)

Bristol-Myers Squibb Company (BMY)

Brooklyn Union Gas Company (BU)

Brown-Forman Corp. (Class B) (BFB)

Browning-Ferris Industries Inc. (BFI)

Capital Holding Corp. (CPH)

Carolina Power & Light Company (CPL)

Carter-Wallace, Inc. (CAR)

Central Fidelity (CFBS)

Central & South West Corp. (CSR)

Chubb Corp. (CB)

Church & Dwight Company (CHD)

CIPSCO Inc. (CIP)

Clorox Company (CLX)

Coca-Cola Company (KO)

Comerica (CMA)

Conagra, Inc. (CAG)

Consolidated Edison Company of New York (ED)

Consolidated Natural Gas Company (CNG)

Cooper Industries, Inc. (CBE)

Cooper Tire & Rubber Company (CTB)

Corning Inc. (GLW)

CPC International, Inc. (CPC)

Crawford & Company (CRDB)

Crompton & Knowles Corp. (CNK)

Dayton Hudson Corp. (DH)

Dean Foods Company (DF)

Deluxe Corp. (DLX)

Disney (Walt) Company (DIS)

Dominion Resources, Inc. (D)

Donaldson Company (DCI)

Donnelley (R.R.) & Sons Company (DNY)

Dover Corp. (DOV)

Dow Jones & Company (DJ)

Dreyfus Corp. (DRY)

Dulce Power

FIGURE 1.3   Blue Chip Companies—A to Z (Continued)

Duke Power Company (DUK)

Du Pont (E.I.) DeNemours & Company (DD)

Dun & Bradstreet Corp. (DNB)

E-Systems Inc. (ESY)

Edwards (A.G.), Inc. (AGE)

EG&G, Inc. (EGG)

Emerson Electric Company (EMR)

Ennis Business Forms, Inc. (EBF)

Equifax Inc. (EFX)

Ethyl Corp. (EY)

Federal Signal Corp. (FSS)

First Alabama Bancshares (FABC)

First of America Bank Corp. (FOA)

First Union Corp. (FTU)

First Virginia Banks, Inc. (FVB)

Fleming Companies, Inc. (FLM)

Florida Progress Corp. (FPC)

Flowers Industries (FLO)

FPL Group, Inc. (FPL)

Gannett Company (GCI)

General Electric Company (GE)

General Mills, Inc. (GIS)

General Re Corp. (GRN)

Genuine Parts Company (GPC)

Giant Food Inc. (GFSA)

Gillette Company (G)

Grainger (W.W.), Inc. (GWW)

Handleman Company (HDL)

Hannaford Bros. Company (HRD)

Harcourt General, Inc. (H)

Harland (John H.) Company (JH)

Hartford Steam Boiler Inspection and Insurance
Company (HSB)

Hawaiian Electric Industries, Inc. (HE)

Heinz (H.J.) Company (HNZ)

Hershey Foods Corp. (HSY)

Hewlett-Packard Company (HWP)

Hillenbrand Industries, Inc. (HB)

Hormel (Geo. A.) & Company (HRL)

Houghton Mifflin Co. (HTN)

Hubbel, Inc. (Class B) (HUBB)

Hunt Manufacturing Company (HUN)

Illinois Tool Works Inc. (ITW)

International Flavors & Fragrances, Inc. (IFF)

Interpublic Group of Companies, Inc. (IPG)

Jefferson-Pilot Corp. (JP)

Johnson & Johnson (JNJ)

Jostens, Inc. (JOS)

Kmart Corp. (KM)

Kellogg Company (K)

Kelly Services (KELY)

KeyCorp (KEY)

Keystone International, Inc. (KII)

Kimball International (Class B) (KBALB)

Kimberly-Clark Corp. (KMB)

Knight-Ridder Inc. (KRI)

KU Energy Corp. (KU)

La-Z-Boy Chair (LZB)

Lance Inc. (LNCE)

Lee Enterprises, Inc. (LEE)

Leggett & Platt, Inc. (LEG)

Lilly (Eli) & Company (LLY)

The Limited Inc. (LTD)

Lincoln Telecom (LTEC)

Longs Drug Stores Corp. (LDG)

Lowe's Companies (LOW)

Luby's Cafeterias, Inc. (LUB)

Marion Merrell Dow Inc. (MKC)

Marsh & McLennan Companies (MMC)

Marshall & Ilsley (MRIS)

Martin Marietta Corp. (ML)

May Department Stores (MA)

McCormick & Co. (MCCR)

McDonnell Douglas Corp. (MD)

FIGURE 1.3   Blue Chip Companies—A to Z (Continued)

McGraw Hill, Inc. (MHP)

Medtronic, Inc. (MDT)

Melville Corp. (MES)

Merck & Company (MRK)

Millipore Corp. (MIL)

Minnesota Mining and Manufacturing
   Company (MMM)

Morrison Restaurants (RI)

Motorola, Inc. (MOT)

Nacco Industries Inc., (Class A) (NC)

Nalco Chemical Company (NLC)

National Service Industries, Inc. (NSI)

NBD Bancorp. (NBF)

New England Business Service (NEBS)

New England Electric System (NES)

Newell Company (NWL)

Nordstrom Inc. (NOBE)

Norfolk Southern Corp. (NSC)

Northern States Power Company (NSP)

Norwest Corp. (NOB)

Oklahoma Gas & Electric Company (OGE)

Old Kent Financial (OKEN)

Owens & Minor, Inc. (OMI)

Parker-Hannifin Corp. (PH)

Pennsylvania Power & Light Company (PPL)

Pep Boys (PBY)

Pepsico (PEP)

Pfizer Inc. (PFE)

Philip Morris Companies (MO)

Pitney Bowes Inc. (PBI)

Potomac Electric Power Company (POM)

PPG Industries Inc. (PPG)

Premier Industrial Corp. (PRE)

Procter & Gamble Company (PG)

Quaker Oats Company (OAT)

Questar Corp. (STR)

Ralston Purina Company (RAL)

Raytheon Company (RTN)

Rite Aid Corp. (RAD)

Roadway Services (ROAD)

Rockwell International Corp. (ROK)

Royal Dutch Petroleum Company (RD)

RPM Inc. (RPOW)

Rubbermaid, Inc. (RBD)

Russell Corp. (RML)

St. Paul Companies (SPC)

San Diego Gas & Electric Company (SDO)

Sara Lee Corp. (SLE)

Scana Corp. (SCG)

Schering-Plough Corp. (SGP)

Seagram Company (VO)

Servicemaster (SVM)

Shell Transport & Trading Company (SC)

Smucker (J.M.) Company (SJMA)

Sonoco Products (SONO)

Southern Company (SO)

Southern New England Telecommunications Corp. (SNG)

Southwestern Public Service Company (SPS)

Standard Register (SREG)

Stanhome Inc. (STH)

Stanley Works (SWK)

Star Banc Corp. (STRZ)

State Street Boston (STBK)

Stride Rite Corp. (SRR)

Supervalu Inc. (SVU)

Syntex Corp. (SYN)

Sysco Corp. (SYY)

TECO Energy, Inc. (TE)

Texas Utilities Company (TXU)

Textron Inc. (TXT)

Tootsie Roll Industries (TR)

Torchmark Corp. (TMK)

UJB Financial Corp. (UJB)

Union Electric Company (UEP)

FIGURE 1.3   Blue Chip Companies—A to Z (Continued)

Union Pacific Corp. (UNP)	Walgreen Company (WAG)
Universal Corp. (UVV)	Wallace Computer Services, Inc. (WCS)
Universal Foods Corp. (UFC)	Warner-Lambert Company (WLA)
Upjohn Company (UPJ)	Washington Gas Light Co. (WGL)
U.S. Bancorp (USBC)	Weis Markets, Inc. (WMK)
UST Inc. (UST)	Winn-Dixie Stores, Inc. (WIN)
UtiliCorp United Inc. (UCU)	Wisconsin Energy Corp. (WEC)
Valspar Corp. (VAL)	Wisconsin Public Service (WPS)
VF Corp. (VFC)	Woolworth Corp. (Z)
Vulcan Materials Company (VMC)	Worthington Industries (WTHG)
Wachovia Corp. (WB)	Wrigley (Wm.) Jr. Company (WWY)
Wal-Mart Stores, Inc. (WMT)	Zurn Industries, Inc. (ZRN)

Abbott Laboratories (NYSE:ABT)

Lou Costello's classic routine, "Who's on first," brings to mind the answer, "Abbott's on first." Not Bud Abbott, but Abbott Labs—a leading worldwide producer of ethical drugs, diagnostic products and hospital instruments. Covering all the bases, the company also doubles as a major hitter in the infant formula and nutritional products segments. Major brand names include Erythrocin, Isomil, Murine, Selsun Blue, Similac and Sucaryl. Headquartered in Abbott Park, Illinois, the company was founded by Dr. William C. Abbott in 1888.

Abbott's wide-range anti-infective, clarithromycin, has gained excellent market acceptance. Initially introduced overseas, the compound is prescribed in the United States under the name of Biaxin. Clarithromycin also is being used for the treatment of specialized infections found in AIDS patients.

Amidst the politics and rhetoric surrounding the nation's health care discussion, all parties agree that the process of identifying and developing innovative products is fundamental to long-term growth in the industry. To that end, Abbott scientists maintain a strategy of diversified research that allows the company to balance the varying degrees of risk against the probability of success as it develops programs. One important program involves a new set of tests

FIGURE 1.4   The Dividend Connection Chart

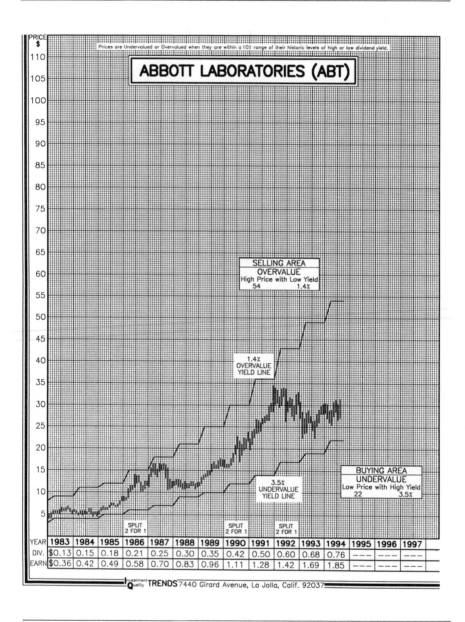

designed to pinpoint strains of viruses that can not be identified with current technology. This AxSYM system has far reaching potential in the areas of AIDS, Alzheimer's disease and cancer research.

Other Interesting Qualities

- Sales mix is 51% drugs and nutritional, 49% hospital and lab products.

- Foreign business accounts for 47% of sales, research and development for 10%.

- Sales are conducted in 132 nations.

- Debt is only 3% of total capitalization.

- Dividends paid since 1926 have been increased in each of the past 21 years.

ABT fluctuates between dividend yield extremes of 3.5% at undervalue and 1.4% at overvalue. The chart reveals an undervalued stock in 1983 and 1984. In 1986, 1987 and 1991 the price rose to overvalue. If an investor had purchased shares of this stock near undervalue in 1989 and sold them at overvalue in 1991, the capital gain would have been 200%, while dividend growth was 66%. In 1992, Abbott began a declining trend that brought the stock near undervalue in mid-1993. Later, the price of ABT swayed with the stock industry group, buffeted by changes in the political winds but never quite falling into the undervalued category. This A+ quality, blue chip stock offers an average annual growth rate of 12%. At undervalue, Abbott offers investors a financially therapeutic investment opportunity.

American Home Products Corp. (NYSE:AHP)

An icon of corporate America with its huge stable of diversified pharmaceuticals and consumer goods, American Home Products has been serving the varied needs of its customers for nearly 100 years. Major brand names include Advil, Anacin, Chap Stick, Chef Boyardee, Clearblue, Dennison, Dimetapp, Dristan, Gulden's mustard, Pam, Primatene and Robitussin. Its subsidiary, Wyeth-Ayerst Laboratories, holds the number one position for pharmaceutical prescriptions in the nation and is the international leader in several therapeutic areas. Whitehall Laboratories develops most of AHP's over-the-counter compounds. Other subsidiaries include Sherwood Medical, acquired in 1982; A. H. Robbins, purchased in 1989; and a 67% holding of Genetics Institute, acquired in 1993.

Through its investment in Genetics Institute, AHP has introduced important products for the treatment of bone marrow and blood diseases. These so-called genetic antibody therapies are the state of the art in cancer treatment and may represent a significant breakthrough in the field of medicine.

American Home Products is the world's leading producer of oral contraceptives and has a significant presence in anti-inflammatories, cardiovascular therapies, psychotropic drugs, anti-infectives and infant formulas. Diversity seems to be the right medicine for AHP, as sales and earnings continue to rise.

Other Interesting Qualities

* Foreign business accounts for 33% of sales.

* Total research and development costs account for 6% of AHP sales.

* Dividends paid since 1919 have been increased in each of the past 42 years.

The chart of AHP is a classic example of blue chip quality. It also profiles the stock's parameters of investment value. When AHP is priced to yield 6%, as it was in 1984 and 1987, it is undervalued and a purchase is recommended. But when the price rises and the yield falls to 3%, as it did in late 1991, AHP is overvalued and a sale should be considered. Although there were intermittent down legs in AHP's profile of value, the consistent trend remained upward from 1982 through 1991. In fact, an investor who purchased shares of AHP at undervalue in 1982 and held the stock for ten years would have realized a 500% capital gain along with a 115% increase in the dividend. In 1992, AHP launched a declining trend, dropping 28% to a price of $55 per share in two years. When AHP penetrates the veil of undervalue, investors who add this blue chip to their core holdings will be home free.

FIGURE 1.5   The Dividend Connection Chart

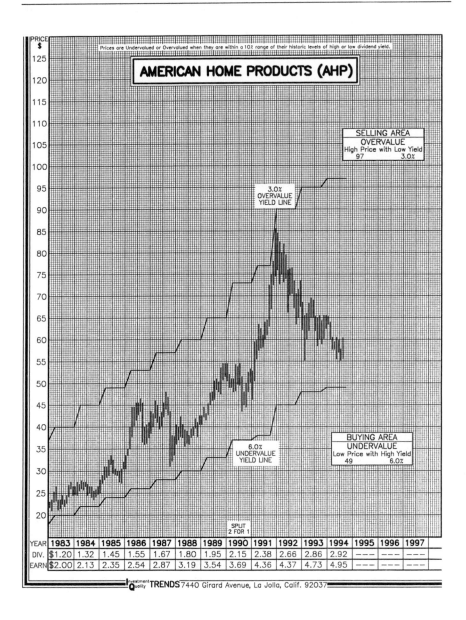

Which Stocks Are the Bluest of the Blue Chips?

Few investors intentionally purchase stocks that have unbecoming investment characteristics. If they do, they generally rationalize their decisions, claiming that the future looks bright for their companies even though the present may be cloudy.

Our research shows that there is just as much profit potential in undervalued blue chip stocks as there is in stocks of lesser quality. The difference lies in the 3 Rs—risk, reliability and return.

These are the companies that command institutional support and sponsorship from powerful money forces. They are the mature, time-tested companies with proven management skills and established marketing techniques. They are experienced industry leaders that have weathered many economic changes and have proven that they can adjust. These are the wealthy companies, with money to attract the most talented managers and capital to invest in research and development from which new and improved products and higher sales and earnings eventually will spring. And these are the companies that seem to be most concerned about their shareholders, especially when it comes to paying and increasing a dividend. Ever mindful of their blue chip status, they are reluctant to lower a dividend except in cases of dire financial misfortune. In good times, these companies generally outperform both the economy and their lesser competitors. In bad times, they resist adversity best. Experience shows that there is no profitable substitute for quality.

But even among blue chips, some are more "blue chip" than others. Safe, successful investing requires attention to both quality and value. We will address value later, but for now let us turn our attention to stocks that offer superb quality. We call those stocks *royal blue chips*. (See Figure 1.6.) When these stocks are priced at undervalue, they offer the best of all possible worlds—outstanding quality and historically attractive value.

Chapter 4 contains a list of blue chip companies that have increased their cash dividends in at least 11 of the past 12 years at compound annual rates in excess of 10%. Working from that list, we distilled those companies that also have very low levels of debt, little or no pension liability and no preferred stock. Such companies obviously are financially strong in addition to being very well managed.

FIGURE 1.6   Royal Blue Chips—Highest Investment Quality (A+)

Abbott Laboratories	International Flavors & Fragrances, Inc.
American Home Products Corp.	Johnson & Johnson
Bandag, Inc.	Kellogg Company
Block (H&R), Inc.	Lilly (Eli) & Company
Bristol-Myers Squibb Company	Marion Merrell Dow Inc.
Coca-Cola Company	Medtronic, Inc.
Crawford & Company	Merck & Company
Deluxe Corp.	Old Kent Financial
Dun & Bradstreet Corp.	RPM Inc.
General Electric Company	Rubbermaid, Inc.
Genuine Parts Company	UST Inc.
Heinz (H.J.) Company	Valspar Corp.
Hershey Foods	Wal-Mart Stores, Inc.
Hormel (Geo. A.) & Company	Walgreen Company
Hubbell Inc.	Winn-Dixie Stores, Inc.

Narrowing the list even further, stocks that have an A+ quality rank in addition to all of the above royal blue chip characteristics are, of course, the bluest of the blue chips.

The Dividend Connection

Genuine Parts
Merck

The stocks profiled on the following pages, Genuine Parts and Merck, are two of the finest quality royal blue chips.

Genuine Parts Company (NYSE:GPC)

George Knutson once said, "Take care of the things that take care of you." This statement might as well have been coined by Genuine Parts, the premier supplier of automotive replacement parts. Founded in 1928, GPC is a service organization that distributes automobile parts for the aftermarket, industrial replacement parts and office products. Headquartered in Atlanta, Georgia, the company serves nearly 6,000 independent outlets and roughly 700 company-owned stores in the United States and Canada.

Steering the largest share of sales is the automotive parts group. Through its more than 5,800 NAPA auto parts stores in the United States, GPC distributes 143,000 items and offers the most complete inventory, accounting, cataloging, marketing and training programs in the automotive aftermarket. This group also operates 65 distribution centers and six plants that rebuild auto parts.

Hammering out the second largest percentage of profits is the industrial parts group, which distributes replacement parts and related industrial supplies. This division stocks more than 200,000 items, including industrial bearings, belts, hoses, mechanical and fluid power transmission equipment. The group distributes products from roughly 300 locations in 36 states and serves more than 150,000 customers in all types of industries located in the United States and Canada. Subsidiaries include Berry Bearing Company, Motion Industries and Oliver Industrial Ltd.

Sealing the third envelope of earnings is the Office Products Group, producing one of the oldest and largest lines of office products in the nation.

Other Interesting Qualities

- Sales mix is 57% automotive, 26% industrial, 17% office.
- GPC is the nation's largest industrial parts distributor.
- There are 17 company-owned Canadian outlets, primarily serving western Canada.
- Debt is only 1% of total capitalization.
- Dividends paid since 1948 have been increased in each of the past 38 years.

FIGURE 1.7   The Dividend Connection Chart

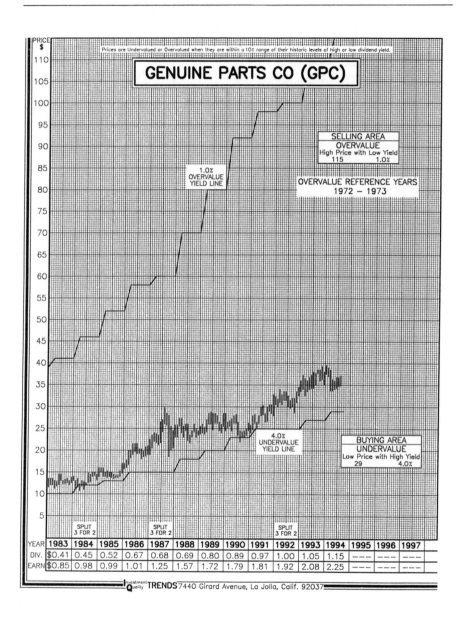

Although for the past ten years the stock has traded within relatively narrow yield parameters, GPC validated its overvalued yield from 1972–1973, when the stock was priced to yield 1%. GPC launched a rising trend in 1985, only to be halted and reversed at the top of the market in 1987. Likewise, a rising trend accelerated from undervalue in 1990, driving the price up for three and a half years until the breaks were applied in early 1994. Still, the price traveled up 170% during the past ten years, while the dividend gained nearly 120%. This A+ quality growth stock meets all six of *I.Q. Trends'* blue chip criteria. Investors are advised to wait at the crosswalk until GPC enters the undervalued zone, where the dividend yield is 4%, which will signal a green light for a genuine buying opportunity.

Merck & Company (NYSE:MRK)

Riding on a rocky road of monumental change, Merck still leads the pack as the nation's premier drug manufacturer. Among the world's top performers in its industry, Merck sells most of its drugs by prescription. Among its largest sellers are Vasotec, for cardiovascular disease; Mevacor, for lowering cholesterol levels; and the break-through compound Proscar, for prostate enlargement. For the seventh year in a row, Merck was rated "America's Most Admired Corporation" by *Fortune* magazine.

During the early 1990s, Merck was a sleeping giant. In the summer of 1993, however, it rose and devoured its most threatening competitor, Medco Containment Services, the nation's largest and fastest growing mail-order drug provider. The price tag was $6 billion. The goal was to create a new kind of company that would take advantage of the industry trend toward wholesaling and managed care. The strategy appears to be sound, and the merger has started a trend of similar alliances in the drug industry.

Merck's past strategy was to focus on so-called annuity drugs. These are prescription medications that patients must take on a daily basis, such as hypertension and cardiovascular drugs. However, with industry pressure mounting to keep a tight rein on health care spending, annuity drugs have been the focus of much cost-cutting effort.

Other Interesting Qualities

- Foreign sales account for 45% of total sales.

FIGURE 1.8   The Dividend Connection Chart

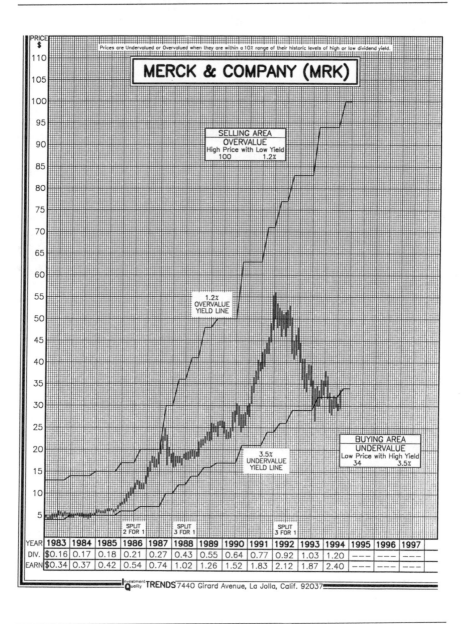

- Research and development costs are 11% of sales.
- Cardiovascular drugs account for about one-half of total revenues.
- Salaries, wages and benefits amount to 26% of sales.
- Dividends paid since 1935 have been increased 17 times in the past 18 years.

A glance at the chart will raise the blood pressure of any MRK shareholder. It shows that when this stock is priced to yield 3.5%, as it was from 1983 through 1985, MRK is undervalued and a purchase can be made. However, when the price rises and the yield falls to 1.2%, Merck is overvalued. Since its peak in early 1993, the stock's price was pulverized by almost 50%. Nearly 10% of the decline occurred after the Medco announcement, leading some analysts to question the deal. Still, we believe that the Merck/Medco marriage merits a mighty "mazel tov!"

This A+ quality growth stock meets all six of *I.Q. Trends'* blue chip criteria. The generous dividend is easily covered by earnings and based on the strength of existing sales plus the projected increase from Medco's intervention, earnings should remain in a healthy uptrend. For investors who are sick at heart from a shortage of good value in the stock market, Merck may be the right medicine.

What Is a Faded Blue Chip?

Standard & Poor's ranks the relative quality of stocks on a scale ranging from A+ (highest) to C (lowest), with D indicating that a company is in reorganization. Growth and stability of earnings and dividends are key elements in establishing the various rankings, although a variety of other factors also are considered. Over the past 30 years, we have found the S&P quality rankings to be a reliable guideline in determining investment quality.

A stock must carry an S&P quality ranking in the A category (A+, A or A–) when it first earns the title of blue chip. If the ranking subsequently falls to B+, we allow it to remain on our list. B+ indicates average quality, and since the rankings are based on a numerical standard, a stock can easily return to the rank of A–.

But if the designation later falls to B, which signifies below-average quality, we feel compelled to delete the stock from our blue chip roster and transfer it to our list of faded blue chips. More than 100 stocks have been deleted from our blue chip list over the last 30 years, many because their S&P rankings fell below acceptable standards of quality. Some were removed because they were acquired by another company, others because they omitted a dividend.

The number of deletions has averaged about three stocks per year. In 1991, however, we saw an unusually large reshuffling of blue chips, due primarily to a shakeup in the banking industry. That year, we lost and replaced 25 stocks, or about 7% of our entire roster of 350.

We currently list 76 stocks as faded blue chips (see Figure 1.9). These stocks at one time were select blue chips but were deleted when their S&P quality rankings were lowered to B. They will be eligible for blue chip reinstatement if their quality rankings return to A– (above average). Although their investment quality has been tarnished, the yields at undervalue and overvalue for these stocks remain valid.

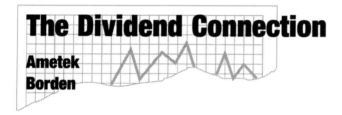

Recent dividend reductions have moved two well-respected companies, Ametek and Borden, to our list of faded blue chips.

Ametek, Inc. (NYSE:AME)

On the cutting edge of today's technology while carving solutions for tomorrow, Ametek products are as diverse as the global community it serves. Operations are in three primary groups: precision instruments, electromechanical and industrial materials. Headquartered in Paoli, Pennsylvania, the company owns more than three dozen facilities in North America, Europe and Asia. Myriad products are sold domestically and in more than 90 nations around the world. Major

FIGURE 1.9   Faded Blue Chips

Aetna Life	Harsco
Alcoa	Hercules
Allied Signal	Honeywell
American Express	IBM
Ametek Inc.	James River
Amoco	Kerr McGee
Atlantic Richfield	Maytag Corp.
Baker-Hughes	Mellon Bank
BankAmerica	Mobil Corporation
Beneficial Corp.	Morrison Knudsen
Black and Decker	Nashua Corp.
Borden Inc.	Northeast Utilities
Briggs & Stratton	Northrop Grumman
Campbell Soup	NY State Electric
Caterpillar	Ogden Corp.
CBS Inc.	Ohio Edison
Centerior Energy	Pacific Gas & Electric
Chase Manhattan	Panhandle Eastern
Chemical Bank	Peco Energy
Chevron Corp.	Perkin Elmer
Cincinnati G&E	Phillips Petroleum
Colgate Palmolive	Rochester Gas
Commonwealth Edison	Sears Roebuck
Dow Chemical	Signet Banking
Dresser Industries	Sonat
Eastman Kodak	Sprint Corp.
Ecolab	Texaco
Edison Brothers	Texas Instruments
Enron Corporation	Time Warner
Ensearch	Times Mirror
Ford Motor Company	Tultex
FPL Group	Union Camp
General Motors	Union Carbide
Georgia Pacific	United Technologies
Goodrich	Unocal
Goodyear Tire	US Shoe
Grace-WR	Westinghouse Electric
Halliburton	Xerox Corp.
Harris Corp.	

FIGURE 1.10   The Dividend Connection Chart

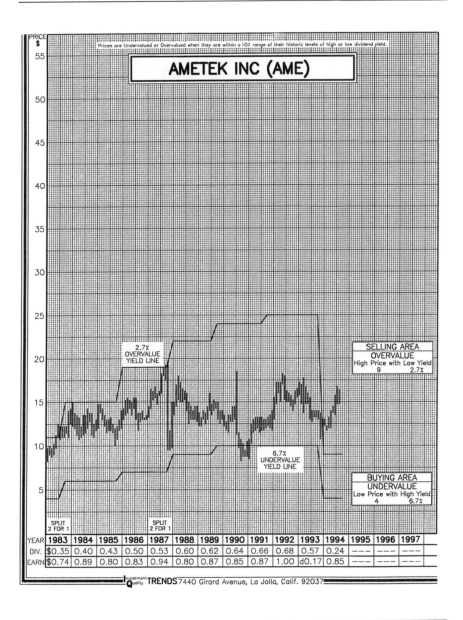

AMETEK INC (AME)

Prices are Undervalued or Overvalued when they are within a 10% range of their historic levels of high or low dividend yield.

2.7%
OVERVALUE
YIELD LINE

6.7%
UNDERVALUE
YIELD LINE

SELLING AREA
OVERVALUE
High Price with Low Yield
9   2.7%

BUYING AREA
UNDERVALUE
Low Price with High Yield
4   6.7%

SPLIT
2 FOR 1

SPLIT
2 FOR 1

YEAR	1983	1984	1985	1986	1987	1988	1989	1990	1991	1992	1993	1994	1995	1996	1997
DIV.	$0.35	0.40	0.43	0.50	0.53	0.60	0.62	0.64	0.66	0.68	0.57	0.24	---	---	---
EARN	$0.74	0.89	0.80	0.83	0.94	0.80	0.87	0.85	0.87	1.00	d0.17	0.85	---	---	---

Investment
Quality TRENDS 7440 Girard Avenue, La Jolla, Calif. 92037

products include vacuum cleaner motors, power tools, car bumpers and side panels, water purification systems, specialty metals, airplane instruments, furnaces, photocopiers, personal computers and industrial plant monitoring equipment. The diversity is mind-boggling, but with an experienced management team, Ametek performs well in all of its market sectors.

Accelerated demand for Ametek motors has made the electromechanical group the largest and most profitable division. Accounting for about one-half of revenues, this sector stands in the boot of Italy, where there are three major manufacturing facilities. Thousands of motors of all shapes and sizes are made at these plants and sold for various floor care products worldwide.

The second largest division is precision instruments. The main frame of the division is U.S. Gauge, which consists of four groups: aerospace, automotive, general gauge and pressure movement technology.

The industrial materials group manufactures products for advanced water treatment and liquid filtration, high-purity engineered metals and high-temperature plastics. This division is leading the way into the future with the development of metal matrix composites. These multiuse materials are combinations of ceramics, plastics, metals and graphite.

Other Interesting Qualities

- Revenue mix is 50% electromechanical, 28% precision instruments, 22% industrial materials.

- Foreign markets account for more than 30% of sales.

- Insiders own 8% of the common stock.

- Dividends paid since 1942 were increased 40 times in 42 years until 1993.

The chart reflects AME's dividend yield profile. When this stock is priced to yield 6.7%, as it was in late 1990 and early 1991, it is undervalued and a purchase is recommended. But when the price rises and the yield falls to 2.7%, as it did from mid-1983 through 1984 and at the top of the market in 1987, AME is overvalued and a sale should be considered. In 1991, the stock launched a rising trend, gaining almost 100% in one and a half years. AME became a faded blue chip in 1993, when its dividend was cut dramatically and Standard & Poor's subsequently lowered its quality rank from B+ to B. Ametek may someday motor its way back to an electrocharged future as a select blue chip.

Borden, Inc. (NYSE:BN)

As one of the most widely recognized brand names, Borden dominates store shelves at home and around the world. Founded in 1857, Borden is the world's number one maker of pasta, wall coverings and food wrapping material, as well as the nation's leading dairy company. Among dozens of Borden products, major brand names include Borden, Cracker Jack, Classico, Creamette, Eagle Brand, Elmer's Krazy Glue and Krunchers.

The company's three greatest assets are the Borden name, its slogan and Elsie the Cow. Research indicates that virtually every consumer in America recognizes the Borden name. And, despite years of underexposure, Elsie still is recognized by more than half of the adult American population.

Judging by the stock's 1993–1994 performance, it appeared that Borden's milk had soured. The company hopes that the worst is over as it continues to adjust to restructuring changes. During the profitable 1980s, Borden typically paid out 35% to 40% of its earnings in dividends. Then came two dividend reductions in 1993. The division restructuring seems to be the key to making Borden a leaner, meaner milking machine.

Other Interesting Qualities

- Foreign operations account for 32% of sales.

- The world's number one pasta, Creamette, is the only major wholly American pasta brand.

- Borden is the leading seller in North America of snack foods.

- The company is the nation's number one supplier to the food service industry.

- Borden is the number one milk producer in America and the number two producer overseas of milk powder.

FIGURE 1.11   The Dividend Connection Chart

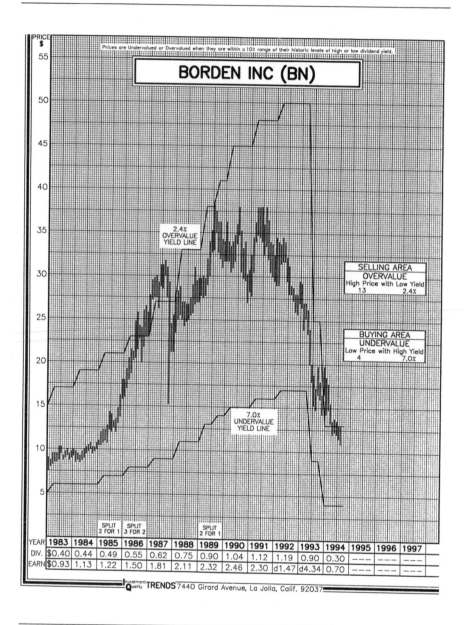

BORDEN INC (BN)

Prices are Undervalued or Overvalued when they are within a 10% range of their historic levels of high or low dividend yield.

2.4%
OVERVALUE
YIELD LINE

SELLING AREA
OVERVALUE
High Price with Low Yield
13   2.4%

BUYING AREA
UNDERVALUE
Low Price with High Yield
4   7.0%

7.0%
UNDERVALUE
YIELD LINE

SPLIT 2 FOR 1   SPLIT 3 FOR 2   SPLIT 2 FOR 1

YEAR	1983	1984	1985	1986	1987	1988	1989	1990	1991	1992	1993	1994	1995	1996	1997
DIV.	$0.40	0.44	0.49	0.55	0.62	0.75	0.90	1.04	1.12	1.19	0.90	0.30	---	---	---
EARN	$0.93	1.13	1.22	1.50	1.81	2.11	2.32	2.46	2.30	d1.47	d4.34	0.70	---	---	---

Investment Quality TRENDS 7440 Girard Avenue, La Jolla, Calif. 92037

- Dividends paid since 1899 were maintained or increased every year from 1938 to 1993.

BN is undervalued when its dividend yield is 7%, as it was in 1981 and 1982. The chart reveals an overvalued yield of 2.4% in 1986, 1987 and 1989. Since its high in 1991, BN has been in a major declining trend. In mid-1993, Borden's stock really curdled, falling a full 20% to a low price of $20 per share. Value investors watched and waited for the signal to move in and buy Borden but were disappointed when the dividend was cut twice in 1993. This, of course, led to a reduction in its S&P quality rank. Hence, Elsie was temporarily put to pasture as Borden battles to regain its status as a true blue.

When Should I Sell a Faded Blue Chip?

The only certainty in the stock market is change. Sometimes an investor buys a blue chip stock, only to find that the quality has slipped and the stock is no longer true blue. Is it time to abandon the stock, or should the stock owner hang on?

Regardless of a change in the quality of a stock, the dividend yields at undervalue and overvalue will remain the same. If, for example, the blue chip was undervalued when the dividend yield was 4% and overvalued when the yield was 2%, the faded blue chip will continue to fluctuate between those same extremes. Quality and value are separate characteristics. One has little to do with the other.

A reduction in the quality rank of a stock indicates that the company is probably suffering hard times, which are reflected in declining sales, earnings, profits and even perhaps a reduced dividend. A stock becomes a faded blue chip when the quality of the company falls below our standards. Whether or not to replace the stock in your portfolio is a personal decision that will depend on your own investment position in the company, possible tax consequences or your desire to maintain a strictly blue chip portfolio. Our suggestion is to put the stock on a list of candidates to sell when the time and the circumstances are right.

If a blue chip is acquired by another company, it is then followed through the takeover company. A case in point is Bergen Brunswig, which acquired Durr-Fillauer Inc. in 1993. At the time, both stocks were listed in our blue chip ranks. Now, only Bergen Brunswig is noted.

A stock also is deleted from our blue chip list when a dividend is omitted. When there is no dividend, there is no dividend yield on which to construct a profile of undervalue and overvalue. Therefore, the stock can not be evaluated according to our approach.

Just as we praise the management of a company that has amassed a long history of uninterrupted dividend payments and dividend increases, so we must blame the management that disappoints its stockholders by failing to maintain a cash dividend. If a dividend increase denotes success, a canceled dividend screams failure. Although a dividend omission usually comes at the end of a long line of bad news and the stock generally is priced as low as it is likely to go, there is no reason to hold a stock that no longer offers a return on your investment. The safety net has been removed, and any further bad news can result in a free fall, as you can see in Figure 1.11 of National Medical Enterprises. When a dividend is canceled, the event generally is viewed as a failure of management, a betrayal of stockholders who may be financially dependent on the dividend income. In our opinion, the stock should be replaced.

Sometimes a company will argue that its dividend must be suspended in order to support internal growth. We say no. All excuses aside, there really is only one reason why a dividend is omitted: bad management. A poorly managed company does not deserve to remain in a portfolio of blue chip stocks.

The Dividend Connection
National Medical Enterprises
Sears, Roebuck

National Medical Enterprises became a faded blue chip when it omitted a dividend. Sears, Roebuck & Company joined those ranks when its Standard & Poor's quality rank fell from B+ to B. Although we would not advocate an initial purchase of those stocks, a current shareholder is justified in holding them for their recovery potential.

National Medical Enterprises (NYSE:NME)

Swimming in a tumultuous tide of heightened public concern, National Medical Enterprises operates one of the nation's largest health care companies, with general hospitals, psychiatric clinics, physical rehabilitation centers and substance abuse facilities in 34 states, the District of Columbia and abroad. International operations include Europe, Australia and the Pacific Rim. Headquartered in Santa Monica, California, the company was founded in 1969.

National Medical Enterprises is likely to benefit from the current political climate, which calls for the use of managed health care providers. In anticipation of the changing political climate, both general and rehabilitation hospitals are strengthening their managed care operations to serve the numerous patients enrolled in health maintenance organizations (HMOs) and preferred provider organizations (PPOs).

There has been a shrinkage in psychiatric operations lately, due largely to negative publicity regarding the business practices of the company's psychiatric division. Widespread hostility has broken out between insurance companies and health care providers. In response to public concern, the company has strengthened physician involvement at its facilities and has taken steps to improve profitability. Speaking of steps, the growth of 12-step substance abuse recovery programs has contributed to the expansion of NME facilities.

Other Interesting Qualities

- NME has 6,560 general hospital beds, 6,590 psychiatric beds and 2,700 physical rehab beds.

- The company operates 32 physical rehab facilities in 11 states.

- Dividends, paid since 1973, were increased 30 times from 1974 to 1992, after which the dividend was omitted in 1993.

The vital stats on the chart show that when this stock was priced to yield 3.5%, as in 1987 and 1988, NME was undervalued and the prognosis was good for a healthy buying opportunity. When the price rose and the yield fell to 1.3%, the sale of an ailing, overvalued stock was advisable. In mid-1991, NME began a sharp decline amid industry pressures and congressional inquiries.

FIGURE 1.12   The Dividend Connection Chart

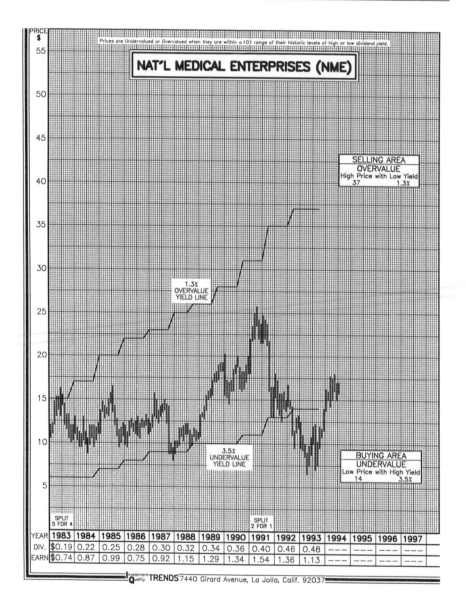

With the psychiatric hospital troubles now in plain view, profits appear to be improving, but suspension of the dividend precludes NME from consideration as a blue chip stock. We hope that NME will soon reinstate its cash dividend. As the trend toward managed health care providers increases, NME should be well positioned to lead the way with healing profits for a company in recovery.

Sears, Roebuck & Company (NYSE:S)

From humble beginnings as a small, Chicago-based catalog mail-order business, Sears, Roebuck has become a leading retailer of general merchandise through department stores and catalog outlet stores. For more than 100 years, the company has enjoyed a reputation for practical affordability and customer confidence. Key subsidiaries are Allstate Insurance (life, health and property) and Coldwell Banker (real estate).

Despite the company's financial strength and industry leadership, Sears has endured a trying decade. Over the past ten years, the company lost $416 million in market value, earning an average of 2.5% less than its cost of capital. While adverse economic conditions can be blamed for some of its recent troubles, there are broader strategic issues that the company still must face. The company has cut many jobs from the merchandise group and frozen management salaries. The next phase of its strategy is a concept called "Sears Brand Central," featuring more than 80 brands including names like Amana, General Electric, Hoover, Singer and Whirlpool. These national brands are expected to complement the company's private Kenmore brand and enable Sears to enhance its number one market share position in appliances and electronics.

Other Interesting Qualities

- There are 863 Sears department stores nationwide.
- The company owns more than 800 auto centers.
- In 1993, Sears spun off Dean Witter/Discover Card.
- Dividends have been paid for 57 consecutive years.

The chart of Sears illustrates four significant yield lines. If this chart were extended back to the early 1970s, it would reveal that Sears

FIGURE 1.13   The Dividend Connection Chart

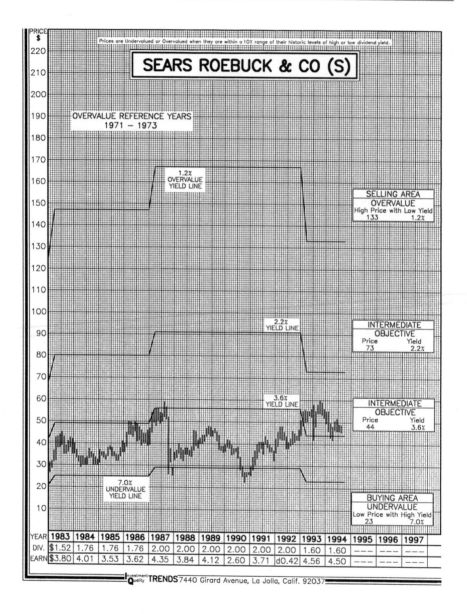

was overvalued at a yield of 1.2% from 1971 through 1973. During the mid- to late 1970s, the stock encountered resistance at a yield of 2.2%, but for the past 12 years, it has traded within a relatively narrow range. Whenever the stock has been priced to yield 7%, as it was in 1982, 1987 and 1990, it has been undervalued and a purchase was recommended. But when the price rose and the yield fell to an intermediate yield objective of 3.6%, as it did in 1986 and early to mid-1987, Sears encountered formidable selling pressure and the trend was reversed.

Sears was a longtime stock on our favored blue chip list until its Standard & Poor's quality rank declined to B in 1993. Sears is fighting back to regain its leadership position. The goal is to reclaim its market share from megarivals Wal-Mart and Kmart. The success of this effort will depend on the stores' ability to respond to change. We hope that Sears will be upgraded to an A quality rank, where at undervalue investors will have a green light for a Sears "red tag special."

Understanding Value in the Stock Market

How Is Value Measured in the Stock Market?

Most investors agree that it is much better and safer to buy good value in the stock market than to speculate in new issues or overvalued securities. But how is value measured in the stock market? How does an investor know when the price of a stock represents good value or when it should be bypassed? There are three fundamental tools that investors use to measure value in the stock market.

Price-Earnings Ratio

The most commonly used measure of value is the price-earnings ratio, which is the relationship of a stock's price to the company's most recent 12-month earnings. To determine the ratio, divide earnings per share into the price of the stock. The resulting figure produces a ratio of the price to the earnings. For example, if the 12-month earnings for a company are $1.85 per share and the stock price is $23 per share, by dividing $1.85 into $23, we find that the PE ratio is 12 to 1. This is considered low. In fact, depending on rates of growth within the stock industry group, any ratio below 15 to 1 is thought to represent fair value.

A low price-earnings ratio indicates that the price is relatively inexpensive. A high price-earnings ratio is already discounting future earnings growth. There is far greater risk in a stock that sports a high price-earnings ratio because if earnings falter, the price of the stock will tumble. The higher the price-earnings ratio, the longer it will take for earnings to justify the price.

A price-earnings ratio of 15 to 1 or less generally indicates good value. A ratio above 20 to 1 suggests that the stock price may be overvalued. However, stocks do have their own personalities, and a high price-earnings ratio for one stock may be an acceptable ratio for another, depending on the company's growth characteristics. Still, as a general rule, low is better than high.

The following stocks are blue chips with relatively low price-earnings ratios, representing one measure of good investment value.

Stock	Price	12-Month Earnings	Price-Earnings Ratio
American Brands, Inc.	31	$3.20	10 to 1
Block Drug	32	2.68	12 to 1
Boeing Company	45	3.66	12 to 1
Clorox Company	50	3.74	13 to 1
EG&G Inc.	16	1.41	11 to 1
Handleman Company	11	1.00	11 to 1
Harland (John H.) Company	23	1.62	14 to 1
Johnson & Johnson	39	2.74	14 to 1
Philip Morris Companies	48	6.04	8 to 1
Super Food Sevices	12	.89	13 to 1

Price-Book Value Ratio

Book value is the net asset value of a company, less debt, less intangibles, less preferred stock, at liquidation or redemption value. The book value figure, when divided by the number of common shares outstanding, theoretically tells you how much money each share would be worth if the company were to go out of business, liquidate all of its assets and pay off all of its debts. We emphasize the word "theoretically" because if a forced sale occurs, the full value of the assets may not be received. Book value figures can be misleading, but they are just as likely to be understated as overstated. Years of inflation have boosted the value of many assets that are carried on the corporate books at original cost, less depreciation. Real estate is one example of an asset that is likely to have appreciated over the years. Many blue chip companies have large real estate holdings purchased decades ago.

Some investors look at the relationship of a company's price to its book value as an indication of investment value; others dispute the importance of that relationship. They argue that book value figures ignore such intangible assets as a company's good name, the established reputation of its products and services, its marketing expertise, quality of management, earnings potential, dividend growth and other measures of financial performance. Book value reflects only the bare bones worth of a company. While that certainly is true, it is still a useful tool in analyzing stock market values.

Benjamin Graham, the father of modern security analysis, based many of his valuation models and techniques on those relationships. In his books, *Security Analysis* and *The Intelligent Investor*, Graham tells investors to purchase stocks as if they were buying the entire business. He advises buying the stock as close to the net asset value (book value) as possible, and no more than 30% above book value. A company generally becomes overvalued when it is priced 100% or more above book. Therefore, a 30% premium still gives the buyer an attractive profit potential.

When the Dow Jones Industrial Average was undervalued in 1974 and 1982, more than 70% of blue chip stocks were priced at or below book value. The Dow Jones Industrial Average itself was priced below book value. In later years, book value bargains were fewer and farther between. Still, if Benjamin Graham were alive today, these are the ten stocks he probably would buy.

Stock	Price	Book Value	Percent
American General Corp.	26	21	+24%
American National Insurance	52	70	Below
Angelica Corp.	26	20	+30
Ball Corp.	25	23	+ 9
Baltimore Gas & Electric	23	18	+28
Comerica	26	35	Below
Handleman Company	11	9	+18
SCE Corp.	17	3	+30
Texas Utilities	38	30	+26
Woolworth Corp.	19	15	+27

Dividend Yield

We believe that the most important measure of investment value is the dividend yield, which is calculated by dividing the price of the stock into the current annual dividend. For example, if the stock is priced at $20 per share and the indicated annual dividend is $1 per share, by dividing $20 into $1, we find that the dividend yield is 5%.

Because dividends represent current income, many investors base their buying and selling decisions on the dividend yield. Unlike interest income, dividends are alive and can grow over time, thereby increasing a stockholder's income stream and providing support under the price of a stock.

Some investors look for yields that are higher than rates of return in the money market. If CDs or money market accounts are paying annual returns of 4%, they might look for dividend yields of 4.5% or more. Other investors look at historically established yield profiles to determine if a stock should be bought or sold.

Dividend yield provides a valid reason for risking capital in the stock market. Price appreciation is every investor's hope, but dividends provide the reality of a cash return.

There is no one measure of dividend yield at undervalue or overvalue that can be applied to every stock. Consumer products companies generally have higher yields at undervalue and overvalue than companies that deal in electronics or exotic technologies; and growth stocks usually have lower yields at undervalue and overvalue than so-called mature stocks. The fact is that each stock establishes its own profile of undervalue and overvalue and must be evaluated individually.

The Dividend Connection
American Brands
Heinz

Even within the same industry group, profiles of value will differ. For example, in the consumer products industry, American Brands is undervalued when the dividend yield is 8% and overvalued when the yield falls to 3.5%, while Heinz has a profile of value between yield extremes of 4.5% at undervalue and 2.2% at overvalue.

American Brands, Inc. (NYSE:AMB)

A global consumer products holding company, American Brands' businesses include tobacco, distilled spirits, life insurance, home improvement products, office supplies and golf equipment. Cigarette sales provide the largest percentage of profits. Major domestic brands include Carlton, Lucky Strike, Misty, Montclair, Pall Mall and Tareyton. Gallaher Tobacco, the company's international division, is the market leader in the U.K. and Ireland, burning up the competition with its top-selling brand, Benson & Hedges.

Alcoholic beverages distill the second largest share of profits. Major brands include DeKuyper, Gilby's, Jim Beam, Kamchatka, Lord Calvert, Ron Rico and Windsor Canadian. Through its acquisition of Invergorden Distillers, American Brands has become the third largest Scotch whisky company in the world. Its flagship product, Jim Beam, is the world's leading bourbon.

It may seem ironic, but after cigarettes and booze the company's third most profitable division is life insurance. The Franklin Life Insurance Company is one of the most successful insurance groups in the industry, with exceptional ratings for financial strength and stability.

Where there's smoke there's fire, and when it comes to cigarette sales, American Brands has taken its share of the heat. Although the media generate a great deal of negative publicity regarding tobacco

FIGURE 2.1   The Dividend Connection Chart

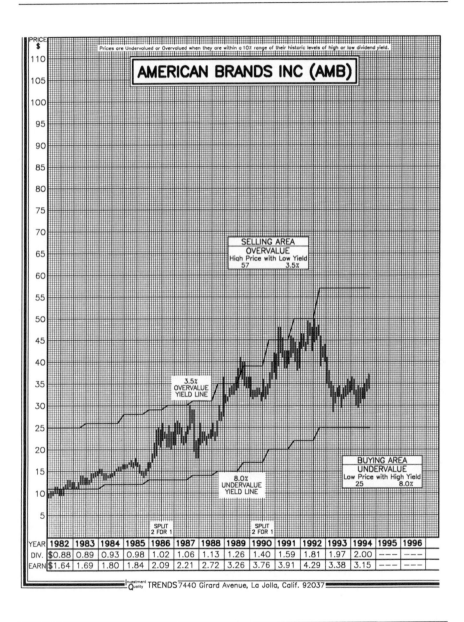

Prices are Undervalued or Overvalued when they are within a 10% range of their historic levels of high or low dividend yield.

AMERICAN BRANDS INC (AMB)

SELLING AREA
OVERVALUE
High Price with Low Yield
57   3.5%

3.5%
OVERVALUE
YIELD LINE

BUYING AREA
UNDERVALUE
Low Price with High Yield
25   8.0%

8.0%
UNDERVALUE
YIELD LINE

SPLIT 2 FOR 1

SPLIT 2 FOR 1

YEAR	1982	1983	1984	1985	1986	1987	1988	1989	1990	1991	1992	1993	1994	1995	1996
DIV.	$0.88	0.89	0.93	0.98	1.02	1.06	1.13	1.26	1.40	1.59	1.81	1.97	2.00	---	---
EARN	$1.64	1.69	1.80	1.84	2.09	2.21	2.72	3.26	3.76	3.91	4.29	3.38	3.15	---	---

Investment Quality TRENDS 7440 Girard Avenue, La Jolla, Calif. 92037

sales, most of the earnings pressure comes from competitive forces within the industry. While American Tobacco holds only 7% of the total domestic market share, its low-priced brands account for 37% of the total industry volume. And even though cigarette smoking is declining in America, worldwide sales are booming. The company's low-tar brands are big sellers in the market segment that would "rather fight than switch"—or quit.

Other Interesting Qualities

- Revenue mix is 56% tobacco, 12% liquor, 10% life insurance, 9% office, 9% home, 5% golf products.

- American Brands is the second largest spirits company in the United States.

- Benson & Hedges accounts for 42% of the U.K. market share.

- Dividends paid since 1905 have been increased in each of the past 28 years.

When this stock is priced to yield 8%, as it was in 1982 and 1985, AMB is undervalued and a purchase is recommended. However, when the price rises and the yield falls to 3.5%, as it did in 1987, 1989 and 1991, AMB is overvalued and a sale should be considered. Even though the price of AMB continued to rise at overvalue from 1989 through 1991, the declining trend that began in 1992 destroyed all of the gain from the previous five years in just six months. This underscores the importance of selling a stock at overvalue. The risk of a severe decline far outweighs the reward of a limited upside potential.

Heinz (H.J.) Company (NYSE:HNZ)

Few products are as inextricably bound to brand-name recognition as Heinz and ketchup. Founding father Henry J. Heinz invented the zesty red condiment in 1869 by adapting and bottling his mother's secret recipe. Considered to be one of the century's marketing geniuses, Heinz promoted his "57 Varieties" using all manner of display advertising. One hundred and twenty-five years later, other widely recognized Heinz brand names include 9-Lives, Ore-Ida, Star-Kist and Weight Watchers. With more than 3,000 varieties, Heinz spreads itself across 200 nations throughout every continent of the globe.

FIGURE 2.2   The Dividend Connection Chart

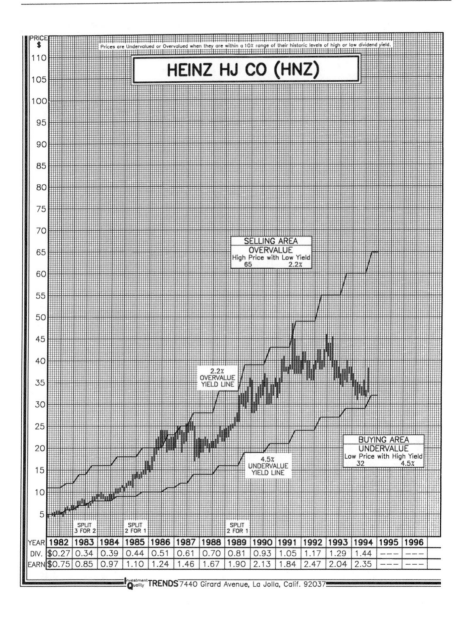

After two decades of expansion, the company has been forced to tighten its belt following weak performance results from the Weight Watchers division. Purchased in 1979, Weight Watchers first succeeded in a decade when thin was in. Nowadays, Americans appear to be more comfortable with their girth. As a result, the entire weight loss industry is thinning out. Still, Weight Watchers is the undisputed heavyweight in its division, accounting for half of the total market share.

The food service division is an unsung hero of the Heinz story. Through acquisition and geographic expansion, the company has created a formidable presence in a market that is growing at about 5% per year. Also adding nutrition to a corporate rebound is the baby food division, with more than $630 million in annual sales worldwide.

Other Interesting Qualities

- Foreign business accounts for 42% of revenues.

- The Heinz family and other insiders control about 30% of the common stock.

- Dividends paid since 1911 have been increased 14 times in the past 12 years.

The chart chronicles the impressive growth of HNZ over the past decade. When this stock is priced to yield 4.5%, as it was from 1982 through 1984, it is undervalued and a buying opportunity is at hand. When the price rises and the yield falls to 2.2%, as it did in 1986, 1987 and briefly in 1991, the stock is overvalued and a sale should be considered. The chart reflects a magnificent total return realized by HNZ shareholders during the past decade. If an investor had purchased shares at undervalue in 1982 and sold them at overvalue in 1991, the capital gain would have been nearly 900%, while dividend growth amounted to 300%. Since then, a worldwide recession has chewed away at the food industry. In 1993, Heinz shares lost about 20% of their value, while comparable stocks in the industry declined 10%. Investors should wait with anticipation for Heinz to reenter the undervalued category, where it offers a delicious investment opportunity.

What Is a Dividend?

How sweet it is. The mail arrives, and there you have it—a check from the company in which you hold stock, the quarterly dividend.

A company ordinarily pays cash dividends to shareholders out of net earnings, after it has met its operating and financial obligations. The dividend is palpable proof to shareholders that their company is making profitable progress. Earnings are figures on a balance sheet, which can be misleading due to tax considerations and extraordinary expenses. But dividends are real money. Cash must be in the coffers for a dividend to be paid.

If earnings are insufficient, a company may dip into its cash flow to meet a dividend payment. However, no company can borrow from cash flow to pay dividends forever. Ultimately, it is earnings that drive the dividend. Dividends also may be paid in the form of additional shares of stock, but the most common form of a dividend is in cash—hence the term *cash payout*.

When a dividend is paid, the price of each share of stock is reduced by the amount of the payout. For example, if a stock is priced at $20 per share, a $.25 per share dividend payout will reduce the price to $19.75. Soon after the dividend payment, the stock generally rebounds to the predividend price.

When a stock dividend is paid, the price is reduced by the amount of the additional shares. For example, if a 50% stock dividend is declared, the price will fall by 50%, but the stockholder then will own twice as many shares. The effect is similar to a two-for-one stock split. A stock dividend does not really improve the value of the holding. A cash dividend does, as it provides a tangible return on the investment dollar.

Some companies have dividend-paying preferred stock as well as dividend-paying common stock. The difference between the two in regard to the dividend is that the preferred stock dividend is fixed, whereas the dividend on the common stock can be increased. However, the dividend on the preferred stock takes precedence over the common stock in case there is difficulty in meeting the indicated payout.

Not all stocks pay a dividend, but most major companies do. Approximately 75% of the companies traded on the New York Stock Exchange pay cash dividends to their shareholders. It is perhaps the most sacred of all corporate financial components, and the measure of value we hold in the highest regard.

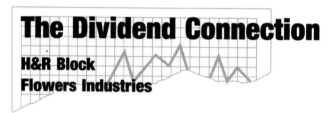

H&R Block and Flowers Industries are highlighted here for their record of hefty dividend increases spanning more than 20 years.

Block (H&R), Inc. (NYSE:HRB)

For nearly 50 years, H&R Block has helped private citizens withstand the scrutiny of the tax man. Its roots stretch back to 1946, when Henry and Richard Bloch opened the United Business Company. In 1955, the partners dropped their bookkeeping accounts to concentrate solely on tax preparation and changed the name to H&R Block. Since then, H&R has expanded to become one of the world's largest tax preparation firms.

In 1980, the company added an important building block to its operations by acquiring CompuServe Inc. The unit consists of three divisions: information services, networking and commercial. The largest division is information, which consists of 2,000 data-bases, on-line discussion forums and relationships with a multitude of hardware and software manufacturers.

Both units (tax preparation and CompuServe) stack up to make Block a formidable worldwide corporation. The tax preparation segment characterizes Block as an industry leader in a mature business. The information services segment exemplifies the company's growth quality and sensitivity to changing trends.

FIGURE 2.3   The Dividend Connection Chart

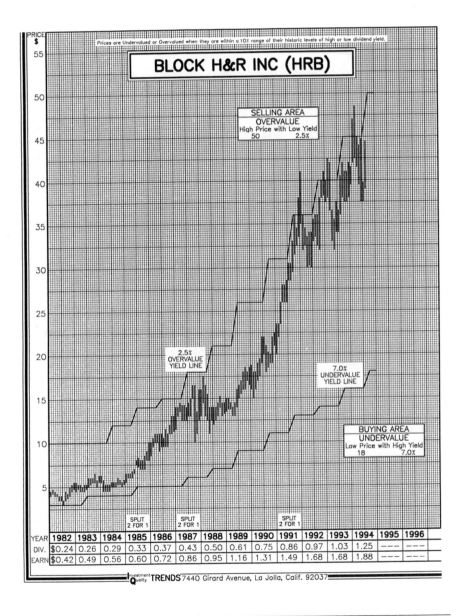

YEAR	1982	1983	1984	1985	1986	1987	1988	1989	1990	1991	1992	1993	1994	1995	1996
DIV.	$0.24	0.26	0.29	0.33	0.37	0.43	0.50	0.61	0.75	0.86	0.97	1.03	1.25	---	---
EARN	$0.42	0.49	0.56	0.60	0.72	0.86	0.95	1.16	1.31	1.49	1.68	1.68	1.88	---	---

Investment Quality **TRENDS** 7440 Girard Avenue, La Jolla, Calif. 92037

Other Interesting Qualities

- Block operates 9,500 company-owned and franchised tax preparation offices worldwide.

- Revenue mix is 62% tax preparation, 35% computer services, 3% financial services.

- Institutions hold 75% of the common stock.

- The company has no debt.

- Dividends paid since 1962 have been increased in each of the past 22 years.

The chart of Block illustrates the vast growth of the tax preparation industry over the past 12 years. When this stock is priced to yield 7%, as it was in 1982 and 1984, Block is undervalued and a purchase is recommended. However, when the price rises and the yield falls to 2.5%, as it did in 1987 and from 1991 to 1994, HRB is overvalued and a sale should be considered. From 1982 to 1994, the price of Block gained 1,500%, while the dividend was boosted by 400%. The chart also illustrates that every time HRB reached its overvalued yield a decline began but was cut short by a dividend increase that raised the relative prices at undervalue and overvalue. Consistent and generous dividend increases add value to the shares of Block and provide ongoing income to its tax-paying shareholders.

Flowers Industries (NYSE:FLO)

Roses are red, violets are blue. The name may be Flowers, but its baking they do. Founded in 1919 as a small, family-owned bakery in Thomasville, Georgia, Flowers Industries has blossomed into a *Fortune* 500 company and one of the largest wholesale bakeries in America. Through acquisitions and expansion, Flowers now delights the palates of customers from regional and national retail food service markets. It provides a wide assortment of fresh-baked and frozen foods, including major brand names such as Bluebird, Cobblestone Mill, Dandee, Danish Kitchens, Dan-Co, European Bakers, Evangeline Maid, Holsum, Nature's Own, Stilwell and Oregon Farm. The Flowers' garden of operations spans 39 profit centers in 16 states.

FIGURE 2.3   The Dividend Connection Chart

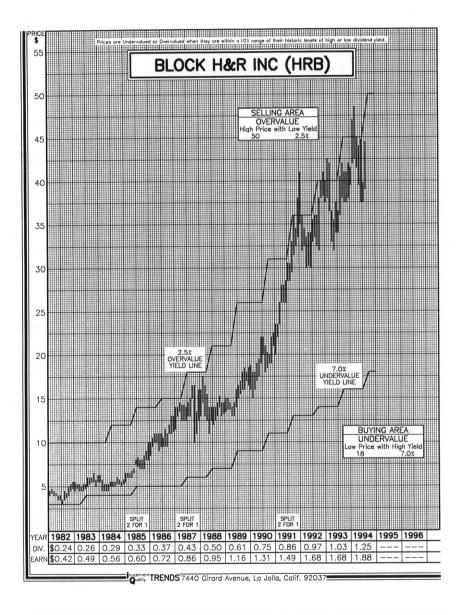

BLOCK H&R INC (HRB)

Prices are Undervalued or Overvalued when they are within a 10% range of their historic levels of high or low dividend yield.

SELLING AREA
OVERVALUE
High Price with Low Yield
50   2.5%

2.5%
OVERVALUE
YIELD LINE

7.0%
UNDERVALUE
YIELD LINE

BUYING AREA
UNDERVALUE
Low Price with High Yield
18   7.0%

YEAR	1982	1983	1984	1985	1986	1987	1988	1989	1990	1991	1992	1993	1994	1995	1996
DIV.	$0.24	0.26	0.29	0.33	0.37	0.43	0.50	0.61	0.75	0.86	0.97	1.03	1.25	---	---
EARN	$0.42	0.49	0.56	0.60	0.72	0.86	0.95	1.16	1.31	1.49	1.68	1.68	1.88	---	---

SPLIT 2 FOR 1   SPLIT 2 FOR 1   SPLIT 2 FOR 1

Investment Quality **TRENDS** 7440 Girard Avenue, La Jolla, Calif. 92037

Other Interesting Qualities

- Block operates 9,500 company-owned and franchised tax preparation offices worldwide.

- Revenue mix is 62% tax preparation, 35% computer services, 3% financial services.

- Institutions hold 75% of the common stock.

- The company has no debt.

- Dividends paid since 1962 have been increased in each of the past 22 years.

The chart of Block illustrates the vast growth of the tax preparation industry over the past 12 years. When this stock is priced to yield 7%, as it was in 1982 and 1984, Block is undervalued and a purchase is recommended. However, when the price rises and the yield falls to 2.5%, as it did in 1987 and from 1991 to 1994, HRB is overvalued and a sale should be considered. From 1982 to 1994, the price of Block gained 1,500%, while the dividend was boosted by 400%. The chart also illustrates that every time HRB reached its overvalued yield a decline began but was cut short by a dividend increase that raised the relative prices at undervalue and overvalue. Consistent and generous dividend increases add value to the shares of Block and provide ongoing income to its tax-paying shareholders.

Flowers Industries (NYSE:FLO)

Roses are red, violets are blue. The name may be Flowers, but its baking they do. Founded in 1919 as a small, family-owned bakery in Thomasville, Georgia, Flowers Industries has blossomed into a *Fortune* 500 company and one of the largest wholesale bakeries in America. Through acquisitions and expansion, Flowers now delights the palates of customers from regional and national retail food service markets. It provides a wide assortment of fresh-baked and frozen foods, including major brand names such as Bluebird, Cobblestone Mill, Dandee, Danish Kitchens, Dan-Co, European Bakers, Evangeline Maid, Holsum, Nature's Own, Stilwell and Oregon Farm. The Flowers' garden of operations spans 39 profit centers in 16 states.

FIGURE 2.4   The Dividend Connection Chart

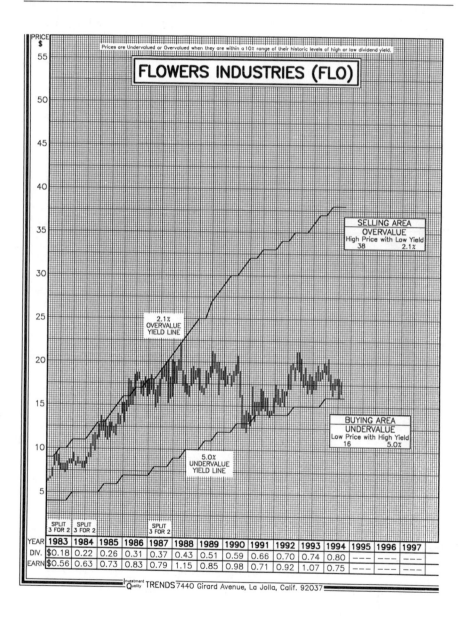

YEAR	1983	1984	1985	1986	1987	1988	1989	1990	1991	1992	1993	1994	1995	1996	1997
DIV.	$0.18	0.22	0.26	0.31	0.37	0.43	0.51	0.59	0.66	0.70	0.74	0.80	— — —	— — —	— — —
EARN.	$0.56	0.63	0.73	0.83	0.79	1.15	0.85	0.98	0.71	0.92	1.07	0.75	— — —	— — —	— — —

Investment Quality TRENDS 7440 Girard Avenue, La Jolla, Calif. 92037

Innovation, efficiency and cost control are the three main reasons why Flowers continues to perform well in the fresh-baked foods business. Flowers entered the frozen foods segment in 1976 with the acquisition of Stilwell Foods. The frozen foods market is highly fragmented, and Flowers has succeeded in battling its competitors with lower prices. As a result, this division has grown at a double-digit pace.

Other Interesting Qualities

- The company owns and operates 34 production facilities.
- Flowers is the fifth largest producer of bakery and snack foods in the nation.
- Debt is only 10% of total capitalization.
- Dividends paid since 1971 have been increased in each of the past 60 quarters.

When this stock is priced to yield 5%, as it was in 1990 and 1991, Flowers is undervalued and a purchase is recommended. But when the price rises and the yield falls to 2.1%, as it did from late 1984 through mid-1988, the stock is overvalued and a sale should be considered. When Flowers reestablished its overvalued yield in 1984, frequent dividend increases continued to raise the price at overvalue, allowing the stock additional headroom for more than three years. Even in October 1987, FLO maintained its price and continued to grow. While there were relatively volatile price swings on a monthly basis, the stock moved mostly sideways for the next two years until it was hit in mid-1990 by the onset of a major recession. In just three months, FLO lost 40% of its value.

With sales growing at an annual 6% rate, FLO should be able to continue its remarkable record of dividend increases. Value-hungry investors are advised to shop for Flowers at undervalue, where the price will bloom and the yield will flourish.

Why Do Companies Pay Dividends?

Companies pay cash dividends because shareholders expect them, even demand them. One might say that the dividend is a cornerstone of capitalism—to pay back profits to shareholders who originally breathed financial life into the company. Dividends also act as an additional inducement to potential investors who are looking for a return on their capital.

Dividends are alive. They grow along with the growth and development of the company. By so doing, dividends can provide ongoing income streams that will help stock owners keep pace with inflation.

Companies that do not pay dividends often claim to need all of their capital to invest in growth. That may be true, especially when a company is just getting started. But if the company has been around for a while and is generating sales, earnings and profits, stockholders will not tolerate that excuse for long. Although stock owners want their company to grow, they also want some spendable return on their investment. Most investors would rather sacrifice a little growth for a little income. Capital gains are in the future and only can be enjoyed after the stock is sold. Dividends are here and now. A bird in the hand is worth two in the bush. That also applies to cash dividends versus capital gains that may or may not materialize.

As the owners of a business, stockholders are entitled to a share of the profits. They are the folks who put their money at risk when the company first came to market. They supplied the capital with which to operate, invest or develop new products and services. Once a company is established in its industry, the owners deserve a return on their investment. Dividends provide that return, rewarding investors for their confidence in the original concept of the corporation and their patience during the company's years of growth and development. An investment that aims only for capital gains is a speculation. A true investment must provide some income. Dividends are the key to satisfying that requirement.

The Dividend Connection
John H. Harland
Johnson & Johnson

Two well-managed companies, John H. Harland and Johnson & Johnson, have not sacrificed dividend in the name of growth. Both have formed strategic alliances with other companies to strengthen their product lines, and both enjoy an impressive record of dividend payment.

Harland (John H.) Company (NYSE:JH)

One thing every business transaction has in common is the paper that binds it. Whether it be a check, contract, clerical form or computer document, Harland supplies the appropriate paper product to seal a deal. As the nation's second largest financial stationer, Harland's primary business is check printing. The Georgia-based company holds 32% of the total U.S. market share, with production facilities in the United States, Puerto Rico and Switzerland.

Although Harland's stock has traded in a relatively narrow range for more than six years, the company moved to repurchase 1.5 million shares of its common stock with a market value of roughly $32 million in 1994. This followed a 3.4 million share repurchase program. The total represented about 5% of Harland's outstanding shares. These repurchase programs bear witness to Harland's confidence that its stock represents excellent value.

Sales in 1994 rose for the 44th consecutive year. Still, earnings were not as robust as expected. In 1994, Harland announced strategic alliances with Telecheck Services Inc., the world's leading check acceptance company, and Cardpro Services Inc., a leading provider of magnetic strip cards. These new affiliations should increase the top line, while ongoing operations will continue to improve the bottom line.

FIGURE 2.5   The Dividend Connection Chart

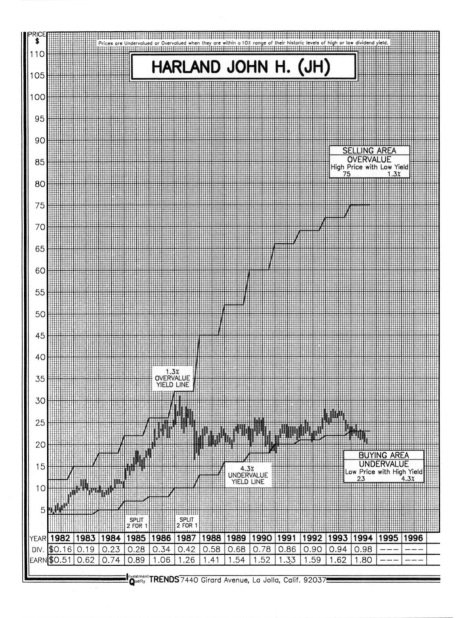

Prices are Undervalued or Overvalued when they are within a 10% range of their historic levels of high or low dividend yield.

HARLAND JOHN H. (JH)

SELLING AREA
OVERVALUE
High Price with Low Yield
75   1.3%

1.3%
OVERVALUE
YIELD LINE

4.3%
UNDERVALUE
YIELD LINE

BUYING AREA
UNDERVALUE
Low Price with High Yield
23   4.3%

SPLIT
2 FOR 1

SPLIT
2 FOR 1

YEAR	1982	1983	1984	1985	1986	1987	1988	1989	1990	1991	1992	1993	1994	1995	1996
DIV.	$0.16	0.19	0.23	0.28	0.34	0.42	0.58	0.68	0.78	0.86	0.90	0.94	0.98	---	---
EARN	$0.51	0.62	0.74	0.89	1.06	1.26	1.41	1.54	1.52	1.33	1.59	1.62	1.80	---	---

Investment Quality TRENDS 7440 Girard Avenue, La Jolla, Calif. 92037

Other Interesting Qualities

- Average annual return on shareholder equity is 21% since 1982.
- Debt is only 6% of total capitalization.
- Directors own about 9% of the common stock.
- Dividends paid since 1932 have been increased in each of the past 41 years.

When this stock is priced to yield 4.3%, as it was in 1982, 1990 and 1992, it is undervalued and offers an attractive buying opportunity. However, when the price rises and the yield falls to 1.3%, as it did from 1986 to 1987, JH is overvalued and a sale should be considered. From undervalue in 1982 to overvalue in 1987, the price of Harland stock appreciated 675% while the dividend rose 165%—an impressive five-year total return. Harland's exemplary record of annual dividend increases bodes well for continued growth of investment income in addition to price protection and long-term capital gains. At undervalue, JH should be able to withstand additional downside pressure while writing its own check for shareholder value.

Johnson & Johnson (NYSE:JNJ)

Serving its customers literally from head to toe with everything from shampoo to athlete's foot powder, Johnson & Johnson reigns as the world's leading manufacturer of health care products. With roughly $14 billion in annual sales, Johnson & Johnson operates 168 companies in 53 nations worldwide. Sales are divided into three segments: consumer (baby care, first aid, toiletries and hygienic), pharmaceutical (therapeutics, contraceptives and veterinary) and professional (medical equipment, surgical products and dental instruments). Some of its leading proprietary products include Band-Aid, Johnson's Baby Shampoo, Modess, Mylanta, Shower to Shower, Stayfree, Sure and Tylenol.

Health care reform tops the list of Johnson & Johnson's investment concerns, and the company is well positioned to adapt to whatever proposals may lie ahead. First, because its pharmaceuticals are so widely diversified, both geographically and in terms of product mix, price limits should have a minimal impact. Second, since only about one-third of its sales are generated by pharmaceutical products,

FIGURE 2.6   The Dividend Connection Chart

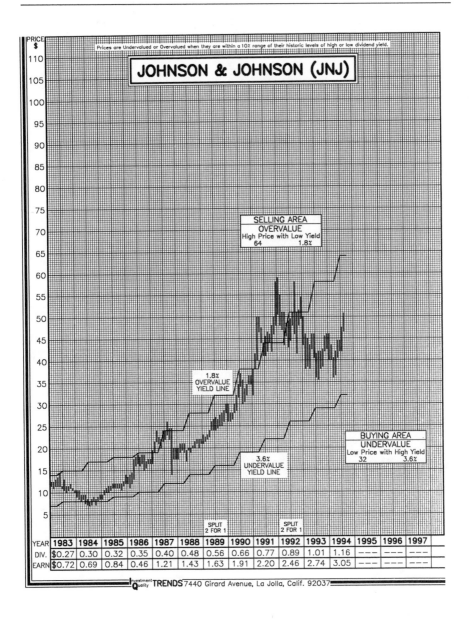

JOHNSON & JOHNSON (JNJ)

Prices are Undervalued or Overvalued when they are within a 10% range of their historic levels of high or low dividend yield.

SELLING AREA
OVERVALUE
High Price with Low Yield
64   1.8%

1.8%
OVERVALUE
YIELD LINE

BUYING AREA
UNDERVALUE
Low Price with High Yield
32   3.6%

3.6%
UNDERVALUE
YIELD LINE

SPLIT 2 FOR 1

SPLIT 2 FOR 1

YEAR	1983	1984	1985	1986	1987	1988	1989	1990	1991	1992	1993	1994	1995	1996	1997
DIV.	$0.27	0.30	0.32	0.35	0.40	0.48	0.56	0.66	0.77	0.89	1.01	1.16	———	———	———
EARN	$0.72	0.69	0.84	0.46	1.21	1.43	1.63	1.91	2.20	2.46	2.74	3.05	———	———	———

Investment Quality TRENDS 7440 Girard Avenue, La Jolla, Calif. 92037

most of its total income will remain unaffected by proposed restrictions. Finally, with Johnson & Johnson's vast commitment to R&D, many new products will enter the pipeline and add to the company's revenues. If anything, J&J is likely to profit from changes in the current system, considering the potential negative impact on smaller companies.

Other Interesting Qualities

- Foreign sales account for 51% of revenues.

- Johnson & Johnson is among the top 20 U.S. corporations in R&D spending.

- Johnson & Johnson entered a joint venture with Merck to develop Dolormin for pain relief.

- Dividends paid since 1905 have been increased in each of the past 29 years.

When this stock is priced to yield 3.6%, as it was in 1984, it is undervalued and a purchase is recommended. However, when the price rises and the yield falls to 1.8%, as it did in 1987, JNJ is overvalued and a sale should be considered. During 1991, the stock penetrated the established yield at overvalue and topped out at a slim 1.5%. A purchase of JNJ at the bottom of the 1987 decline would have resulted in a capital gain of 321% by 1991, while the dividend more than doubled. This A+ quality growth stock meets all six of *I.Q. Trends'* blue chip criteria. With relatively little debt and an abundance of new products in the pipeline, an undervalued purchase of Johnson & Johnson stock will offer value-oriented investors "no more tears."

Why Are Dividends Important?

Don't underestimate the importance of cash dividends. Dividends contribute significantly to shareholder value. When a dividend is increased, the stock becomes more valuable and more highly rated. Conversely, when a dividend is reduced, value is drained from the source of the investment and the stock becomes less attractive to investors.

Dividends not only instill shareholder confidence, they also attract new investors to the company and provide cash rewards that can compensate for the ever-present risks.

Value-oriented investors depend on cash dividends not only to keep pace with inflation and improve their standard of living, but also as an indication of good corporate management. A company that pays cash dividends year after year and increases those dividends regularly is well managed. An ongoing dividend stream proves that a company is generating sufficient capital to cover expenses, pay the interest on its debt and reward its owners. When a dividend is increased, the stock owner knows without reading a balance sheet or an annual report that their company is doing well.

Some investors live or die by earnings reports. Earnings are important, but who knows if the reported earnings are accurate? Earnings can be distorted for income tax purposes. They can be hidden or disguised behind vague bookkeeping terms such as cash flow, depreciation or inventory reserves. A clever accountant can make earnings appear good or not so good, depending on the season or the objective.

There can be no subterfuge about a cash dividend. It is either paid or it is not paid. If it is paid, the shareholder knows that the company is making money. If it is not paid, no rhetoric can disguise the circumstances.

The Dividend Connection

Kmart
Teleflex

Although they serve different markets, Kmart and Teleflex have shown an ability to change in response to new competitive challenges. Both are solid growth stocks.

Kmart Corp. (NYSE:KM)

Attention Kmart shoppers: The second largest retailer in the world continues to build its business by transforming the way America shops. The company's retailing roots began as Kresge in 1899, with the first Kmart store opening in 1962. The company reigned as the world's number one retailer for more than ten years, but for the past three years, its back has been pushed against the wall by its greatest competitor, Wal-Mart.

In the early 1990s, the company embarked on a $4 billion mission to modernize its battalion of beleaguered retail stores. The intent was to enlarge existing stores and upgrade its tarnished dime store image. Results from the stores it renovated are so impressive that the company has started to lift the faces of all the remaining retail stores. The new stores show a 17% increase in sales and a 6% boost in the amount spent per transaction.

Internationally, the company operates stores in Canada and Australia. It has entered the eastern European market by purchasing a 76% interest ($11.8 million) in a Czechoslovakian department store called Maj. It will invest $100 million in the Prague-based chain and plans to buy 11 more stores—five in the Czech Republic and six in Slovakia. These acquisitions offer Kmart a unique opportunity to capitalize on markets formerly closed to U.S. commerce.

Other Interesting Qualities

- There are more than 4,000 retail Kmart outlets.

- Kmart stores account for about 80% of the company's sales.

- Kmart sold 25% of its underperforming units in 1994.

- Net profit margin is a narrow 2%.

- Dividends paid since 1913 have been increased in each of the past 29 years.

Kmart has established yield parameters of 6% at undervalue and 2.5% at overvalue. The chart illustrates an overvalued price in 1986 and 1987 and undervalue in 1982 and 1990. In 1991, KM launched a rising trend that was halted in 1992. This represented a 133% capital gain; the dividend rose 12%. In 1994, while consumer confidence was weak and company focus appeared blurred, KM slipped back to an

FIGURE 2.7   The Dividend Connection Chart

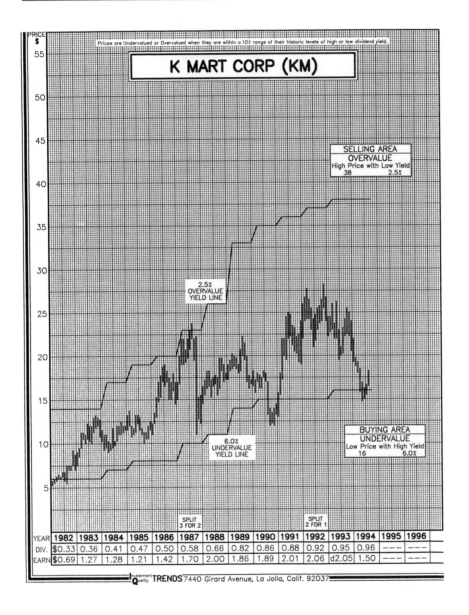

K MART CORP (KM)

Prices are Undervalued or Overvalued when they are within a 10% range of their historic levels of high or low dividend yield.

SELLING AREA
OVERVALUE
High Price with Low Yield
38   2.5%

2.5%
OVERVALUE
YIELD LINE

6.0%
UNDERVALUE
YIELD LINE

BUYING AREA
UNDERVALUE
Low Price with High Yield
16   6.0%

SPLIT
3 FOR 2

SPLIT
2 FOR 1

YEAR	1982	1983	1984	1985	1986	1987	1988	1989	1990	1991	1992	1993	1994	1995	1996
DIV.	$0.33	0.36	0.41	0.47	0.50	0.58	0.66	0.82	0.86	0.88	0.92	0.95	0.96	---	---
EARN	$0.69	1.27	1.28	1.21	1.42	1.70	2.00	1.86	1.89	2.01	2.06	d2.05	1.50	---	---

Investment Quality TRENDS 7440 Girard Avenue, La Jolla, Calif. 92037

undervalued price of $16 per share. With capital expenditures in the rear and increased sales ahead, Kmart should be in the express lane for a profitable future.

Teleflex Inc. (NYSE:TFX)

Founded 50 years ago in historic Plymouth Meeting, Pennsylvania, Teleflex is a leading, modern-day manufacturer of products and services for the automotive, marine, industrial and medical markets worldwide. Operating more than 60 facilities in 13 states and 16 foreign countries, Teleflex bridges its technology throughout North America, Europe and Asia.

The single largest segment is aerospace, for which Teleflex supplies precision controls, coatings, blades and specialized repair services for gas turbine engines. In this highly competitive industry, Teleflex has made an effort to emphasize its commercial businesses over its defense business. Unlike many defense-oriented firms attempting to make the transition into the commercial aerospace arena, Teleflex already is a top gun in this high-flying industry.

Driving the second largest share of profits is the automotive group, which manufactures a number of specialized products such as automatic transmission shifter controls and automotive cable length adjusters. Overseas, Teleflex is involved in a European joint venture that was awarded the transmission controls business for a line of 1997 Volkswagens. Growth in U.S. car production is also adding mileage to company sales.

Because Teleflex has nurtured a diversified portfolio of businesses, it is not so vulnerable to any one external force. Hence, even though the U.S. defense industry is in retreat and the commercial airline industry is largely grounded, Teleflex manages to weather the winds of change.

Other Interesting Qualities

- Sales mix is 30% aerospace, 27% medical, 43% commercial.

- Foreign business accounts for 30% of sales.

- Institutions hold nearly 60% of the common stock.

- Insiders own about 26% of the common stock.

FIGURE 2.8   The Dividend Connection Chart

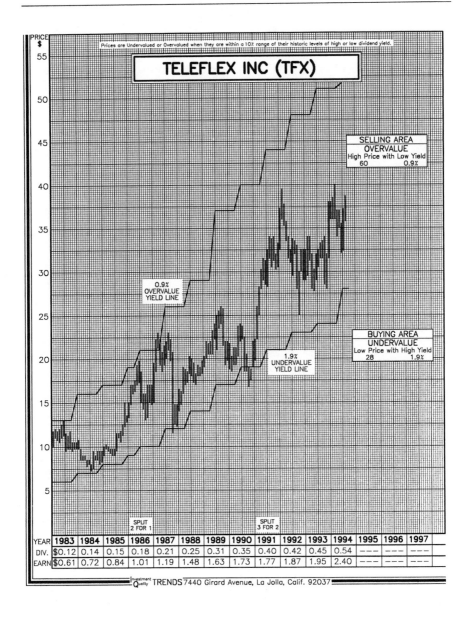

Prices are Undervalued or Overvalued when they are within a 10% range of their historic levels of high or low dividend yield.

TELEFLEX INC (TFX)

SELLING AREA
OVERVALUE
High Price with Low Yield
60   0.9%

0.9%
OVERVALUE
YIELD LINE

1.9%
UNDERVALUE
YIELD LINE

BUYING AREA
UNDERVALUE
Low Price with High Yield
28   1.9%

SPLIT
2 FOR 1

SPLIT
3 FOR 2

YEAR	1983	1984	1985	1986	1987	1988	1989	1990	1991	1992	1993	1994	1995	1996	1997
DIV.	$0.12	0.14	0.15	0.18	0.21	0.25	0.31	0.35	0.40	0.42	0.45	0.54	---	---	---
EARN	$0.61	0.72	0.84	1.01	1.19	1.48	1.63	1.73	1.77	1.87	1.95	2.40	---	---	---

Investment
Quality TRENDS 7440 Girard Avenue, La Jolla, Calif. 92037

• Dividends paid since 1977 have been increased every year.

The chart illustrates the extremely volatile nature of Teleflex. Still, within its wide price range TFX has established a consistent profile of value. When this stock is priced to yield 1.9%, as it was in 1984, 1987 and 1990, it is undervalued and a purchase is recommended. However, when the price rises and the yield falls to 0.9%, as it did in 1983, 1986 and early 1987, TFX is overvalued and a sale should be considered. In late 1990, the stock launched an impressive rising trend but halted 20% short of its overvalued destination.

Although its yield at undervalue is relatively low, Teleflex is a growth stock with a 14% compound annual growth rate over the past ten years. At undervalue, these flexible shares will reward patient, long-term investors.

Comparing the Stock Price to Value

What Is an Undervalued Stock?

"How low can you go?" is the question most often asked of limbo dancers and undervalued stocks.

Undervalue is identified by a relatively high dividend yield that in the past has coincided with the bottom of a major price decline. The term can apply to an individual stock, a group of stocks or the overall market. As an investment tool, it is the green light that signals a buying opportunity.

An undervalued stock should not be purchased without considering other factors. Perhaps there are serious fundamental problems within the company that have forced the price to drop to undervalued levels. Perhaps the dividend is in jeopardy. The reasons why the price of a stock is undervalued should be investigated, especially if the market in general is overvalued. However, if the stock is a blue chip and its dividend is well protected by earnings, at undervalue a purchase merits consideration.

It would be nice if there were one high yield that identified an undervalued price for every stock. Unfortunately, it is not that easy. Each stock has established its own profile of value based on repetitive extremes of high and low dividend yield. Undervalue is not simply a very low price. Rather, it represents a relatively high yield in relation to a currently low price. This makes the purchase of an undervalued stock a bargain—good value and good quality at a low price.

Some stocks are undervalued when their yields are 5% or 6% or 7%. Others may be equally undervalued on the basis of their historic profiles of dividend yield when their yields are 2% or 3% or 4%. The point is that each stock has established its own profile of value, its own individual parameters of dividend yield, and each stock must be evaluated individually.

The identification of undervalue and overvalue based on historic profiles of dividend yield is the basis of our approach to value in the stock market. It is the primary factor by which we determine when to buy and when to sell a stock. It is, in fact, our dividend connection to value.

The Dividend Connection
Knight-Ridder
Upjohn

The following two blue chips are examples of undervalued stocks. Notice that one stock, Upjohn, has a high, 5% yield at undervalue. The other stock, Knight-Ridder, offers historically good value when the yield is 3.5%. At those price-yield levels, these two stocks are equally undervalued according to their individual records of dividend yield. The yields at undervalue and overvalue tend to be repetitive, as the charts clearly illustrate.

Knight-Ridder Inc. (NYSE:KRI)

Catch a ride on the information superhighway and you will be bound to make several stops at the crossroads of Knight-Ridder. The company was formed by a merger of Knight newspapers and Ridder publications two decades ago. Headquartered in Miami, Florida, Knight-Ridder chose a path of diversification in 1983, when it formed

FIGURE 3.1   The Dividend Connection Chart

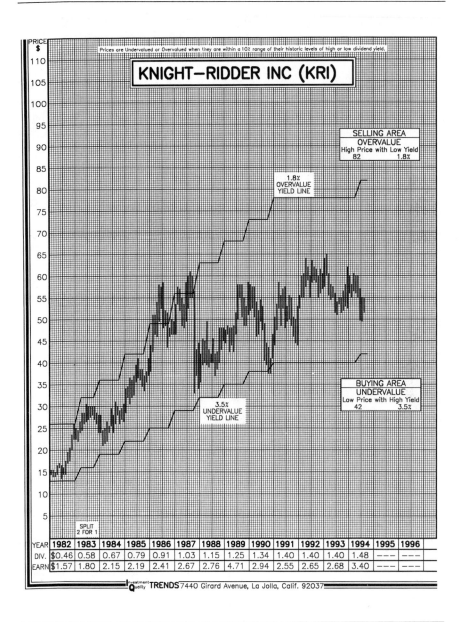

YEAR	1982	1983	1984	1985	1986	1987	1988	1989	1990	1991	1992	1993	1994	1995	1996
DIV.	$0.46	0.58	0.67	0.79	0.91	1.03	1.15	1.25	1.34	1.40	1.40	1.40	1.48	– – –	– – –
EARN	$1.57	1.80	2.15	2.19	2.41	2.67	2.76	4.71	2.94	2.55	2.65	2.68	3.40	– – –	– – –

the business information services division. It moved into the fast lane of that field in 1988, when it acquired Dialog Information Services.

Generating the largest percentage of profits is its newspaper publishing business, with 29 daily varieties in 15 states. Major newspapers include the *Philadelphia Inquirer, Miami Herald, San Jose Mercury News* and *Detroit Free Press*. Knight-Ridder also owns 49% of the voting shares and 65% of the nonvoting shares of the *Seattle Times*.

The business information division comprises three operating groups: Dialog, the world's leading on-line source for global business and professional information, *Knight-Ridder Financial News*, a worldwide provider of immediate and archival financial market news, and the *Journal of Commerce*, which produces printed and electronic data about transportation and world trade.

The next area in which Knight-Ridder plans to scoop the competition is cable transmission. The company has made large investments in cable TV and worldwide media communications. TKR Cable, a fifty-fifty joint venture with Liberty Media Corp., owns and operates eight cable systems in New York and New Jersey. Press-Link, KRI's electronic on-line media services company, broadened its technophonic connections by adding ABC-TV, White House photo office, Standard & Poor's and United Press International to its global network.

Other Interesting Qualities

- Revenue mix is 83% newspaper publishing, 17% business information.
- Labor costs amount to 43% of sales.
- Knight-Ridder has been awarded 62 Pulitzer Prizes.
- Dividends paid since 1941 have been increased ten times in the past 12 years.

When this stock is priced to yield 3.5%, as it was in 1982, 1987 and 1990, KRI is undervalued and a purchase is recommended. However, when the price rises and the yield falls to 1.8%, as it did in 1983 and from 1986 to 1987, KRI is overvalued and a sale should be considered. In 1987, the stock fell 46% to undervalue in just one month. Soon after the October crash, KRI began moving upward, regaining nearly 90% of that loss in two years. Still, the stock has never recaptured its 1987 high, and volatile price swings have crippled the upward momentum.

KRI increased its dividend each year from 1972 to 1992. The payout was unchanged for two years thereafter. The company argued that additional capital was required to fuel internal growth. Happily, dividend growth is back on track, with an increase of 5.7% in 1994. With dividends and earnings in an uptrend as well as steady growth in its core and noncore businesses, a purchase of Knight-Ridder should go to press at undervalue for the promise of a Pulitzer Prize-winning total return.

Upjohn Company (NYSE:UPJ)

Treading on a bridge over troubled water, Upjohn is a world leader in the rapidly changing drug industry. In its 107th year of continuous operation, the company discovers, develops, manufactures and markets human and animal pharmaceuticals as well as specialty chemicals and agricultural seeds. Headquartered in Kalamazoo, Michigan, it has more than 200 manufacturing and sales facilities worldwide.

Eight new FDA-approved Upjohn drugs are an essential part of the company's strategy for new sales growth. Over the past several years, the company has increased its ability to bring new products quickly through the pipeline. The average time to develop a drug from discovery to market now is about 12 months.

For more than 50 years the company has been a major player in the control of infectious diseases. Upjohn scientists now are applying their knowledge to advance the battle against AIDS, with an important new compound currently undergoing clinical trials. New products are contributing a healthy dose of potent profits.

Other Interesting Qualities

- Major products include Cortaid, Halcion, Kaopectate, Rogaine and Xanax.

- Foreign business accounts for 38% of sales.

- Research and development costs amount to 15% of revenues; labor, 24%.

FIGURE 3.2   The Dividend Connection Chart

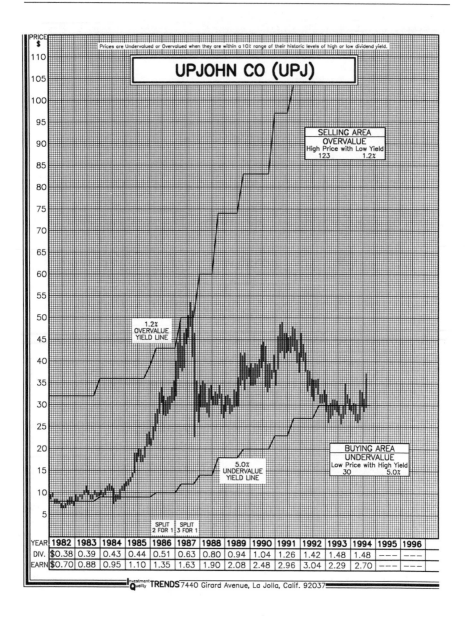

UPJOHN CO (UPJ)

Prices are Undervalued or Overvalued when they are within a 10% range of their historic levels of high or low dividend yield.

SELLING AREA
OVERVALUE
High Price with Low Yield
123   1.2%

1.2%
OVERVALUE
YIELD LINE

5.0%
UNDERVALUE
YIELD LINE

BUYING AREA
UNDERVALUE
Low Price with High Yield
30   5.0%

SPLIT
2 FOR 1

SPLIT
3 FOR 1

YEAR	1982	1983	1984	1985	1986	1987	1988	1989	1990	1991	1992	1993	1994	1995	1996
DIV.	$0.38	0.39	0.43	0.44	0.51	0.63	0.80	0.94	1.04	1.26	1.42	1.48	1.48	---	---
EARN	$0.70	0.88	0.95	1.10	1.35	1.63	1.90	2.08	2.48	2.96	3.04	2.29	2.70	---	---

Investment
Quality TRENDS 7440 Girard Avenue, La Jolla, Calif. 92037

- Dividends paid since 1908 have been increased in each of the past 18 years.

The chart illustrates the vital signs for UPJ. When this stock is priced to yield 5%, as it was from 1982 to 1984 and again in 1993 to 1994, UPJ is undervalued and a purchase is recommended. However, when the price rises and the yield falls to 1.2%, as it did in 1987, UPJ is overvalued and a sale should be considered. An investor who purchased shares of UPJ at undervalue in 1984 and held them to the top of the bull market in 1987 saw a capital gain of 575%. Meanwhile, the dividend rose 244%. The decline from overvalue is attributed primarily to a controversy surrounding Halcion and industrywide political pressure. Now that the industry's worst fears of health care reform have been reduced, most pharmaceutical stocks have started to rebound. Future dividend increases will further extend the upside potential and provide layers of therapeutic safety under the price of Upjohn.

When Should I Sell an Extremely Undervalued Stock?

Rarely is there a valid reason to sell an undervalued stock.

The prices designating undervalue and overvalue are neither exact nor inviolate. They reflect historically repetitive extremes of high dividend yield at depressed, undervalued levels and low dividend yield at inflated, overvalued levels. Prices often violate the limits by a few points, and a stock sometimes moves an extraordinary distance beyond the confines of undervalue or overvalue. As investors well know, nothing restricts price movement within precise frontiers. Logical, psychological and even irrational factors sometimes motivate investors to buy and sell in sufficient numbers to move prices to extremes.

However, in most instances, overvalued and undervalued designations come within 10% of the high or low in a major price move. Therefore, we have determined that prices are undervalued or overvalued when they are within a 10% range of their historic levels of high or low dividend yield.

Current events or extraordinary circumstances sometimes batter a company's stock well below the established parameter of undervalue. The shareholder must then determine why the price of the stock has been so adversely affected. A prolonged period of depressed earnings usually raises doubts in the minds of investors about the safety of the dividend, causing the stock to fall below undervalued price levels. A perceived dividend decrease is often factored into the price of an extremely undervalued stock.

Even when a dividend is omitted, some time should be given for a stock to regain its equilibrium. Once the deed is done, the cloud of uncertainty is lifted, and the stock frequently moves upward. After the rebound, however, a sale should be made because that stock no longer meets the criteria of blue chip quality or long-term investment value.

When bad things happen to good companies, it must be viewed as a buying opportunity rather than a bailout. As long as a stock's dividend is maintained, even an extremely undervalued stock merits investment consideration.

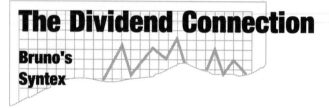

The Dividend Connection
Bruno's
Syntex

The two stocks profiled here, Bruno's and Syntex, illustrate the risk of holding an overvalued stock versus the wisdom of buying or holding one that is undervalued.

Bruno's Inc. (OTC:BRNO)

Bruno's is a leading regional food and drug retailer operating 257 supermarkets in Alabama, Georgia, Mississippi, Florida, South Carolina and Tennessee. Store names include: Bruno's, Consumer Warehouse, Food Max, Food World and Piggly Wiggly. After flourishing throughout the 1980s, Bruno's has tightened its belt as it battles the unforeseen circumstances of the 1990s.

FIGURE 3.3   The Dividend Connection Chart

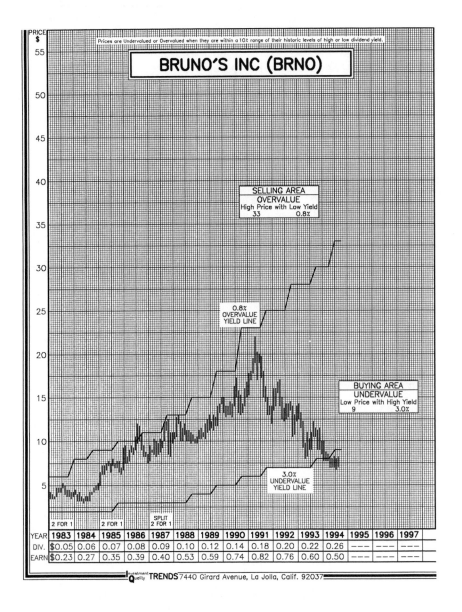

A family-owned and operated business, Bruno's was dealt a devastating blow in December 1991, when an airplane crash killed several key managers, including cofounding brothers Angelo and Leo Bruno. Ronald Bruno, Angelo's son, has served as CEO for the past two years and has fought valiantly to turn the company around. He consolidated southern divisional offices into a single operating unit and streamlined distribution services, resulting in annual cost savings of $5 million.

Nineteen ninety-four marked the beginning of a three-year strategic plan that includes opening 12 to 15 new stores and remodeling 20 existing stores. Still, the trend of its strategy is to scale back expansion. The intent is to focus on bettering the performance of existing outlets, reducing operating costs and paring debt and related interest expenses.

Profitability continues to be a problem as a result of weak regional economic trends and competitive dynamics. The net effect is that of a well-managed company making the best of a difficult economic situation. A more robust economy should produce improved sales, pulling earnings out of deep freeze and into the express lane.

Other Interesting Qualities

- Bruno's has 229 stores in Alabama and Georgia; 28 are divided among the four other states.

- Profit margin is a slim 2%.

- The company is one of the nation's 20 largest supermarket chains.

- Bruno's family owns 10% of common stock; other insiders own 15%.

- Dividends paid since 1974 have been increased every year since they were initiated.

Let's turn to the chart to see the yields this stock produces. A 3% dividend yield identifies historically good value where a purchase is recommended. At 0.8% BRNO is overvalued and a sale should be considered. Frequent dividend increases from 1986 through 1991 continued to boost the price and allowed the stock additional headroom to rise within an overvalued area. Still, extensions of overvalue do not last forever. From an overvalued price peak in 1991, BRNO lost 65% of its value in just two years. That decline destroyed the entire gain that was accomplished over the previous five years.

Syntex Corp. (NYSE:SYN)

Syntex is an international health care company whose stock had been in limbo since 1992. With roots literally reaching to the deepest jungles of Mexico in the 1940s, this manufacturer of prescription pharmaceuticals and diagnostic products initially gained recognition from its use of the native yam plant root. This research and development led to Syntex pioneering a wide range of steroid hormones, including compounds for the treatment of skin disease and the first birth control pill.

There were three major questions on the minds of Syntex investors.

First, they wondered what would happen at the end of 1993, when the company's flagship product, Naprosyn, a nonsteroid anti-inflammatory drug, went off patent? Many other pharmaceutical companies were standing in the wings waiting to capture a share of the market with competitive alternatives. To counter this threat, Syntex applied for and received FDA approval of an over-the-counter version of Naprosyn, developed as a joint venture with Procter & Gamble. The company also developed a generic version of the drug, which enabled it to maintain a significant market share.

Second, investors questioned the strength of Syntex's pharmaceutical pipeline. To address this concern, Syntex changed its research strategy. Rather than develop many new compounds, the company decided to focus on a smaller number of promising new drugs. Four drugs were given priority status.

The final question concerned the safety of the dividend. We saw no reason to abandon our prior recommendation of Syntex as an undervalued stock that simply had become excessively undervalued due to the above concerns. After declining to a price of $13 per share, where the dividend yield was 8%—double the historic 4% yield at undervalue—the payoff came in 1994, when it was announced that the company would be acquired by Roche Holding Ltd. for $24 per share. Needless to say, the announcement delighted Syntex stockholders who had purchased the stock any time in the prior two and a half years. True to management's word, the dividend was not

FIGURE 3.4   The Dividend Connection Chart

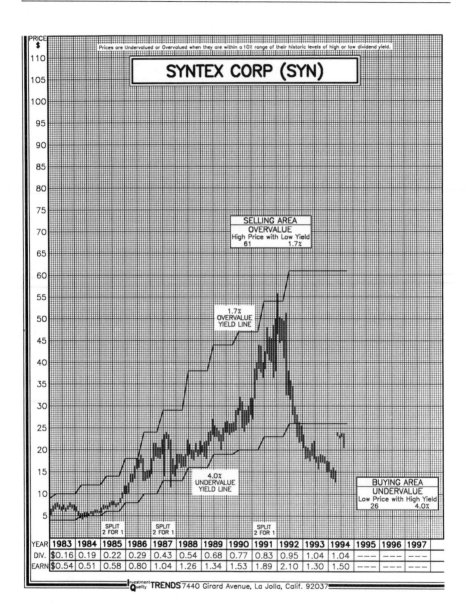

Prices are Undervalued or Overvalued when they are within a 10% range of their historic levels of high or low dividend yield.

SYNTEX CORP (SYN)

SELLING AREA
OVERVALUE
High Price with Low Yield
61   1.7%

1.7%
OVERVALUE
YIELD LINE

4.0%
UNDERVALUE
YIELD LINE

BUYING AREA
UNDERVALUE
Low Price with High Yield
26   4.0%

SPLIT
2 FOR 1

SPLIT
2 FOR 1

SPLIT
2 FOR 1

YEAR	1983	1984	1985	1986	1987	1988	1989	1990	1991	1992	1993	1994	1995	1996	1997
DIV.	$0.16	0.19	0.22	0.29	0.43	0.54	0.68	0.77	0.83	0.95	1.04	1.04	———	———	———
EARN	$0.54	0.51	0.58	0.80	1.04	1.26	1.34	1.53	1.89	2.10	1.30	1.50	———	———	———

Investment-
Quality TRENDS 7440 Girard Avenue, La Jolla, Calif. 92037

reduced, and the over-the-counter version of Naprosyn is meeting with much success.

The chart shows the dramatic impact that fears about Naprosyn sales and weak earnings had on SYN. When this stock was priced to yield 1.7%, as it was in mid-1986 and early 1992, it was overvalued and a sale should have been made. However, when this prime quality blue chip became undervalued, a purchase was in order. There are those who say, "Why buy a stock with problems—isn't that simply inviting trouble?" The other side of that argument is value investing. When stocks are extremely undervalued, an extraordinary investment opportunity may be at hand.

What Is an Overvalued Stock?

Overvalue is identified by a relatively low dividend yield that in the past has coincided with the top of a major rising price trend. The term can apply to an individual stock, a group of stocks or the overall market.

As an investment tool, it is the alarm bell that signals the sale of a stock holding. An overvalued stock can continue to rise, but the upside potential is far outweighed by the downside risk. However, if an overvalued company increases its dividend, the price at overvalue also will rise, creating further room on the upside.

Unfortunately, many investors, perhaps motivated by greed or so-called loyalty, are blinded to the dangers of an overvalued stock until it is too late. An overvalued stock often generates excitement on Wall Street, but by the time good news is out about the rising star, it already has lost its brilliance. That's the time when inexperienced investors rush in where angels and value-oriented investors fear to tread.

A charming story is attributed to Wall Street mogul Bernard Baruch, who narrowly escaped the stock market crash in 1929. Baruch was on his way to work one day in early October of that infamous year when he stopped at a street corner to get his shoes shined. During the exchange, the young man said to the venerable Baruch, "It's a great time to buy stocks." Baruch immediately went to his broker and sold every stock he owned. When asked why, Baruch responded, "By the time a shoeshine boy says to buy, it's undoubtedly time to sell."

Whether the story is fact or fiction, it underscores a basic truth. Investing in the stock market must be based on value, not perception, news or "hot tips." Just as it takes courage to purchase a stock at undervalue, it takes wisdom to sell at overvalue and protect those well-earned profits.

The Dividend Connection
American Greetings
Johnson Controls

The two stocks on the following pages, American Greetings and Johnson Controls, are excellent examples of overvalued situations. Here, too, you will see vastly different profiles of value.

American Greetings (Class A) (OTC:AGRE)

With the appropriate salutation for every occasion, American Greetings is the world's largest publicly owned manufacturer of greeting cards and related products of social expression. Polish immigrant Jacob Sapirstein started his business in 1906 by selling handmade postcards from a horse-drawn wagon in Cleveland, Ohio. The company now produces postcards, greeting cards, gift wrap, specialty boxes and bags, tissue paper, party goods, stationery, calendars, candles, hair accessories and picture frames. Its products are distributed through 97,000 retail stores in 68 countries.

In terms of sales, AGRE runs a close second to privately owned Hallmark, which dominates specialty card stores. AGRE is gaining fast on Hallmark due to the company's top-selling status among mass retail chains. For years, 90% of card buyers purchased their cards from specialty stores. Now, roughly 65% of greeting cards are bought at mass retail outlets.

FIGURE 3.5   The Dividend Connection Chart

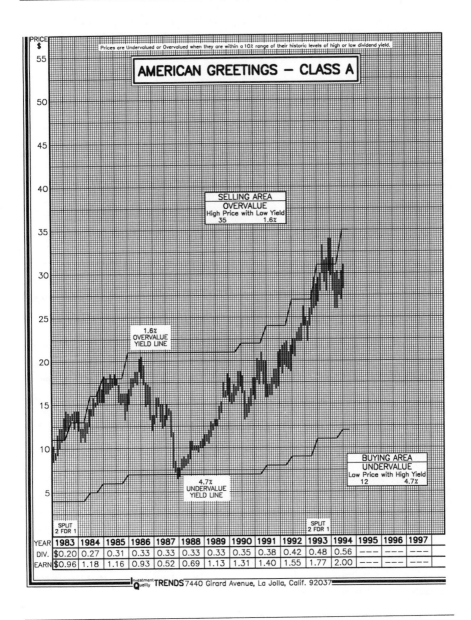

American Greetings – Class A

Prices are Undervalued or Overvalued when they are within a 10% range of their historic levels of high or low dividend yield.

SELLING AREA
OVERVALUE
High Price with Low Yield
35   1.6%

1.6%
OVERVALUE
YIELD LINE

4.7%
UNDERVALUE
YIELD LINE

BUYING AREA
UNDERVALUE
Low Price with High Yield
12   4.7%

SPLIT 2 FOR 1

SPLIT 2 FOR 1

YEAR	1983	1984	1985	1986	1987	1988	1989	1990	1991	1992	1993	1994	1995	1996	1997
DIV.	$0.20	0.27	0.31	0.33	0.33	0.33	0.33	0.35	0.38	0.42	0.48	0.56	---	---	---
EARN	$0.96	1.18	1.16	0.93	0.52	0.69	1.13	1.31	1.40	1.55	1.77	2.00	---	---	---

Investment Quality TRENDS 7440 Girard Avenue, La Jolla, Calif. 92037

The United States is the most important market for American Greetings, followed by Canada, the U.K., Mexico and France. The company is focusing its marketing efforts internationally by printing cards in 16 languages to meet the diverse needs of sentimentalists around the world.

Other Interesting Qualities

• Foreign sales account for 17% of the total.

• Labor and advertising costs amount to 45% of sales.

• Debt is only 8% of total capitalization.

• Insiders control 64% of the votes.

• Dividends paid since 1950 have been increased eight times in the past 12 years.

When this stock is priced to yield 4.7%, as it was in late 1987, it is undervalued where a purchase is recommended. However, when the price rises and the yield falls to 1.6%, as it did from 1983 to 1985 and again in 1993, AGRE is overvalued and a sale should be considered. Although dividend increases supported a rising price trend at over-value, weak value began to take its toll in late 1985 and eventually brought the price to its knees in late 1987.

In 1988, AGRE launched a spectacular rising trend that soared to overvalue by 1993—gaining 385%. A short price decline was touched off in 1994, but the stock remained in overvalued territory. When a declining stock market catches up with this stock, seasons greetings will be in order for an undervalued purchase of AGRE.

Johnson Controls, Inc. (NYSE:JCI)

A global giant in four important business segments, Johnson Controls holds worldwide leading market positions in facilities services and control systems, automotive seating, plastic packaging and automotive batteries. Founded in 1885 in Milwaukee, Wisconsin, Johnson now operates from more than 500 locations worldwide.

The controls segment is a leading provider of facilities management and services to education, health care, office, government, industrial and retail buildings.

FIGURE 3.6   The Dividend Connection Chart

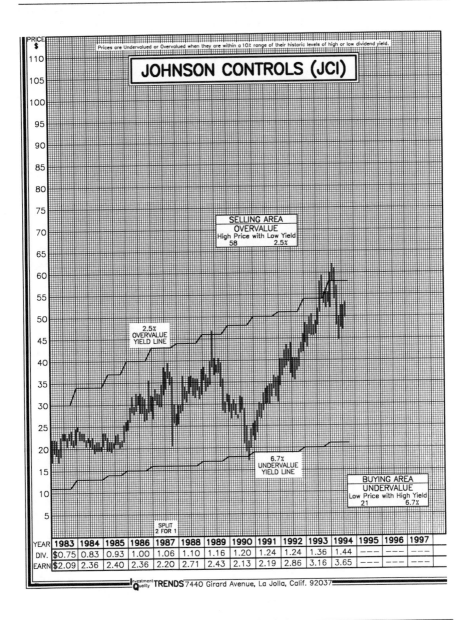

Prices are Undervalued or Overvalued when they are within a 10% range of their historic levels of high or low dividend yield.

JOHNSON CONTROLS (JCI)

SELLING AREA
OVERVALUE
High Price with Low Yield
58   2.5%

2.5%
OVERVALUE
YIELD LINE

6.7%
UNDERVALUE
YIELD LINE

BUYING AREA
UNDERVALUE
Low Price with High Yield
21   6.7%

SPLIT
2 FOR 1

YEAR	1983	1984	1985	1986	1987	1988	1989	1990	1991	1992	1993	1994	1995	1996	1997
DIV.	$0.75	0.83	0.93	1.00	1.06	1.10	1.16	1.20	1.24	1.24	1.36	1.44	---	---	---
EARN	$2.09	2.36	2.40	2.36	2.20	2.71	2.43	2.13	2.19	2.86	3.16	3.65	---	---	---

Investment Quality TRENDS 7440 Girard Avenue, La Jolla, Calif. 92037

Johnson is the world's largest independent supplier of automotive seating systems. Complete seats and seating components are sold to nearly every major automobile manufacturer in the world. About 75% of sales go to North American operations, and the balance is sold to Europe.

Another worldwide leading segment is Johnson's plastic packaging division. The popularity of bottled water represents an excellent growth opportunity for this segment. Plastic packaged juices are another growth area for Johnson, with 2 billion bottles sold annually.

A dependable car battery is a necessity, so Johnson's automotive battery division has a built-in market. It is the largest supplier to the North American auto battery market, providing both original and replacement batteries. Major customers include Caterpillar, Chrysler, Ford, Honda, Mazda, Nisson, Sears, Toyota and Wal-Mart.

Other Interesting Qualities

- Revenue mix is 33% control, 41% seats, 15% plastics, 11% batteries.

- Institutions hold 60% of the common stock; insiders hold 11%.

- Dividends paid since 1885 have been increased in each of the past 18 years.

When this stock is priced to yield 6.7%, as it was in 1990, it is undervalued and a purchase is recommended. However, when JCI is priced to yield 2.5%, as it was in 1993, it is overvalued and a sale should be considered. A fully completed cycle of value may be seen for the stock from 1989 to 1993. During that time, JCI descended from an overvalued price of $47 per share to an undervalued price of $17 per share in just 16 months, illustrating the importance of selling at overvalue. The stock then turned around immediately, but it took more than two years to regain the points it lost. By mid-1993, JCI once again was in overvalued territory. It stayed aloft in overvalue for almost one year, until it began to lose footing in mid-1994. Investors were wise to sell these shares at the top of the market in early 1994, but even wiser to repurchase them when they become undervalued.

Why Should I Sell My Overvalued Stock When It Keeps Going Up?

Although reason generally prevails when it comes to buying an undervalued stock, many investors find it very difficult to sell, even at overvalued levels. After a stock has moved from undervalue to overvalue, increasing a shareholder's income, improving his or her lifestyle, perhaps allowing that person to finance a house, a car or a college education, a bond of loyalty develops that makes the thought of selling the stock seem like an act of betrayal.

This is especially true of conservative, long-term investors who are patient by nature and are more used to buying stocks than selling them. They will look for reasons to hold their stock, even though the price is statistically overvalued. There is no doubt about it. Buying is easy. Selling is hard.

How can an investor overcome the inclination to hold the stock even after it has become overvalued?

The charts in this book offer convincing proof that stocks generally fluctuate between repetitive extremes of undervalue and overvalue—if not immediately, eventually. Unfortunately, once a stock becomes overvalued, there is no way to determine if subsequent dividend increases and economic strength will continue to lift the overvalued price higher and keep the stock in overvalued territory or if the price is due to turn down. Just as some stocks remain undervalued for long periods of time, others linger at overvalued levels for equally long periods of time before the trend is reversed. Still, many stocks do turn down (or up) almost immediately after reaching overvalue (or undervalue).

One way to handle the uncertainty of selling an old friend at overvalue is through the use of a stop loss order placed 12% to 15% below the overvalued price. In this way, the market will decide if a stock should be sold or not. Although you will surrender some profit by subjecting the investment to a stop loss order, there should be plenty of profit to spare. A stock that is purchased at undervalue will gain at least 100% by the time it reaches overvalue. If dividend increases have been frequent, the journey from undervalue to overvalue will be far greater than 100%.

Even if a sale at overvalue proves to be premature, you might feel better if you compare the downside risk at overvalue to the very limited and uncertain upside potential. It really is better to be safe than sorry. Overvalued stocks eventually return to undervalued price levels where they can be repurchased. Meanwhile, the capital can be reinvested in stocks of similar quality but better value. Undervalued stocks already have experienced the historical extent of their bear market declines and are unlikely to fall much further.

Sooner or later, undervalued blue chip stocks rise to overvalued price levels. And overvalued stocks do not remain overvalued forever. At the top of the market in 1987, 40% of our 350 blue chip stocks were overvalued. It gives one pause to know that when the Dow Jones Industrial Average was making new highs in 1990, only 19% of our total still appeared in the overvalued category. And at the market peak in January 1994, with the Dow Jones Industrial Average nearly 50% higher than it was at the peak in 1987, only 24% of our stocks appeared in the overvalued category.

Some investors take a cavalier attitude about such warnings. They say that prices that decline will later rise, and they are willing to ride out the hills and valleys. Well and good; but do they realize how much the ride will cost? A stock that loses 70% of its value must rise vastly more than 70% to make up for that loss. For example, if a stock is overvalued at a price of $50 per share and loses 70% of its value in a declining trend, the price will drop to $15 per share. However, a rise back to $50 per share would represent an up move of 233%. Hence, downside percentage moves are much more devastating than they may appear. An up move of 233% typically takes years to accomplish.

This chapter underscores the importance of continually reviewing one's portfolio to weed out stocks that no longer satisfy the requirements of good value.

Figure 3.7 lists 47 overvalued and declining trend stocks with devastating downside risks of 70% or more.

The Dividend Connection

AAR Corp.
Walt Disney

Let's take a closer look at two declining trend companies from Figure 3.7—AAR Corp., in the aviation industry, and Walt Disney Company, in the entertainment field.

AAR Corp. (NYSE:AIR)

AAR is a leading supplier of products and services to the global aviation industry. The company serves domestic and international passenger and cargo airlines as well as other worldwide aerospace manufacturers. American and foreign governments are among its largest customers. The company's operations are divided into three primary activities: trading, overhaul and manufacture.

AAR's trading activities form a comprehensive worldwide network. The company sells and leases aircraft and engines as well as engine parts and airframe components. Its supply network also distributes a broad line of aviation hardware.

The company's overhaul activities include the maintenance and repair of airframe and engine components such as landing gear, hydraulic systems and control instrumentation. It also provides custom modifications and finishing services.

The manufacturing segment uses advanced concepts and materials to produce specialized aviation components and systems. Primary custom products include cargo systems, containers, pallets and interior design elements. The division also supplies products for the industrial market, which include floor maintenance equipment, industrial handling products and nuclear shielding materials. All three segments are growing at a healthy rate, and AAR's leading industry position attracts major long-term contracts.

FIGURE 3.7   Blue Chip Stocks with Downside Risks of 70% or More (Mid-1994)

Stock	Price	Div.	Yield	Down	Undervalued Price	Undervalued Yield
AFLAC Inc.	31	.40	1.3%	84%	5	8.0%
Alberto-Culver Company	22	.28	1.3	82	4	7.0
Albertson's, Inc.	30	.44	1.5	70	9	5.0
Alco Standard Corp.	55	1.00	1.8	71	16	6.2
Armstrong World Industries, Inc.	54	1.20	2.2	72	15	7.9
Carter-Wallace, Inc.	22	.33	1.5	77	5	6.5
Cooper Tire & Rubber Company	27	.22	0.8	89	3	8.0
Crompton & Knowles Corp.	23	.40	1.7	74	6	6.7
Disney, Walt Company	45	.30	0.7	73	12	2.5
Donaldson Company	48	.56	1.2	71	14	4.0
Dreyfus Corp.	49	.76	1.6	76	12	6.5
Foster Wheeler Corp.	41	.66	1.6	76	10	6.3
Gap, Inc.	47	.40	0.9	72	13	3.0
Gillette Company	64	.84	1.3	81	12	7.0
Great Lakes Chemical Corp.	75	.38	0.5	71	22	1.7
Hannaford Bros. Company	25	.38	1.5	76	6	6.5
Heilig-Meyers Company	33	.20	0.6	76	8	2.5
Hillenbrand Industries	42	.57	1.4	74	11	5.0
Houghton Mifflin Co.	45	.86	1.9	73	12	7.3
Illinois Tool Works Inc.	43	.52	1.2	72	12	4.5
Interpublic Group, Inc.	31	.50	1.6	74	8	6.0
La-Z-Boy Chair	31	.68	2.2	71	9	7.5
Leggett & Platt, Inc.	46	.60	1.3	74	12	5.0
Lowe's Companies, Inc.	65	.32	0.5	83	11	3.0
Manor Care, Inc.	28	.09	0.3	89	3	2.8
Martin Marietta Corp.	45	.90	2.0	76	11	8.5
May Department Stores	43	1.04	2.4	70	13	8.0
McDonnell Douglas Corp.	115	1.40	1.2	73	31	4.5
Medtronic, Inc.	83	.68	0.8	72	23	2.9
Morrison Restaurants	24	.33	1.4	71	7	5.0
Motorola, Inc.	102	.56	0.5	81	19	3.0
Newell Company	40	.72	1.8	78	9	7.7
Nordstrom Inc.	43	.34	0.8	74	11	3.0
Newcor Corp.	63	.18	0.3	79	13	1.4
Owens & Minor, Inc.	24	.21	0.9	71	7	3.0
Reynolds & Reynolds Company	23	.34	1.5	74	6	6.0
Shaw Industries	21	.22	1.0	81	4	5.0
Sherwin-Williams Company	32	.56	1.8	75	8	6.6
Smucker (J.M.) Company	25	.46	1.8	72	7	6.4
Tootsie Roll Industries	70	.38	0.5	89	8	5.0
Tyco International Ltd.	53	.40	0.8	89	6	6.5

FIGURE 3.7   **Blue Chip Stocks with Downside Risks of 70% or More (Mid-1994) (Continued)**

Stock	Price	Div.	Yield	Down	Undervalued Price	Undervalued Yield
UJB Financial Corp.	28	.84	3.0	71	8	9.9
Universal Foods Corp.	34	.92	2.7	71	10	9.0
Valspar Corp.	44	.52	1.2	80	9	6.0
Walgreen Company	41	.68	1.7	76	10	6.7
Whirlpool Corp.	65	1.22	1.9	74	17	7.3
Wrigley (Wm.) Jr. Company	51	.48	0.9	75	13	3.6

Other Interesting Qualities

- Sales mix is 53% trade, 28% overhaul, 19% manufacture.

- U.S. government sales account for 15% of revenues.

- Insiders own 13% of the common stock.

- Dividends paid since 1973 have been increased seven times in the past 12 years.

When this stock is priced in the 6.5% yield area, as it was in 1983, it is undervalued and a purchase is recommended. But when the price rises and the yield falls to 1.3%, as it did in 1987 and 1989, AIR is flying high in overvalued territory and a sale should be considered. The stock experienced outstanding growth from 1983 through 1989 with a capital gain of 825% and dividend increases of more than 100%. While moderate growth was seen from mid-1987 to late 1989, the devastating nosedive of 1990 underscores the importance of selling at overvalue. The AIR crash of 1990 also put a five-year hold on dividend growth, but improved earnings should promote future dividend increases. At undervalue, investors can confidently board AIR before the price again takes flight.

Disney (Walt) Company (NYSE:DIS)

In some ways, Disney's Oscar-winning movie and musical Broadway hit, *Beauty and the Beast*, can be viewed as a metaphor for the parent company. Like the French fable, the company's central character is a

FIGURE 3.8   The Dividend Connection Chart

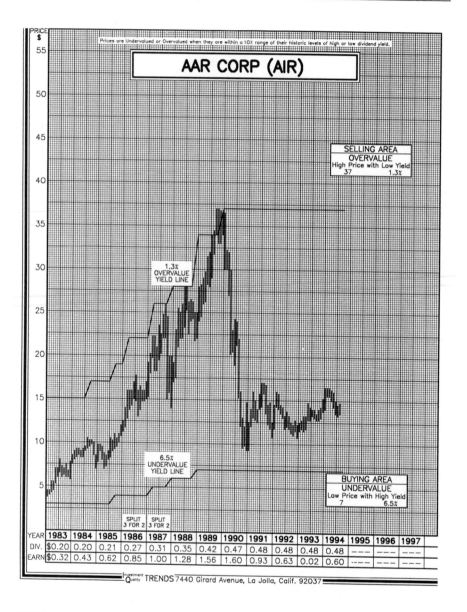

FIGURE 3.9   The Dividend Connection Chart

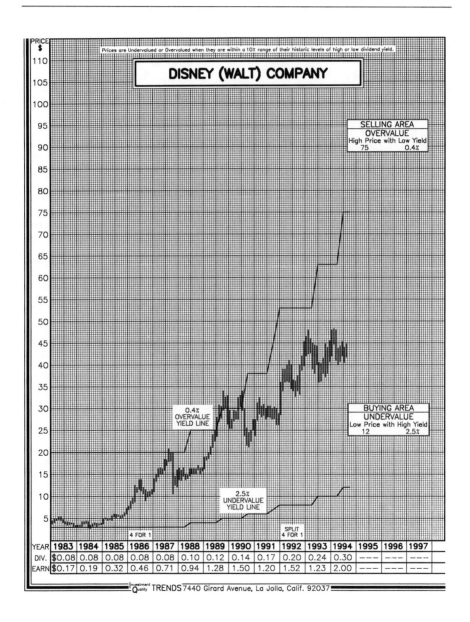

Prices are Undervalued or Overvalued when they are within a 10% range of their historic levels of high or low dividend yield.

DISNEY (WALT) COMPANY

SELLING AREA
OVERVALUE
High Price with Low Yield
75   0.4%

0.4%
OVERVALUE
YIELD LINE

BUYING AREA
UNDERVALUE
Low Price with High Yield
12   2.5%

2.5%
UNDERVALUE
YIELD LINE

4 FOR 1

SPLIT
4 FOR 1

YEAR	1983	1984	1985	1986	1987	1988	1989	1990	1991	1992	1993	1994	1995	1996	1997
DIV.	$0.08	0.08	0.08	0.08	0.08	0.10	0.12	0.14	0.17	0.20	0.24	0.30	---	---	---
EARN	$0.17	0.19	0.32	0.46	0.71	0.94	1.28	1.50	1.20	1.52	1.23	2.00	---	---	---

Investment
Quality TRENDS 7440 Girard Avenue, La Jolla, Calif. 92037

presence bigger than life. Like the fairy tale, Disney operates in an enchanted world of make believe. And, perhaps most important, the moral of both is that true value must be found from within. Disney is a leading worldwide entertainment business that owns and operates theme parks, motion picture studios, TV networks, retail stores, Broadway theatre properties and a National Hockey League team. The company's history parallels that of its timeless mascot, Mickey Mouse, who is nearly 70 years old. Mickey-licensed merchandise set all-time records in 1994.

A dozen years ago, Disney's movie production was pushed to the bottom of its industry, but its box office receipts have topped the competition in five of the past six years. *Beauty and the Beast* started a string of full-length animated blockbusters. It was followed in 1993 by *Aladdin*, the top-grossing animated film of all time. Then came *The Lion King* which captured the throne of 1994 animated film revenues. One potential threat to Disney's continued dominance in the movie business comes from the recent resignation of studio chairman Jeffrey Katzenberg, who is considered to be the genie in Disney's lamp of success. In a bid to seize more power from reining CEO Michael Eisner, Katzenberg negotiated himself out of a job. This could be even worse news for Disney, since Katzenberg is considered to be the genie in Disney's lamp of success.

Everything Disney touches seems to turn to gold, but that is not true in Toontown. Attendance at the California theme park was down significantly in 1994, and after completing its first full year of operation in France, Euro Disney results were disastrous. Still, the theme parks are at the top of the Matterhorn of Disney revenues.

Other Interesting Qualities

- Disney's *Beauty and the Beast* broke all sales records in its New York debut.

- *Home Improvement, Blossom, Empty Nest* and *Nurses* all are top-rated Disney TV shows.

- Disney has produced the five top-grossing home videos of all time.

- Dividends paid since 1957 have been increased seven times in the past 12 years.

When this stock is priced to yield 2.5%, as it was in 1983 and 1984, it is undervalued and a purchase is recommended. But when the price rises and the yield falls to 0.4%, as it did in 1987 and 1989, DIS is overvalued and a sale should be considered. The stock's slim yield at overvalue is enough to make any income-oriented investor grumpy. When the roller coaster on Wall Street brings it back to undervalue, investors are encouraged to purchase shares of Disney for much more than a Mickey Mouse return.

Do Interest Rates Affect Yields at Undervalue and Overvalue?

Surprisingly, changes in interest rates have very little effect on the established yield parameters at undervalue and overvalue—for most stocks. They do, however, affect so-called interest-sensitive securities such as banks, insurance companies and utilities.

When interest rates rose to historically high levels in 1973 and 1981, interest-sensitive stocks declined to prices that produced new levels of high dividend yield, breaking through previously established yield lines at undervalue. We represent this by identifying three significant yield levels on the charts that illustrate these stocks. Generally, when interest rates are high, the price of interest rate-sensitive stocks will fall to extraordinarily high yields, which are identified on those charts. When interest rates are in a low range (3% to 6%), the prices of these stocks fluctuate within the normal parameters of undervalue and overvalue.

History has shown that the established profiles of dividend yield at undervalue and overvalue for most stocks are relatively stable, regardless of fluctuations in money rates. In determining yield parameters at undervalue and overvalue, we research the dividend yield history for each stock as far back as there is available data. Our informational journey covers a minimum of 25 years and sometimes extends back to the turn of the century. The fact that these yields are repetitive throughout all economic cycles and interest rate changes validates them as accurate measures of investment value.

There are some aberrations that may violate our established parameters of undervalue and overvalue, but interest rate swings are not usually among them.

The Dividend Connection

IPALCO
Millipore

IPALCO and Millipore illustrate both conditions. The first is a utility stock that has established a three-tiered profile of value. The second is an industrial stock that weathered the vicissitudes of fluctuating interest rates but held fast to its long-standing profile of value.

IPALCO Enterprises (NYSE:IPL)

In its 68th year of continuous operation, IPALCO's core business, Indianapolis Power & Light, provides electric and steam utility service to about 400,000 customers in Indianapolis and Marion County. IPALCO also owns Mid-America Capital Resources, Inc., a holding company for nonregulated operations, including Mid-America Energy Resources and Cleveland Energy Resources.

Due largely to effective cost-control efforts, IPL's rates are among the lowest in the nation. The company plans to remain a low-cost producer and to compete with independent power producers, cogenerators and other utilities. Growth in IPALCO's region continues to outpace the nation's and supports the company's strategy. IPALCO is seeking to expand its business by pursuing new, nonregulated energy products and services that have the potential to produce even greater returns than its electric utility operations. And even though IPALCO charges customers some of the lowest rates in the nation, its profit margin remains ample.

Other Interesting Qualities

- Revenue mix is 95% electricity, 5% steam.
- Electric mix is 35% residential, 33% industrial, 31% commercial, 1% other.
- Generating sources are 99% coal, 1% oil.

FIGURE 3.10   The Dividend Connection Chart

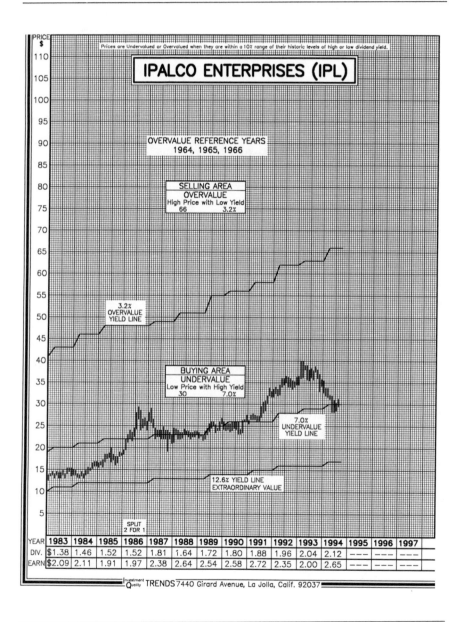

IPALCO ENTERPRISES (IPL)

Prices are Undervalued or Overvalued when they are within a 10% range of their historic levels of high or low dividend yield.

OVERVALUE REFERENCE YEARS
1964, 1965, 1966

SELLING AREA
OVERVALUE
High Price with Low Yield
66   3.2%

3.2%
OVERVALUE
YIELD LINE

BUYING AREA
UNDERVALUE
Low Price with High Yield
30   7.0%

7.0%
UNDERVALUE
YIELD LINE

12.6% YIELD LINE
EXTRAORDINARY VALUE

SPLIT
2 FOR 1

YEAR	1983	1984	1985	1986	1987	1988	1989	1990	1991	1992	1993	1994	1995	1996	1997
DIV.	$1.38	1.46	1.52	1.52	1.81	1.64	1.72	1.80	1.88	1.96	2.04	2.12	---	---	---
EARN	$2.09	2.11	1.91	1.97	2.38	2.64	2.54	2.58	2.72	2.35	2.00	2.65	---	---	---

Investment
Quality TRENDS 7440 Girard Avenue, La Jolla, Calif. 92037

- IPALCO's equity ratio is 53%, substantially higher than the industry average.

- Dividends paid since 1938 have been increased 15 times in the past 16 years.

When this stock is priced to yield 7%, as it was from 1987 through 1990, it is undervalued and represents an attractive buying opportunity. IPL established its overvalued yield at 3.2% in the mid-1960s, when virtually all electric utilities stocks were selling at top prices. The chart also reveals the "extraordinary yield" of 12.6%, present from 1983 through 1984. That yield is unlikely to be seen again until interest rates return to historically high levels. However, a 7% yield at undervalue appears sustainable under normal circumstances.

IPALCO has a long tradition of producing superior returns for its investors. The dividend has been increased nearly 5% each year during the past decade. Over the past five years, the average annual total return has been more than 18%. At undervalue, IPL offers a high-voltage investment opportunity, regardless of fluctuating interest rates.

Millipore Corp. (NYSE:MIL)

When patients report to the hospital with a strange disease contracted by contaminants in the local drinking water, where do scientists turn for answers? They turn to Millipore, the world's leading supplier of products used to separate, analyze and purify fluids. This is just one critical application in a wide range of industries that rely on the $3.5 billion multinational company for support. Pharmaceutical, environmental, microelectronics, health care, food, beverage and a host of other markets all are served by Millipore's technology. Headquartered in Bedford, Massachusetts, the company has 12 manufacturing sites in 31 nations.

AIDS and HIV-related diseases have sparked a revolution in the field of vaccine development. Millipore scientists are now designing strategies for promising antiviral therapies. This, along with Millipore's already leading chromatography segment, adds up to exciting innovation in an area of health care, that has long awaited some meaningful strains of hope.

FIGURE 3.11   The Dividend Connection Chart

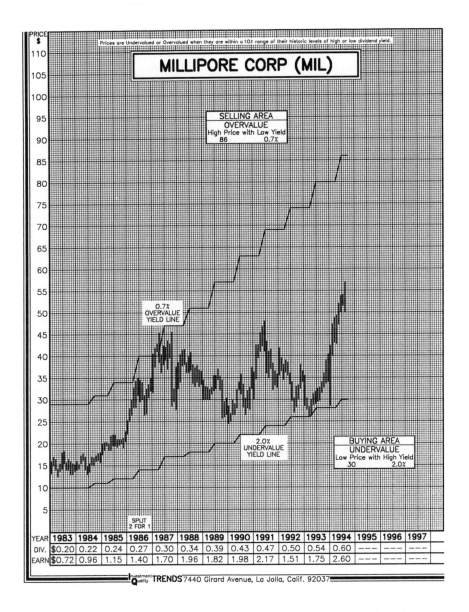

The focus is on the future. Untapped and developing market opportunities hold the greatest hope for Millipore's progress. Even though health care sales have been weak, industry trends prescribe an increased need for the company's pharmaceutical technology. Bioscience is another major market opportunity for Millipore's products and research. The company has seeded significant investments in this area, and it expects a harvest in the future.

Other Interesting Qualities

- Sales mix is 70% food, drug and chemical; 22% government and universities; 8% medical.

- Foreign sales account for 63% of revenues.

- Labor costs account for 25% of sales; research and development, 9%.

- Dividends paid since 1966 have been increased in each of the past 22 years.

When MIL is priced to yield 1.7%, as it was in 1992 and 1993, it is undervalued and a purchase is recommended. However, when the price rises and the yield falls to 0.7%,as it did in 1986 and 1987, MIL is overvalued and a sale should be considered. In 1990, the stock launched a rising trend from an undervalued price of $24 per share. The trend halted 18 months later at a price of $48 per share when the ravages of a worldwide recession began taking its toll on the fluid purification industry. MIL became undervalued in 1992 but almost immediately bounced back into a rising trend. Still, weak foreign markets depressed MIL back into undervalued territory. The relatively slim yield of 1.7% looks more attractive when one considers the dividend growth record—a compound average annual rate of 11% over the past decade. At undervalue, MIL should rise to the top of investment considerations.

The Dividend Connection

How Do Dividends Connect with Stock Prices?

The oldest cliche in the stock market is Baron Rothschild's advice to investors, "Buy low and sell high." But how do we know when a stock is priced low or high? What determines the relative measures of high and low in the stock market?

In fact, Rothschild did not tell investors to buy low and sell high. What he said was, "Buy cheap and sell dear," advice that has been misquoted for many years. While the words "low" and "high" by themselves have little meaning in the stock market, the words "cheap" and "dear" are relative terms that refer to value. Investors who follow Rothschild's advice to buy cheap and sell dear understand the meaning of the market.

Dividends connect with stock prices in specific ways. In addition to providing income, they are the most reliable tool by which value is measured. By dividing the current price of a stock into the annual dividend, we can determine the dividend yield. And by relating the dividend yield to the high and low yields that have occurred repeatedly at peaks and valleys in the price cycle of that stock, we can determine whether the current price is cheap or dear.

For example, suppose that a stock priced at $30 per share pays a dividend of $1.50 per share. By dividing 30 into 1.50, we see that the current dividend yield is 5%. If that 5% yield repeatedly has marked a low point in the price trend of the stock in question, we know it is cheap and historically good value is available. When that dividend is increased, the value of the stock rises.

Using this same example, if research shows that a 2.5% yield has occurred repeatedly at the top of a rising price trend after which the stock has declined, we can assume that a 2.5% dividend yield identifies an overvalued area in which a sale should be considered. If the dividend is increased, thus raising the prices at undervalue and overvalue, the stock will be given more headroom and a decline can be averted.

The strong dividend connection to stock prices also is evidenced in other ways. We know that when a dividend is increased, the value of the stock rises. A rising price trend is supported and in fact inspired by frequent dividend increases. However, when a dividend is cut, the price of a stock generally falls as the value of the holding is reduced. Even the suggestion that a dividend may be lowered will result in a declining price, as investors anticipate a loss of value.

When the dividend yield is historically high, the price will be low, the stock will be cheap, and a purchase can be made. But when the dividend yield is historically low, the price will be high, the stock will be dear, and a sale should be made.

The Dividend Connection

Avery Dennison
Handleman

The following two stocks illustrate the connection between price trends and dividend increases.

Avery Dennison Corp. (NYSE:AVY)

It truly can be said that Avery Dennison has succeeded because of its stick-to-itiveness. A leading producer of self-adhesive materials, tapes, labels and office supplies, the company is the result of a merger

FIGURE 4.1   The Dividend Connection Chart

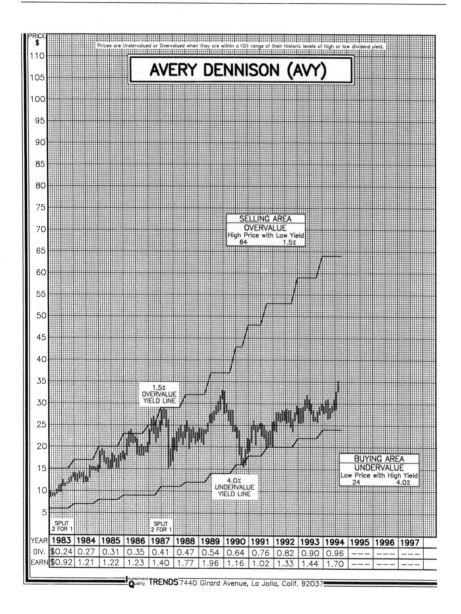

PRICE $

AVERY DENNISON (AVY)

Prices are Undervalued or Overvalued when they are within a 10% range of their historic levels of high or low dividend yield.

SELLING AREA
OVERVALUE
High Price with Low Yield
64   1.5%

1.5%
OVERVALUE
YIELD LINE

BUYING AREA
UNDERVALUE
Low Price with High Yield
24   4.0%

4.0%
UNDERVALUE
YIELD LINE

SPLIT 2 FOR 1

SPLIT 2 FOR 1

YEAR	1983	1984	1985	1986	1987	1988	1989	1990	1991	1992	1993	1994	1995	1996	1997
DIV.	$0.24	0.27	0.31	0.35	0.41	0.47	0.54	0.64	0.76	0.82	0.90	0.96	---	---	---
EARN	$0.92	1.21	1.22	1.23	1.40	1.77	1.96	1.16	1.02	1.33	1.44	1.70	---	---	---

Investment Quality **TRENDS** 7440 Girard Avenue, La Jolla, Calif. 92037

between Avery International and Dennison Manufacturing in 1990. Although the timing of the merger on the eve of a major recession may not have been ideal, most of the restructuring goals have been met, and Avery Dennison has emerged as one of the top three companies in its industry with worldwide operations in more than 30 nations.

In a culture that demands quick response, Avery Dennison has shortened its product development cycle. By using time-saving methods developed over the past few years, the company's Fasson Films division sealed a major Sony Music contract to develop new labeling equipment. It landed the job by guaranteeing Sony a 50% faster delivery than any other vendor. With the sticky task of restructuring nearly completed, Avery Dennison achieved solid growth in 1994.

Other Interesting Qualities

- Sales mix is 50% pressure-sensitive materials, 20% office products, 22% product identification tags.

- Foreign business accounts for about 40% of sales.

- The Avery Dennison merger cost nearly $86 million in pretax charges.

- Dividends paid since 1942 have been increased in each of the past 12 years.

Since Avery International was the dominant company in the merger, commanding nearly three times as many common shares as Dennison, the stock's current profile of value is seen through the history of Avery. When AVY is priced to yield 4%, as it was in 1990 and 1991, it is undervalued and a purchase is recommended. However, when the price rises and the yield falls to 1.5%, as it did from 1985 through the top of the bull market in 1987, AVY is overvalued and a sale should be considered.

Both Avery and Dennison had constructed an excellent history of dividend growth. In the case of Avery, a purchase at undervalue ten years ago would be yielding more than 16% on the original investment capital. Dennison, which was also a blue chip for many years, experienced dividend growth of 70% during the decade prior to the merger. As capital improvement and productivity enhancement programs are completed, earnings should rise substantially. At undervalue, we label Avery Dennison an excellent choice for long-term investment growth.

Handleman Company (NYSE:HDL)

From humble beginnings as a family-owned health and beauty aids company, Handleman has grown steadily over the past 60 years to become the largest and most successful provider of compact discs, music cassettes, videos, books and personal computer software to North America's largest retailers. Some major artist properties include Mariah Carey, Whitney Houston, Janet Jackson and Travis Tritt. Popular videos include *Free Willy, Home Alone 2, Mrs. Doubtfire, Aladdin* and *The Fugitive*. Best-selling books include *The Client, Jurassic Park* and *Without Remorse*. Software packages include MS DOS, Quicken, Mortal Kombat and 3D Home Designer. Now celebrating its diamond anniversary, the company has achieved profitability in each of its 60 years of business.

Historically, the company's two largest accounts have been Kmart and Wal-Mart. Together, these two customers generate roughly 60% of total sales. Still, with the dominance of these and other mass merchants, it is getting harder for Handleman to turn a buck from its shrinking profit margins. Therefore, the company is focusing more of its attention on CD disc production. This represents an important investment for Handleman, since CDs sell for higher prices than cassettes and carry high gross margins.

Geographic diversification and international growth are two important themes of Handleman's strategic melody. In Mexico, a distribution center was opened in 1994. The facility serves the two largest Kmart stores in that country. In the U.K., the company has entered into a joint venture with VCI—that nation's second largest distributor of video products.

Other Interesting Qualities

- Sales mix is 56% music, 34% videos, 6% books, 4% software.
- Handleman services 20,700 retail departments.
- Institutions hold 70% of the common stock.

FIGURE 4.2   The Dividend Connection Chart

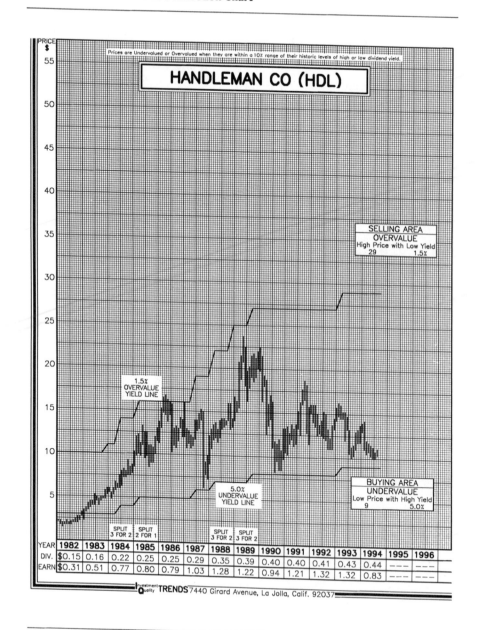

Prices are Undervalued or Overvalued when they are within a 10% range of their historic levels of high or low dividend yield.

HANDLEMAN CO (HDL)

SELLING AREA
OVERVALUE
High Price with Low Yield
29   1.5%

1.5%
OVERVALUE
YIELD LINE

5.0%
UNDERVALUE
YIELD LINE

BUYING AREA
UNDERVALUE
Low Price with High Yield
9   5.0%

YEAR	1982	1983	1984	1985	1986	1987	1988	1989	1990	1991	1992	1993	1994	1995	1996
DIV.	$0.15	0.16	0.22	0.25	0.25	0.29	0.35	0.39	0.40	0.40	0.41	0.43	0.44	---	---
EARN	$0.31	0.51	0.77	0.80	0.79	1.03	1.28	1.22	0.94	1.21	1.32	1.32	0.83	---	---

SPLIT 3 FOR 2   SPLIT 2 FOR 1   SPLIT 3 FOR 2   SPLIT 3 FOR 2

Investment Quality **TRENDS** 7440 Girard Avenue, La Jolla, Calif. 92037

- Dividends paid since 1963 have been increased ten times in the past 12 years.

The chart illustrates the volatile nature of the entertainment industry. When this stock is priced to yield 5%, as it was in 1987 and 1990, it is undervalued and faithfully stages a comeback. However, when the price rises and the yield falls to 1.5%, as it did in 1986 and 1989, HDL is overvalued and a sale should be considered. A classic portrait of the stock's value cycle can be seen from 1987 to 1990. In November 1987, HDL launched a rising trend from undervalue, gaining 300% to overvalue in mid-1989. The stock then made an about-face and lost almost all of its gain, back to undervalue one year later. Another rising trend was launched but halted far short of its upside objective in late 1991. Thereafter, HDL played a melancholy tune. At undervalue, Handleman represents "solid gold" investment opportunity.

What Is the Dividend Yield–Total Return Approach?

Dividends provide a springboard to value in the stock market; and dividend yield is the tool we use to identify attractive buying and selling areas. The term *total return* refers to the combination of dividends and capital gains.

It seems so elementary, but it bears repeating—the only reason why capital is put at risk in any investment vehicle is the opportunity of getting a return on one's investment dollar. In the real estate market, that return takes the form of rent plus long-term capital gains. In the money market, the return is interest paid on bonds or cash equivalents, with very little opportunity for growth of capital and virtually no chance for growth of investment income.

The stock market offers current income plus growth of dividend income plus capital gains. The combination of good value plus attractive long-term investment growth potential is the object of the dividend yield–total return approach.

After many years of witnessing the apparently irrational behavior of the stock market, we have observed some truths to be absolute. One of those truths was best said by Charles Dow, founder of *The Wall Street Journal* and creator of the popular Dow Jones averages: "To know values is to know the meaning of the market."

No one will disagree with that. But just how does one identify value in the stock market? How does an investor know when a stock is undervalued where it can be bought, or overvalued where it should be sold? After all, one investor's idea of good value may be mere speculation to another. For the answer to that question, we look again to the unique barometer of dividend yield.

When all other factors that rate analytical consideration have been digested, the underlying value of dividends, which determines yield, will in the long run also determine price. The key to value, therefore, lies in yield as reflected by the dividend trend. History shows that individual stock prices fluctuate between repetitive extremes of high dividend yield and low dividend yield. These recurring extremes of yield establish what is identified as undervalued and overvalued price levels. When a dividend is raised, the prices at undervalue and overvalue are raised automatically to continue reflecting the histori-cally established yield extremes. Each stock has its own distinctive high and low profile of yield and must be evaluated individually.

If a major rising price trend has ended in a 2% yield area many times, and a major declining price trend repeatedly has ended in a 5% yield area, a profile of value has been established for that stock. In this case, a 2% dividend yield identifies a historically overvalued price where the stock should be sold to preserve capital and protect profits. Conversely, when that stock is priced to yield 5%, it is histori-cally undervalued and a good buying opportunity is at hand.

Thus, a long-term investment strategy comes to light. It is an illuminating concept that offers outstanding potential for growth of capital and growth of dividend income with minimal downside risk.

This approach combines the two most important components of investment value: dividend yield plus the potential for long-term capital gains. Together, this one-two punch of investment power equals the objective of a rewarding total return.

The Dividend Connection

Bristol-Myers Squibb
Longs Drug Stores

Bristol-Myers Squibb and Longs Drug Stores exemplify the dividend yield–total return approach.

Bristol-Myers Squibb Company (NYSE:BMY)

Weighing in as the third largest pharmaceutical company in the world, Bristol-Myers Squibb markets an arsenal of top-selling prescription drugs, over-the-counter products, medical devices, beauty aids and infant formula. Resulting from a merger of two pharmaceutical giants in 1989, the company boasts a medicine chest full of popular brand names including Ban, Bufferin, Clairol, Comtrex, Excedrin, Fisherman's Friend, Gerber, Mum, Nice 'n Easy, NoDoz and Sea Breeze. In medical facilities throughout the world, doctors fill their prescription pads with Bristol-Myers' patented pharmaceuticals for cardiovascular, cancer, infectious disease, central nervous system and dermatological therapies.

The biggest challenge facing drug companies is the perceived threat of health care reform. The truth of the matter is that prescription drugs account for only a small fraction of America's total health care bill. Consequently, few controls, if any, are likely to be imposed in this area of vital public importance.

The company's cancer drug, Taxol, received FDA approval in 1994 for use in the treatment of breast cancer. The drug already had been used to treat ovarian cancer. Studies have shown that Taxol significantly reduces or eliminates 30% to 60% of tumors in breast cancer patients. Standard therapies produce a response rate of about 20%. Taxol is derived from the bark of the rare Pacific yew tree. Although harvesting of the yew tree has been under pressure from environmentalists, Bristol-Myers Squibb is confident that it can

FIGURE 4.3   The Dividend Connection Chart

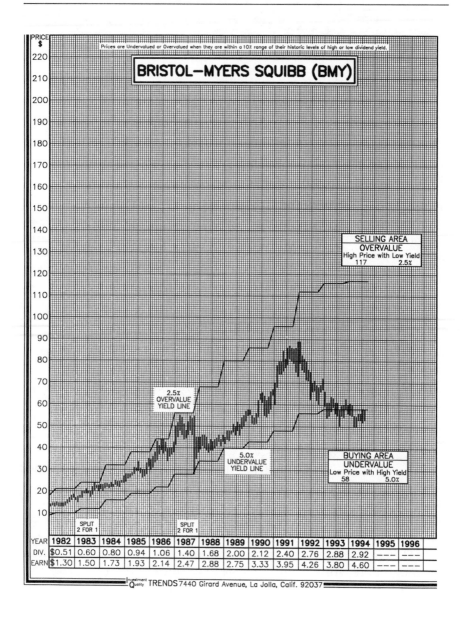

produce a synthetic version when the demand surpasses the current supply.

Other Interesting Qualities

- Bristol-Myers Squibb pharmaceuticals are second largest in the United States.

- Cancer drugs are number one worldwide.

- The company's Clairol hair coloring products are number one in the United States.

- 57% of revenues are derived from sales of pharmaceuticals.

- Dividends paid since 1902 have been increased in each of the past 23 years.

The chart shows that a 5% yield identifies undervalue, as seen in October 1987 and again in 1993. The chart also reveals an overvalued yield of 2.5% in 1986 and 1987. After reaching an all-time high price of $90 per share in early 1992, BMY began a long slide down to a low price of $50 per share in 1994, reflecting the fears and uncertainties that afflicted all pharmaceutical companies.

With an exemplary record of dividend growth, dividends have been boosted in each of the past 24 years, providing a compound annual return of 15%. Due to industry pressure, price growth may be anemic over the next two years, but with its generous yield, BMY offers a prescription for safety with a potent long-term total return.

Longs Drug Stores Corp. (NYSE:LDG)

Living up to its name with a long history of dedicated service, Longs Drugs opened its first store more than a half century ago and now is among the largest drugstore chains in North America. Founded in 1938 by Joe and Tom Long in Oakland, California, the company now has grown to roughly 300 stores, mostly in the Golden State.

Although Longs sells everything from cosmetics to greeting cards, its pharmacy remains at the core of the business, accounting for more than 27% of sales. Beyond that, the company's strategy is one of decentralized structure, giving store managers a free choice of product mix based on the needs and preferences of each individual

FIGURE 4.4   The Dividend Connection Chart

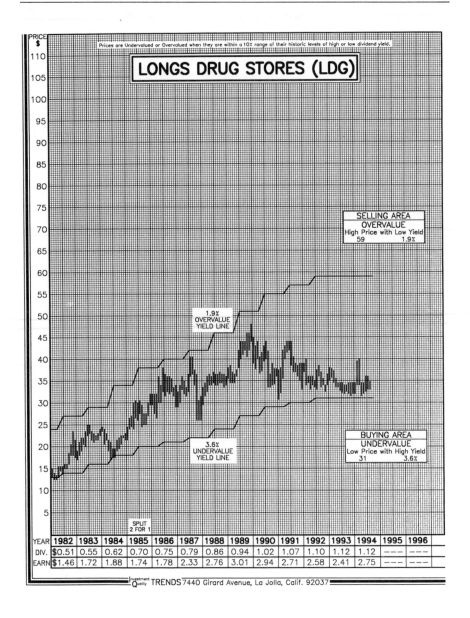

Prices are Undervalued or Overvalued when they are within a 10% range of their historic levels of high or low dividend yield.

LONGS DRUG STORES (LDG)

SELLING AREA
OVERVALUE
High Price with Low Yield
59   1.9%

1.9%
OVERVALUE
YIELD LINE

BUYING AREA
UNDERVALUE
Low Price with High Yield
31   3.6%

3.6%
UNDERVALUE
YIELD LINE

SPLIT
2 FOR 1

YEAR	1982	1983	1984	1985	1986	1987	1988	1989	1990	1991	1992	1993	1994	1995	1996
DIV.	$0.51	0.55	0.62	0.70	0.75	0.79	0.86	0.94	1.02	1.07	1.10	1.12	1.12	---	---
EARN	$1.46	1.72	1.88	1.74	1.78	2.33	2.76	3.01	2.94	2.71	2.58	2.41	2.75	---	---

Investment
Quality TRENDS 7440 Girard Avenue, La Jolla, Calif. 92037

community. Longs sells nationally advertised name-brand merchandise as well as its increasingly popular generic label.

The company's Medi-Link program, which allows customers to obtain prescriptions from any of its stores from third-party providers, has come under some fire. State and federal regulatory agencies conducted an inquiry into their billing procedures in 1990 for Hawaii and 1992 for Nevada. Longs admitted to inaccuracies in some of its billings during that time but claimed that corrections were made and no further penalties were warranted. The reimbursements due to billing corrections were not substantial, but if additional penalties are imposed, Longs' earnings could come up short.

Other Interesting Qualities

- In 1994 there were 260 stores in California, 24 in Hawaii, 6 in Colorado, 6 in Nevada, 2 in Alaska.
- Sales per store average $9 million.
- Longs is the fifth largest U.S. drugstore chain.
- More than 30% of the common stock is owned by the Long family.
- Dividends paid since 1961 have been increased in each of the past 29 years.

The chart shows a long view of LDG stock. Whenever Longs is priced to yield 3.6%, as it was in 1982, 1984 and from 1993 to 1994, the stock is undervalued and a purchase is recommended. However, when the price rises and the yield falls to 1.9%, as it did in 1986, 1987 and 1989, LDG is overvalued and a sale should be considered. The onset of recession in 1990 pulled LDG into a declining trend and landed the stock at undervalue one year later.

A well-managed company, Longs' debt is only 3% of total capitalization, and cost-cutting efforts continue to increase gross margin levels. While pharmacy remains at the heart of the business, photo developing is adding its share of picture-perfect profits. At undervalue, LDG distinguishes itself as a stock that is long on quality and strong on value.

When Is a Dividend Safe and Sound?

There is nothing so demoralizing to a stockholder, and nothing so destructive to our investment approach, than a canceled or suspended dividend. If dividend growth gives us a positive picture of a well-managed company, certainly a reduced dividend underscores hard times and an unsatisfactory financial performance.

According to our investment concept, high and low extremes of dividend yield establish profiles of undervalue and overvalue for dividend-paying stocks. When a dividend is increased, the prices at undervalue and overvalue rise to reflect the historically established yield extremes. A rising dividend trend provides increasingly strong support under the price of a stock. Conversely, when a dividend is reduced, the prices at undervalue and overvalue decline. A stock can be purchased at undervalue on an indicated payout, but if that dividend is cut, the undervalued price may subsequently become the overvalued price.

This happened in 1993 to IBM, a stock that had established its profile of value between dividend yield extremes of 5% at undervalue and 2.5% at overvalue. When the annual dividend for Big Blue was $4.48 per share, as it was from 1988 through 1992, the price at undervalue was $97 per share, where the yield was 5%. The price at overvalue was $194 per share, where the dividend yield was 2.5%. But when the dividend was reduced to $2.16, the price at undervalue became $43 per share, while the price at overvalue fell to $86 per share. Later that year, the dividend was reduced further to $1 per share, shrinking the prices at undervalue to $20 and overvalue to $40 per share. The investor who purchased IBM at $97 per share thinking it was a bargain was distressed by the dividend betrayal. (See chart of IBM in Chapter 7.)

It is critical to investors that the cash dividend be safe and sound. But how can an investor be relatively sure that the dividend will be maintained—perhaps even increased?

Signs of Safety and Potential Growth

Dividends generally are paid out of earnings. If the dividend payout ratio (the dividend as a percent of earnings) is 50% or less, the dividend is quite safe and there is enough room in the equation for it to be increased.

Signs That Dividend Growth May Be Slowing Down

If the dividend payout ratio rises above 50% of earnings, the dividend is not necessarily in danger, but a dividend increase will be more difficult to achieve.

Utilities stocks, typically higher yielding than industrial stocks, sport higher payout ratios. An electric utility stock with a payout ratio of less than 85% probably is safe.

The closer the dividend payout ratio gets to 100%, whether it be an industrial or a utility stock, the more endangered the dividend becomes and the less likely it is to be increased. Rising earnings, however, can support a rising dividend trend regardless of the payout ratio. Dividend growth also may be slowed by the company's decision to funnel more earnings into corporate expansion or to make an acquisition.

Signs of a Dividend in Danger

It is difficult, if not impossible, for a company to pay out more than it takes in. Therefore, if the indicated annual dividend is higher than the company's annual earnings, the dividend may be in jeopardy.

Even when a dividend is not covered by earnings, the payout sometimes can be sustained by a strong cash flow. Cash flow is the amount of money earned before deducting depreciation and other charges that do not involve an outlay of capital. Therefore, we cannot say unequivocally that when a dividend is greater than the most recent 12-month earnings it will not be paid. It stands to reason, however, that an unprotected dividend is in greater danger than one that is covered by earnings.

If the company is a blue chip with a long and proud history of uninterrupted dividends, the dividend probably will be rescued by cash flow and maintained despite a temporary earnings shortfall. Reported earnings that do not cover the dividend could be the result of accounting measures taken to accommodate sales of assets or other one-time charges. In such cases, the dividend may be perfectly safe. Still, it pays to remember that unless the dividend is well protected by earnings, there is some cause for concern, and initial investments in that company should be postponed until the dividend is safe.

The Dividend Connection
Carolina Power & Light
SCEcorp

Despite a high 80% payout ratio, Carolina Power & Light has been able to increase its dividend for the past 12 years. SCEcorp, on the other hand, reduced its payout ratio by slashing dividends 30% this year.

Carolina Power & Light Company (NYSE:CPL)

Providing electric power to more than a million customers throughout North and South Carolina, Carolina Power & Light, founded in 1908, serves a 30,000-square-mile-territory. Its 16 power plants provide a flexible mix of fossil, nuclear and hydroelectric resources with a total generating capacity of roughly 10,000 megawatts. The company is headquartered in Raleigh, North Carolina, one of the nation's most attractive areas for industry location and expansion.

Like all other electric utilities, CPL faces increasing competition from a number of sources, including independent electricity suppliers. The company is responding aggressively by offering attractive customer incentives, increasing sales and maximizing efforts to operate efficiently. It also is attempting to renegotiate existing contracts with its wholesale customers to ensure continued patronage. It signed a 30-year contract with the North Carolina Electric Membership Corporation, which represents 17 wholesale electric companies in its service area. Carolina Power & Light has agreed to develop a new power supply contract with its largest customer, the Fayetteville, North Carolina, Public Works Commission.

Other Interesting Qualities

- Fuel mix is 54% coal, 31% nuclear, 13% purchased, 2% other.

FIGURE 4.5   The Dividend Connection Chart

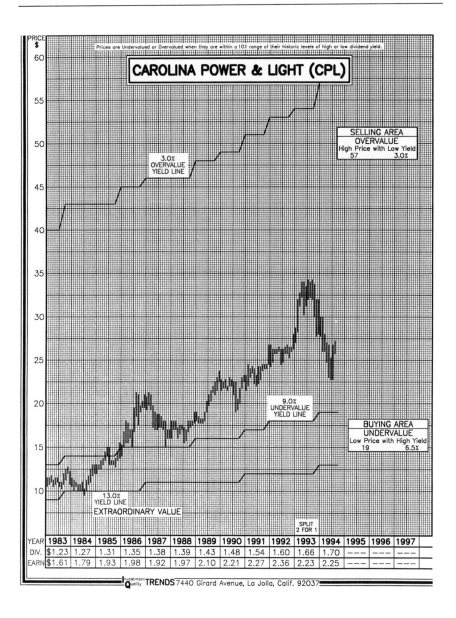

YEAR	1983	1984	1985	1986	1987	1988	1989	1990	1991	1992	1993	1994	1995	1996	1997
DIV.	$1.23	1.27	1.31	1.35	1.38	1.39	1.43	1.48	1.54	1.60	1.66	1.70	---	---	---
EARN	$1.61	1.79	1.93	1.98	1.92	1.97	2.10	2.21	2.27	2.36	2.23	2.25	---	---	---

Investment Quality TRENDS 7440 Girard Avenue, La Jolla, Calif. 92037

- Revenue mix is 33% residential, 26% industrial, 21% wholesale, 20% commercial.

- Geographic mix is 66% North Carolina, 34% South Carolina.

- The dividend payout ratio is roughly 80%.

- Dividends paid since 1937 have been increased 11 times in the past 12 years.

When this stock is priced to yield 9%, as it was in 1987 and 1988, it is undervalued and a purchase is advised. The chart also reveals an extraordinary yield of 13% in 1984, when most interest-sensitive utilities were at bargain basement prices. During the mid-1960s, CPL was priced to yield 3% at overvalue. From its undervalued price in 1988, CPL launched a primary rising trend that lasted for five years. During that time, the price rose 125% and the dividend was increased by 18%. When the stock split two for one in February 1993, the price began to decline. From its 1993 high to its 1994 low price, CPL declined 30%—roughly the same percentage loss as the industry average. Still, we believe that Carolina Power & Light will maintain a position of industry leadership and reward stockholders with an above-average total return.

SCEcorp (NYSE:SCE)

Pulsating mighty megawatts of power throughout central and southern California, SCEcorp dominates the utility scene as the second largest electricity provider in the nation. The parent company of Southern California Edison and the Mission companies, SCE is head-quartered in Rosemead, California, with assets of $19 billion. The 106-year-old utility serves more than 4.1 million customers. Its 50,000-square-mile service area has a population of about 11 million. The Mission companies include Mission Energy, the nation's largest non-utility power producer, Mission First Financial and Mission Land Company.

SCE's San Onofre Unit 1 was terminated in 1992 after 25 years of service, but Units 2 and 3 remain productive. SCE is recovering its $350 million investment in Unit 1 with a 9% return on capital. In addition, San Onofre received the industry's highest performance rating from the Institute of Nuclear Power Operators.

FIGURE 4.6   The Dividend Connection Chart

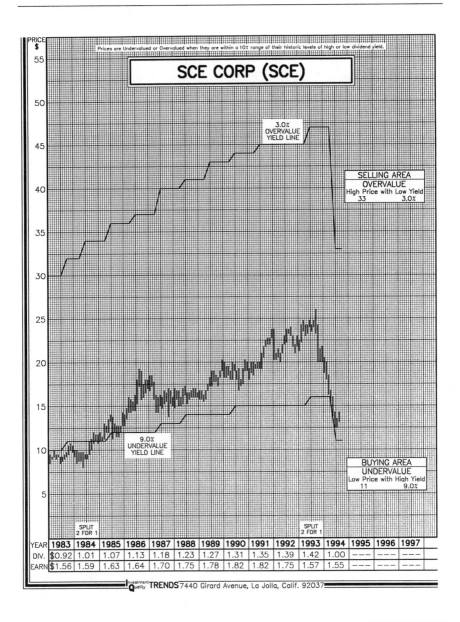

YEAR	1983	1984	1985	1986	1987	1988	1989	1990	1991	1992	1993	1994	1995	1996	1997
DIV.	$0.92	1.01	1.07	1.13	1.18	1.23	1.27	1.31	1.35	1.39	1.42	1.00	---	---	---
EARN	$1.56	1.59	1.63	1.64	1.70	1.75	1.78	1.82	1.82	1.75	1.57	1.55	---	---	---

The Mission subsidiaries are engaged in a number of profitable ventures, including a major contract with the government of Indonesia. However, Mission terminated its involvement in a Mexico project due to assaults by environmentalists who claimed that the carbon 2 coal-fired plant had unacceptable pollution standards. Although short-term earnings appear lackluster, growth in nonutility businesses are plugged into long-term profits.

Other Interesting Qualities

• Revenue mix is 35% residential, 36% commercial, 13% industrial, 16% other.

• Generating sources are 24% gas, 14% coal, 22% nuclear, 37% purchased, 3% hydro.

• Energy costs amount to 39% of revenues; labor costs, 17%.

• Dividends paid since 1909 have been increased in 16 of the past 17 years.

As one of the 15 stocks that make up the Dow Jones Utilities Average, SCE commands a great deal of institutional and individual investor support. Whenever this stock is priced to yield 9.9%, as illustrated on the chart from 1983 through 1984, it is undervalued and a purchase is recommended. If this chart were extended back to the mid-1960s, it would reveal an overvalued yield of 3%, where a sale should be considered. SCE had been in an uptrend for several years, while frequent dividend increases raised the prices proportionately at undervalue and overvalue. Then the dividend was slashed by 30% in August 1994. The dividend cut reduced the company's high payout ratio and signaled the end of a year-long price decline. Although earnings remain a concern, other projects such as overseas investments and alternative energy operations are encouraging. The company's finances are strong, with a retained earnings account of $3.2 billion, one of the highest in the industry.

What Is the Significance of Dividend Growth?

Next to windfall profits, nothing delights a shareholder more than a nice fat dividend check. And nothing provides clearer evidence that a company is serving its shareholders than a rising dividend trend.

Consecutive annual dividend increases indicate in no uncertain terms that the sales, earnings and profits of a company are alive and well.

When a corporation steadily boosts its cash dividend despite economic vicissitudes, political changes or fluctuating interest rates, its management is on track. More reliable than earnings, more accurate than book values, dividends are the single best measure of fundamental value in the stock market.

Capital gains, of course, are desired and eagerly awaited by all investors, but a cash return inspires patience and makes the wait worthwhile. In the stock market, a rising dividend trend produces the best of all investment results. It weaves a safety net under the price of a stock and produces a superior total return.

Let's look at the practical results of a rising dividend trend. Assume that a stock is undervalued when its dividend yield is 5%. If the annual dividend is $1 per share, the price at undervalue is $20 per share, where the yield is 5%. When the annual dividend is increased to $1.20 per share, the price at undervalue becomes $24 per share, where the yield then is 5%. The investor who purchased the stock when it was undervalued at $20 per share is likely to see the price rise at least 20% to conform to the stock's historic profile of yield at undervalue. The increased dividend then produces a 6% cash return on the original investment capital. The next year, if that dividend is increased to $1.40 per share, the price at undervalue will be $28 per share and the yield on the original investment will rise to 7%.

This example illustrates how a company that continuously raises its dividend adds value to the shareholder's investment by increasing the cash return on that invested capital.

By the time the stock in our example rises to a price of $40 per share, if the dividend has kept pace it will have grown to $2 per share. That stock then will offer the same degree of investment value as it did when the price was $20 per share and the annual dividend was $1 per share. But for the investor who bought the stock when it was selling for $20 per share, the price obviously has doubled and the yield on the original price has ballooned to 10%.

The blue chips listed in Figure 4.7 have boosted their cash dividends at least 11 times in the past 12 years at compound annual rates of growth in excess of 10%. With superior records of dividend growth, these stocks obviously merit investment consideration—especially when their prices are undervalued.

FIGURE 4.7 Blue Chips with Compound Annual Growth Rates of More Than 10%

Abbott Laboratories	Johnson & Johnson
AFLAC Inc.	Kellogg Company
American Home Products Corp.	Kimberly-Clark Corp.
AMP Inc.	Lilly (Eli) & Company
Bandag, Inc.	Loctite Corp.
Bankers Trust New York Corp.	Luby's Cafeterias, Inc.
Bard (C.R.), Inc.	Marion Merrell Dow Inc.
Block (H&R), Inc.	Masco Corp.
Bristol-Myers Squibb Company	Medtronic, Inc.
Coca-Cola Company	Melville Corp.
Cooper Tire & Rubber Company	Merck & Company
Deluxe Corp.	Millipore Corp.
Diebold, Inc.	Pall Corp.
Dun & Bradstreet Corp.	Pfizer Inc.
EG&G, Inc.	Philip Morris Companies
Ennis Business Forms, Inc.	Premier Industrial Corp.
General Electric Company	Quaker Chemical
General RE Corp.	Rubbermaid, Inc.
Genuine Parts Company	Sherwin-Williams Company
Harland (John H.) Company	Smucker (J.M.) Company
Hartford Steam Boiler Inspection and Insurance Company	Stanhome Inc.
Heinz (H.J.) Company	Tootsie Roll Industries
Hershey Foods Corp.	UST Inc.
Hormel (Geo. A.) & Company	Valspar Corp.
Hubbell (Class B) Inc.	Walgreen Company
Hunt Manufacturing Company	Wallace Computer Services, Inc.
International Flavors & Fragrances, Inc.	Weis Markets, Inc.
Jefferson-Pilot Corp.	Winn-Dixie Stores, Inc.
	Worthington Industries

The Dividend Connection
Masco Corporation
Quaker Chemical

Masco Corporation and Quaker Chemical are two stocks with an impressive record of dividend growth. Both have a comfortable dividend-to-earnings ratio.

Masco Corp. (NYSE:MAS)

As more Americans make home improvement the leading U.S. pastime, we tip our hard hats to Masco—the nation's leading manufacturer of building, renovation and home furnishing products. Masco companies account for 95% of the market's leadership brands. As the world's largest faucet manufacturer, Masco controls 37% of the domestic market. Brand names include Baldwin, Bowers, Drexel Heritage, Encore, Heartland, KraftMaid, Peerless, Universal, Waste King and Winfield.

Industry dynamics play into the Masco formula for success. The primary factors are the aging supply of homes and low interest rates. With 60% of U.S. homes over 30 years of age, there is a vast market for home improvement. The lowest mortgage rates in a generation are making homes more affordable, and home equity loans are encouraging the remodeling and renovation of existing homes.

Nine years ago, Masco entered the home furnishings market, and the company now is the largest U.S. manufacturer in this segment. In recent years, the recession and start-up costs for new products inhibited profit margins, pulling the rug out from under the bottom line. Long term, however, the home furnishings division should provide wall-to-wall earnings.

Masco has increased both sales and earnings in 34 of the past 37 years. Sales have increased at an average annual rate of 17%, while net income has grown a robust 18% per year. Masco should continue

FIGURE 4.8　The Dividend Connection Chart

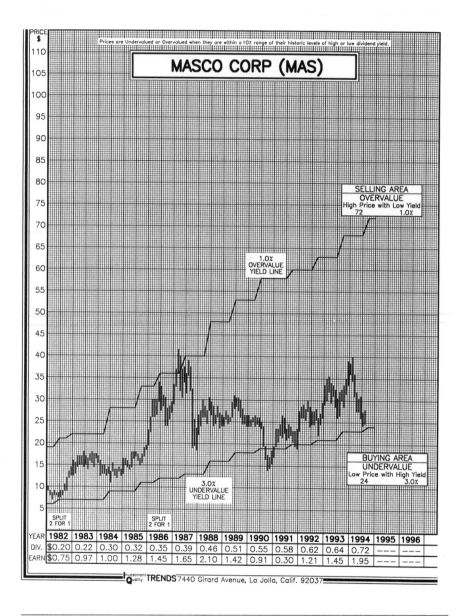

YEAR	1982	1983	1984	1985	1986	1987	1988	1989	1990	1991	1992	1993	1994	1995	1996
DIV.	$0.20	0.22	0.30	0.32	0.35	0.39	0.46	0.51	0.55	0.58	0.62	0.64	0.72	---	---
EARN	$0.75	0.97	1.00	1.28	1.45	1.65	2.10	1.42	0.91	0.30	1.21	1.45	1.95	---	---

Investment Quality TRENDS 7440 Girard Avenue, La Jolla, Calif. 92037

to nail down handsome profits as its business is fueled by an improving economy and increased housing starts.

Other Interesting Qualities

- Sales mix is 46% kitchen and bath, 44% home furnishings, 10% home improvement.

- Institutions hold 65% of the common stock.

- Insiders own 10% of the common stock.

- Dividends paid since 1944 have been increased in each of the past 35 years.

When this stock is priced to yield 3%, as it was in 1982, 1990 and 1991, it is undervalued and a purchase is recommended. However, when the price rises and the yield falls to 1%, as it did in 1986 and 1987, MAS is overvalued and a sale should be considered.

Thirty-five consecutive years of dividend increases have produced average annual income growth of 22%. Record earnings and improving profit margins position Masco for further growth well into the next century. A purchase at undervalue will furnish shareholders with the building blocks for investment success.

Quaker Chemical Corporation (QTC:QCHM)

Whether it is rolled on, lubed up, sealed in or cleaned off, chances are that Quaker Chemical manufactures an appropriate product for the job. Headquartered in Conshohocken, Pennsylvania, Quaker is one of the largest companies in the world devoted to the production of specialty chemicals. Major products include machine lubricants, corrosion preventives, cleaning compounds, hydraulic fluids, resins, sealants and coatings. The largest markets served are the aerospace, automotive, construction, metal-work, paper and steel industries.

The company's 78-year history has been one of change and growth. During that time, Quaker has evolved from a small regional supplier of specialty chemical materials to a diverse, multinational corporation. The company is expanding its corporate infrastructure in Asia with the establishment of a regional office in Hong Kong. A new division has been formed in South America to create affiliates in Brazil and Argentina. The worldwide recession of the early 1990s,

FIGURE 4.9   The Dividend Connection Chart

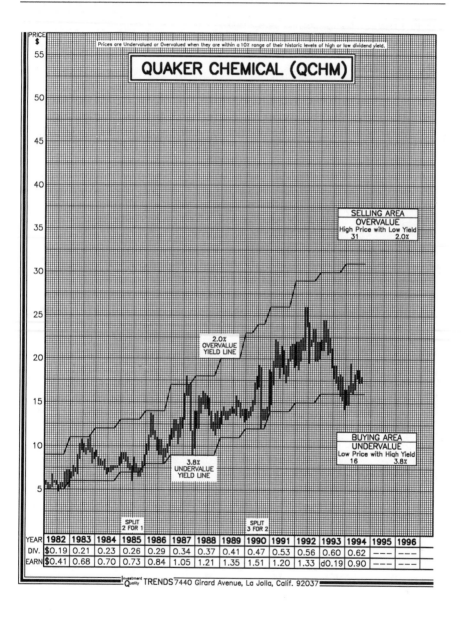

PRICE $

Prices are Undervalued or Overvalued when they are within a 10% range of their historic levels of high or low dividend yield.

QUAKER CHEMICAL (QCHM)

SELLING AREA
OVERVALUE
High Price with Low Yield
31   2.0%

2.0%
OVERVALUE
YIELD LINE

BUYING AREA
UNDERVALUE
Low Price with High Yield
16   3.8%

3.8%
UNDERVALUE
YIELD LINE

SPLIT
2 FOR 1

SPLIT
3 FOR 2

YEAR	1982	1983	1984	1985	1986	1987	1988	1989	1990	1991	1992	1993	1994	1995	1996
DIV.	$0.19	0.21	0.23	0.26	0.29	0.34	0.37	0.41	0.47	0.53	0.56	0.60	0.62	---	---
EARN	$0.41	0.68	0.70	0.73	0.84	1.05	1.21	1.35	1.51	1.20	1.33	d0.19	0.90	---	---

Investment Quality TRENDS 7440 Girard Avenue, La Jolla, Calif. 92037

with crashing car sales, took a toll on Quaker's European steel market. These factors, along with a tentative economic policy in China, make the Quaker expansion in South America and Hong Kong more meaningful.

Other Interesting Qualities

- Foreign sales account for 44% of sales and 70% of profits.

- Sales mix is 44% specialty chemicals, 28% metal fabrication, 21% construction, 7% paper.

- The company is the world's largest manufacturer of can-making chemicals.

- Insiders own 30% of the common stock.

- Dividends paid since 1954 have been increased in each of the past 12 years.

When this stock is priced to yield 3.8%, as it was in 1982, 1985, 1987 and 1990, QCHM is undervalued and a purchase is recommended. When the price rises and the yield falls to 2%, as it did in 1983, 1986 and mid-1987, the stock is overvalued and a signal to sell has been triggered. The chart also bears witness to the volatility of Quaker Chemical. Over the past dozen years, the stock has completed five cyclical price trends. Still, frequent and generous dividend increases have contributed to Quaker's long-term growth. A purchase of QCHM at undervalue in 1982 bore rich fruit by 1992, with a capital gain of almost 225% and dividend growth of nearly 200%.

A growth stock with a compound annual dividend growth rate in excess of 12%, Quaker has covered its payout comfortably with earnings that exceed the dividend by more than 100%. The company's future success lies in its ability to seize the foreign marketplace. The past few years of overseas operations can be described as the best of times and the worst of times. But as an investment selection, 'tis a far, far better option than most.

Building Your Dividend-Rich Stock Portfolio

How Much Money Should I Have To Start?

An individual investor can become involved in the stock market from virtually any level of financial participation. Do you have at least $1,000 to invest for a period of three to five years? If so, you are ready to launch your portfolio.

The allure of stock mutual funds is that an investor can commit very small sums of money and achieve a level of broad diversification.

Still, we endorse a strategy of saving capital until at least a sum of $1,000 has been accumulated and a meaningful individual investment can be made. An investor with less than $1,000 of discretionary capital should not put money at risk in the stock market. Before investing any capital in common stocks, a person should have enough cash on hand to meet six months of living expenses with a cushion of cash for some unforeseen emergency. One should not have to liquidate stocks for personal expenses or be forced to sell stocks at an inappropriate time. The thrust of our approach demands that the investor be in control of when to buy and when to sell.

Of course, the larger the pool of investment capital, the safer and more diversified a portfolio can be. It takes money to make money. Obviously, the more money one has in the stock market, the greater the potential for capital gain.

There is a common misconception that all blue chip stocks are high priced. Not true. Many quality stocks are priced below $20 per share, well within the range of a small, individual investor. You can begin by buying either one round lot of 100 shares or several odd lots of less than 100 shares and increase your position through dividend reinvestment plans or when additional capital becomes available. Stocks purchased in odd lots carry only a 1/8 point premium over the price of a round lot purchase.

The 45 blue chip stocks listed in Figure 5.1 currently are priced below $20 per share. They offer excellent opportunities for entry-level investors. Do not confuse their low prices with poor performance or inferior quality. Remember, these all are blue chip stocks with excellent histories of growth in capital and dividend income.

The Dividend Connection

Bergen Brunswig
Zero Corp.

While all of these stocks represent high quality at relatively low prices, we recommend purchasing only those that are undervalued based on their historical parameters of dividend yield. Two such stocks are Bergen Brunswig and Zero Corp.

Bergen Brunswig Corp. (CLASS A) (NYSE:BBC)

As the nation's second largest wholesale drug distributor, Bergen Brunswig is at the epicenter of the rapidly changing health care scene. The company distributes the products of pharmaceutical and medical supply manufacturers, including health and beauty aids, from 35 distribution centers and 18 medical supply branches. Its pharmaceutical network includes roughly 13,000 hospitals and pharmacies. The medical and surgical supply division distributes products to some

FIGURE 5.1   Affordable Blue Chips

Stock	Price	Dividend	Yield
AAR Corp.	15	$ .48	3.2%
American Heritage Life	17	.66	3.9
Atlantic Energy, Inc.	19	1.54	8.1
Avemco Corp.	16	.44	2.8
Bergen Brunswig Corp. (Class A)	17	.48	2.8
Bruno's Inc.	7	.24	3.4
Crawford & Company	16	.50	3.1
Delmarva Power & Light Company	18	1.54	8.6
DPL Inc.	19	1.18	6.2
Edwards (A.G.), Inc.	17	.56	3.3
EG&G, Inc.	15	.56	3.7
Ennis Business Forms, Inc.	14	.56	4.0
Ethyl Corp.	12	.50	4.2
Family Dollar Stores, Inc.	15	.35	2.3
Federal Signal Corp.	19	.42	2.2
Flowers Industries	18	.79	4.4
Glatfelter (P.H.) Company	16	.70	4.4
Handleman Company	11	.44	4.0
Hormel (Geo. A.) & Company	19	.50	2.6
Hunt Manufacturing Company	16	.36	2.3
International Multifoods Corp.	16	.80	5.0
Kmart Corp.	16	.96	6.0
Lance Inc.	18	.96	5.3
The Limited Inc.	19	.36	1.9
Lincoln Telecom	15	.52	3.5
Marion Merrell Dow Inc.	18	1.00	5.6
New England Business Service	19	.80	4.2
Pacificorp	17	1.08	6.4
Pall Corp.	16	.37	2.3
Quaker Chemical	18	.62	3.4
Rite Aid Corp.	19	.60	3.2
RPM Inc.	19	.52	2.7
Ryland Group, Inc.	19	.60	3.2
Safety-Kleen Corp.	15	.36	2.4
San Diego Gas & Electric Company	19	1.52	8.0
SCEcorp	15	1.42	9.5
Southern Company	18	1.18	6.6
Stride Rite Corp.	13	.38	2.9
Super Food Services	12	.36	3.0
Tasty Baking	15	.52	3.5
TECO Energy, Inc.	19	1.01	5.3
Universal Corp.	19	.96	5.1
Washington Water Power Company	16	1.24	7.8
Woolworth Corp.	17	1.16	6.8
Zero Corp.	13	.40	3.1

FIGURE 5.2   The Dividend Connection Chart

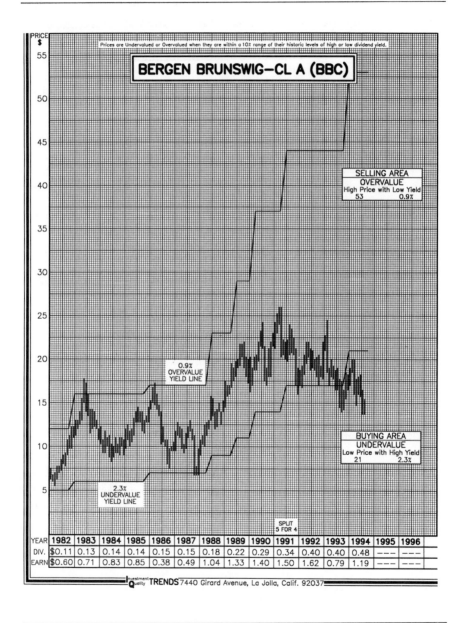

25,000 hospitals, clinics, nursing homes, veterinary facilities and physician offices.

The company is increasing its market share by dividing and conquering the competition. First came the successful acquisition of Durr-Fillauer Medical Inc. of Montgomery, Alabama. With $1 billion in annual sales, Durr-Fillauer consists of six regional drug distribution centers and 18 medical supply branches. Bergen Brunswig then purchased the Big B Inc. chain of 306 drugstores, Southwestern Hospital Supply Group, Dr. T.C. Smith Company and Healthcare Distributors of Indiana Inc. to strengthen its mighty grip on the industry.

Although increased competition is shrinking profit margins, Bergen Brunswig has advanced the bottom line by improving its operating efficiency. The company has restructured its administrative operations, curbed many related expenses and consolidated four distribution centers into one larger, more efficient facility.

Universal coverage will add roughly 40 million Americans to the current health care system. Since any universal plan will rely heavily on the volume provided by wholesale drug distributors, Bergen Brunswig stands to profit handsomely.

Other Interesting Qualities

- Bergen Brunswig is the nation's largest supplier of pharmaceuticals to hospitals and managed care facilities.

- Institutions hold 57% of the common stock.

- Insiders own 10% of Class A shares.

- Dividends paid since 1978 have been increased ten times in the past 12 years.

When BBC is priced to yield 2.3%, as it was in 1986, 1987 and various times from 1991 to 1994, the stock is undervalued and a purchase is recommended. However, when the price rises and the yield falls to 0.9%, as it did in 1983 and 1986, BBC is overvalued and a sale should be considered. A rising trend was launched in 1988, but it was reversed in 1991, far short of its overvalued objective. The stock then returned to undervalue, where it remained through 1994, offering a prescription for long-term investment growth.

Zero Corp. (NYSE:ZRO)

Contrary to its name, Zero is the nation's number one manufacturer of air cargo containers and systems. In a simple case of mistaken identity, Zero was named by founder John Gilbert, who bought the Zierold Sheet Metal Company in 1953. For years, the name was mispronounced as Zero; so, to simplify matters, Gilbert officially renamed the corporation. Under the Halliburton and Anvil brand names, Zero produces two premium lines of aluminum luggage and carrying cases. Cosmetics, moon rocks and million-dollar satellite parts are stored and transported in Zero's protective cases. From the astronauts at Kennedy Space Center to the basketball players of the Los Angeles Lakers, Zero's customers are as diverse as the cases it produces.

Although Zero is headquartered in Los Angeles, the company has transplanted two of its major manufacturing facilities to Utah. By so doing, it cut its workers' compensation expenses by 30%, health care costs by 25% and wages by 20%. Restructuring also took place within the borders of California, as Zero consolidated several of its factories in that state. These actions were taken in response to poor earnings.

Earnings began to improve in 1994, mostly as a result of cost-cutting efforts. There were signs of rebounding revenues as orders improved from the semiconductor and airline industries. As the economy improves, sales should climb in Zero's other divisions, particularly telecommunications and computer cooling systems.

Other Interesting Qualities

- Revenue mix is 30% instrumentation, 24% computer, 16% consumer, 15% airline, 15% government.
- Zero supplies mainframe cooling systems to IBM.
- Zero has zero debt.
- Dividends paid since 1974 have been increased 21 times in the past 19 years.

The price of Zero's stock is contained within yield extremes of 4% at undervalue and 1.3% at overvalue. The 4% yield was tested in 1990 and reconfirmed twice in 1991 and again in 1992. During the past 12 years, the overvalued yield was seen in 1983, 1984 and 1986. Although

FIGURE 5.3   The Dividend Connection Chart

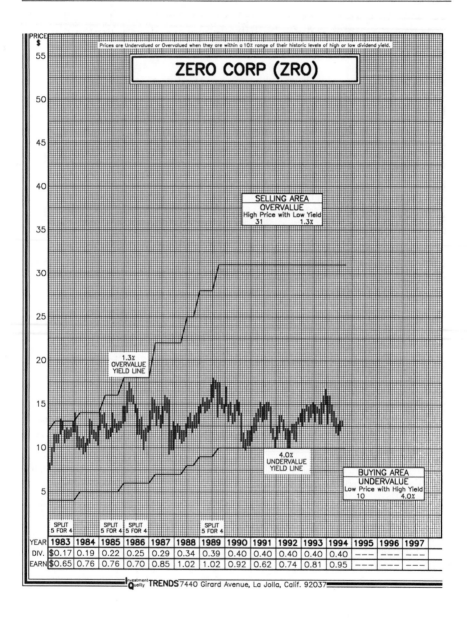

Prices are Undervalued or Overvalued when they are within a 10% range of their historic levels of high or low dividend yield.

ZERO CORP (ZRO)

SELLING AREA
OVERVALUE
High Price with Low Yield
31   1.3%

1.3%
OVERVALUE
YIELD LINE

4.0%
UNDERVALUE
YIELD LINE

BUYING AREA
UNDERVALUE
Low Price with High Yield
10   4.0%

YEAR	1983	1984	1985	1986	1987	1988	1989	1990	1991	1992	1993	1994	1995	1996	1997
DIV.	$0.17	0.19	0.22	0.25	0.29	0.34	0.39	0.40	0.40	0.40	0.40	0.40	———	———	———
EARN	$0.65	0.76	0.76	0.70	0.85	1.02	1.02	0.92	0.62	0.74	0.81	0.95	———	———	———

SPLIT 5 FOR 4 (1983), SPLIT 5 FOR 4 (1985), SPLIT 5 FOR 4 (1986), SPLIT 5 FOR 4 (1989)

Investment Quality TRENDS 7440 Girard Avenue, La Jolla, Calif. 92037

dividend increases have been on hold for the past four years, Zero is a growth stock with a compound annual growth rate of 10% over the past 12 years. If earnings continue to trend up, the payout too should begin to rise. With zero debt and ample cash available for attractive acquisitions, Zero is in position to stage a formidable comeback. A purchase of this stock at undervalue, should add many zeros to the assets of its shareholders.

How Should I Allocate My Investment Capital?

By now it should be clear that our favorite investment vehicles by far are undervalued blue chip stocks, where much money can be made with a modicum of risk. Still, depending on the prevailing market climate, not all of one's investment capital can be invested confidently in the stock market at any given time. So the question of capital allocation comes into play.

Under ideal investment circumstances, when the market is undervalued, the vast majority (90% to 95%) of capital will be best served in common stocks. Numerous studies have confirmed this. Long-term investments in dividend-paying common stocks far outperform any other investment vehicles.

Investors should never commit 100% of their capital to the stock market. Unforeseen circumstance might demand immediate cash. It also is good to have some available capital to take advantage of unexpected investment opportunities. When the stock market is overvalued, nothing frustrates an investor more than the inability to place capital in investments that produce a reasonable return. But when the market is overvalued or in a primary declining trend, preservation of capital is more important than appreciation of capital. The return *of* capital is more critical than the return *on* capital.

Investment capital should be divided into four equal portions. When the market is overvalued, only the first portion (approximately 25%) should be invested. Even then, investments should be restricted to undervalued blue chips. The other three portions (approximately 75%) should be placed in a variety of short-term money market vehicles. True, the return will not be as great as that of a long-term fixed holding, but the cash will be readily available when better stock market values are present.

As the Dow Jones Industrial Average declines from overvalue and finds support in a historically validated 4% yield area (see Chapter 9), the second of the four portions can be invested. The balance again should remain in short-term money market accounts.

At the 5% yield area, the third portion of capital should be allocated to undervalued blue chips. And when the market reaches undervalued levels, where the dividend yield on the Dow Jones Industrial Average is 6%, the remaining capital can enter the stock market.

The following table illustrates this model for capital allocation. Our model does not include investments in bonds or annuities, which render an investor unable to guard against inflation by locking in long-term fixed rates of return. We also do not endorse so-called REITS (real estate investment trusts), which are too heavily tied to the speculative real estate market.

Table of Sample Capital Allocation

Investment Capital—$400,000

Dow Jones Industrial Average yields 3%
$100,000 invested in common stocks
$300,000 in short-term money market instruments

Dow Jones Industrial Average yields 4%
$200,000 invested in common stocks
$200,000 in short-term money market instruments

Dow Jones Industrial Average yields 5%
$300,000 invested in common stocks
$100,000 in short-term money market instruments

Dow Jones Industrial Average yields 6%
$400,000 invested in common stocks

Note: These percentage figures are based on the assumption that 5% to 10% of total capital remains uninvested at all times

Should I Favor Dollar Cost Averaging?

Dollar cost averaging is a method of buying securities at regular intervals with a fixed amount of money. Those intervals are generally monthly, quarterly or annually.

When a stock is undervalued, dollar cost averaging is a very good idea. Regular incremental purchases of an undervalued stock build a potentially powerful position. It takes the emotion out of a decision to buy and moderates the risk with an additional chance of reward.

This method works especially well in a bear market, when prices are falling. As prices decline, the same number of dollars will purchase more shares, thereby reducing the average price per share. When the bear market eventually ends and a bull market begins, the position becomes profitable in a relatively short time.

Another way to dollar cost average is to buy a similar number of shares at regular intervals, thereby averaging the higher prices with the lower prices.

There is nothing wrong with either of these approaches, except that brokerage costs resulting from numerous purchases will boost the average price per share, perhaps higher than if a single purchase is made at an undervalued price.

Reinvesting quarterly dividends is another way to dollar cost average into a stock automatically without additional brokerage costs. This should be a consideration when the cash return from that investment is not needed for current income.

In any event, the stockholder should keep an eye on value. The routine of averaging dollars into a stock should be stopped and reversed when an overvalued area is approached. Then the stock owner should dollar cost average out of the holding, selling regular incremental shares to minimize potential losses.

Averaging out of a stock at overvalue has even greater appeal than averaging in at undervalue. Stocks are more likely to linger at overvalue and can move even higher when dividends are increased, disappointing investors who may have sold their entire position when a stock first became overvalued.

Averaging into a stock at undervalue and out of a stock at overvalue puts a refinement on the principle of dollar cost averaging that investors are wise to consider.

The Dividend Connection

EG&G, Incorporated
Kimberly-Clark

The following two stocks, EG&G, Inc. and Kimberly-Clark, lingered respectively at undervalue and overvalue, where dollar cost averaging was best served.

EG&G, Inc. (NYSE:EGG)

Your mission, if you choose to accept it, is to analyze and understand the high-tech world of EG&G, a worldwide provider of mind-boggling, advanced scientific products and services. Although it's not an impossible mission, a lay person could be intimidated by the scope of this toy store to the think tanks. Its divisions include:

- Instruments—providing mechanisms for precise measurement on an atomic level, high-tech equipment for airport and industrial security and fiber optics to assist in astrophysics research.

- Components—providing parts for sophisticated imaging systems, laser equipment and electronic cooling apparatus.

- Technical services—bringing risk management skills and science to a broad range of industrial, commercial and government contracts.

- Aerospace—providing systems for the 737, 767, Airbus, cruise missiles, stealth aircraft and space vehicles.

- Defense—six divisions involved in the design and maintenance of military programs.

- Department of Energy—providing reactor safety, machinery and waste management products.

Thoroughly involved in an expanding world of change, EG&G is ever-mindful of the need to stay aggressive, agile and responsive. The

FIGURE 5.4   The Dividend Connection Chart

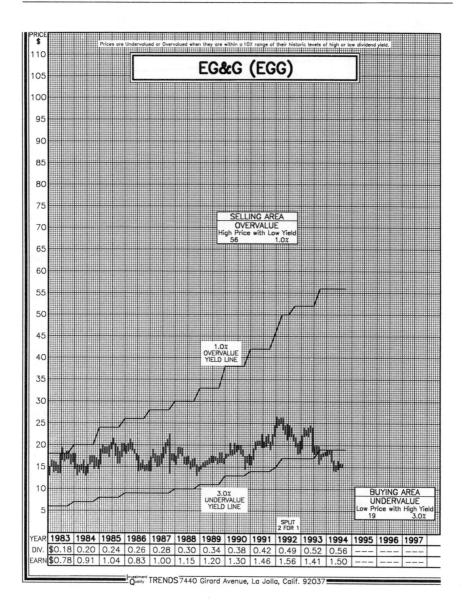

EG&G (EGG)

Prices are Undervalued or Overvalued when they are within a 10% range of their historic levels of high or low dividend yield.

SELLING AREA
OVERVALUE
High Price with Low Yield
56   1.0%

1.0%
OVERVALUE
YIELD LINE

3.0%
UNDERVALUE
YIELD LINE

BUYING AREA
UNDERVALUE
Low Price with High Yield
19   3.0%

SPLIT
2 FOR 1

YEAR	1983	1984	1985	1986	1987	1988	1989	1990	1991	1992	1993	1994	1995	1996	1997
DIV.	$0.18	0.20	0.24	0.26	0.28	0.30	0.34	0.38	0.42	0.49	0.52	0.56	---	---	---
EARN	$0.78	0.91	1.04	0.83	1.00	1.15	1.20	1.30	1.46	1.56	1.41	1.50	---	---	---

Investment Quality TRENDS 7440 Girard Avenue, La Jolla, Calif. 92037

U.S. Food and Drug Administration soon should approve laser surgery to correct nearsightedness. EG&G manufactures the ultra-high-quality light sources for the lasers involved in this procedure. The company also is funding research for the correction of farsightedness and astigmatism. In this way, EG&G is proving itself to be a truly visionary company.

Other Interesting Qualities

- Sales mix is 60% government, 14% technical services, 14% instruments, 12% components.

- Operations are conducted on all seven continents through more than 50 subsidiaries.

- EG&G is a *Fortune* 200 company.

- Insiders own 16% of the common stock; University of California owns 6%.

- Dividends paid since 1965 have been increased in each of the past 16 years.

When this stock is priced to yield 1%, it is overvalued and a sale should be considered. But when the price falls and the yield rises to 3%, as it did numerous times in the past eight years, it is undervalued and a purchase is recommended. Although the capital gains have not been profound over the past 12 years, frequent and generous dividend increases have provided an attractive total return. Also noteworthy is the company's strong balance sheet, which shows only 4% debt. This excellent financial stability enables the company to be on the lookout for potential acquisitions. Long-term projections are favorable. An improving worldwide economy should bring EGGstraordinary value to stock owners.

Kimberly-Clark Corp. (NYSE:KMB)

Wiping the tears and the rears of consumers worldwide is a dirty job, but somebody has to do it. Kimberly-Clark is the second largest manufacturer of facial tissue, toilet paper, feminine napkins and disposable diapers. Its brand names, Kleenex, Kotex and Huggies, are virtually generic to their products. The company also makes newsprint, cigarette paper and specialty paper for the electronics industry.

FIGURE 5.5   The Dividend Connection Chart

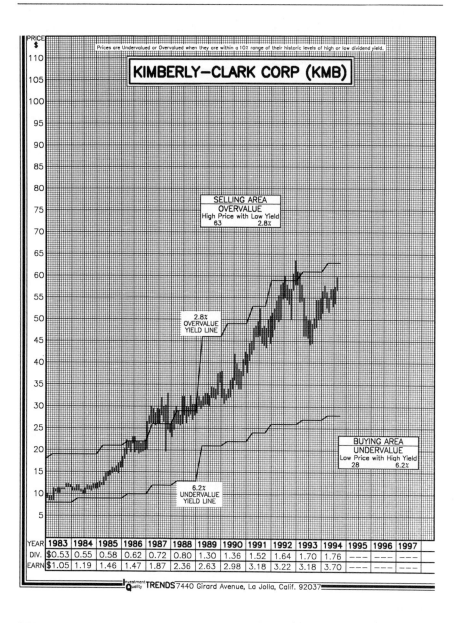

YEAR	1983	1984	1985	1986	1987	1988	1989	1990	1991	1992	1993	1994	1995	1996	1997
DIV.	$0.53	0.55	0.58	0.62	0.72	0.80	1.30	1.36	1.52	1.64	1.70	1.76	---	---	---
EARN	$1.05	1.19	1.46	1.47	1.87	2.36	2.63	2.98	3.18	3.22	3.18	3.70	---	---	---

Investment Quality TRENDS 7440 Girard Avenue, La Jolla, Calif. 92037

It recently diversified into aircraft maintenance and commercial airline services.

Kimberly-Clark's flagship product is disposable diapers. This relatively new item, which came of age in the 1980s, has grown consistently along with America's baby boom. The company commands 32% of the disposable diaper market, second only to Procter & Gamble. But Kimberly-Clark is the innovator of the industry, with improved leakage control and a virtual monopoly on training pants.

Other Interesting Qualities

- Sales mix is 81% consumer paper products, 15% industrial paper, 4% airline industry.

- Kimberly-Clark owns .7 million acres of U.S. timberland.

- Institutions hold more than 60% of the common stock.

- Dividends paid since 1935 have been increased in each of the past 22 years.

When KMB is priced to yield 6.2%, as it was in 1983 and 1984, the stock is undervalued and a purchase is recommended. However, when the price rises and the yield falls to 2.8%, as it did from 1986 through 1988 and again in 1992, KMB is overvalued and a sale should be considered. Driven by the strength of its top-selling products, Kimberly-Clark's past growth has been nothing to sneeze at. Capital gains over the past ten years have amounted to 500%, while the dividend has increased by 220%.

This A+ quality growth stocks meets all six of our blue chip criteria. No wonder it has hovered in overvalued territory for more than three years. Still, the 30% decline in 1993 revealed some vulnerability in the stock and the additional pressure of a full-blown bear market could put a temporary end to the stock's 12-year winning streak. At overvalue, KMB is a strong candidate for dollar cost averaging out of a stock before the onset of a tearful decline.

How Should I Construct My Stock Portfolio

Don't put all your eggs in one basket. That familiar adage also applies to investments. No matter how careful and conservative you may be in your stock selection, no matter how cautiously you steer your investment vehicles, Wall Street is an avenue of potholes. Diversification mitigates risk in the stock market and is the key to a well-constructed stock portfolio.

As a general rule, similar amounts of capital should be invested in a diversified selection of undervalued blue chip stocks. If, for example, you have $10,000 to invest, you might invest $2,000 in each of five different stocks to achieve a well-balanced, diversified portfolio. The number of shares you buy is not as important as keeping the dollar amount similar in each original purchase. By so doing, you will be able to keep track of which stocks are the best performers, and if one selection turns sour, your entire portfolio will not be destroyed. When additional capital becomes available, you can add other stocks to the portfolio in the same $2,000 increments.

If the original sum to be invested is greater than $10,000, the allocation of capital into individual stocks can be proportionally larger. By holding each investment to the same dollar value, you may be purchasing some stocks in odd lots (less than 100 shares). It doesn't matter. You can round up the best positions later or add to your holdings through a dividend reinvestment program. There is no way to determine at the outset which stocks will be the most rewarding.

There is a danger in becoming overdiversified. Research on this subject has concluded that a well-diversified portfolio should aim to include 20 to 25 stocks for maximum safety. It has been determined that 15 to 20 stocks gives a portfolio adequate diversification without being difficult to follow on a regular basis.

At times, there may be little opportunity for diversification among undervalued stocks because relatively few stocks of good quality are bargain priced. In that case, it is best to select a few undervalued stocks and keep the balance of your capital on the sidelines until additional stocks in diverse areas fall into the undervalued category.

There is no need to rush into the stock market just because you have some capital to invest. In fact, the slower you commit your capital, the less likely you are to make mistakes. Stocks are like streetcars. If you miss one, there is always another one just ahead.

We strongly encourage investors to make their own stock selections. It can be financially fatal to put your faith and your capital in the hands of money managers or stock mutual funds. Although they offer diversification, they do not offer individual choice. The opportunity to make specific selections is your earned right as an enlightened investor.

Remember, nobody is as sensitive to your investment objectives as you are. Nobody cares as much about your capital as you do. There is no guarantee—or even likelihood—that stocks in a mutual fund portfolio will be either undervalued or entirely blue chip. Because both of those factors are critical to investment success, we urge investors to fashion their own portfolios, exclusively selecting undervalued blue chip stocks for minimum risk and maximum investment growth potentials.

Figure 5.6 shows one possible example of a diversified portfolio of 20 blue chip stocks that represent five important industry sectors. This list is not meant to exclude other stocks that may be of equal quality and value. But for the patient, long-term investor who desires safety, value and growth, this is one possible portfolio that should produce an above-average total return over the next several years.

The Dividend Connection

Allegheny Power
General Mills

Two of the stocks listed in Figure 5.6, Allegheny Power System and General Mills, are profiled in this section.

Allegheny Power System Inc. (NYSE:AYP)

In an age when most electric utilities are diversifying to weather the storm of industry change, Allegheny Power continues to derive virtually all of its income from the generation of electricity. Incorporated in Maryland in 1925, this holding company performs its services through three major subsidiaries: Monongahela Power Company,

---

FIGURE 5.6   Sample Diversified Portfolio of Blue Chip Stocks

---

Electric Utilities

Allegheny Power System Inc.
Consolidated Edison Company of New York
Detroit Edison Company
Oklahoma Gas & Electric Company

Pharmaceutical and Health Care

Bristol-Myers Squibb Company
Lilly (Eli) & Company
Merck & Company
Upjohn Company

Consumer Goods

Brown-Forman Corp. (Class B)
General Mills
Heinz (H.J.) Company
Philip Morris Companies

Business Products

Avery Dennison Corp.
Deluxe Corp.
Ennis Business Forms, Inc.
Harland (John H.) Company

Retail Stores

Bruno's Inc.
Kmart Corp.
Longs Drug Stores Corp.
Rite Aid Corp.

The Potomac Edison Company and West Penn Power Company. These subsidiaries jointly own Allegheny Generating Company, which sells 840 megawatts of generating capacity to its parents. The service area extends throughout Maryland, Ohio, Pennsylvania, Virginia and West Virginia. This single, integrated system provides electricity to 1.3 million customers in a 30,000-square-mile territory.

Economic development in Allegheny's territory is robust and bodes well for the continuing growth of the utility. Ninety big companies recently either located to or expanded operations in its service area. Low electric rates, skilled labor, proximity to geographic marketplaces, abundant water supply and other natural resources all contribute to attracting and retaining businesses and industries.

Other Interesting Qualities

- Revenue mix is 32% residential, 28% industrial, 17% commercial, 23% other.

- Fuel sources are 89% coal, 10% pumped storage, 1% hydroelectric.

FIGURE 5.7   The Dividend Connection Chart

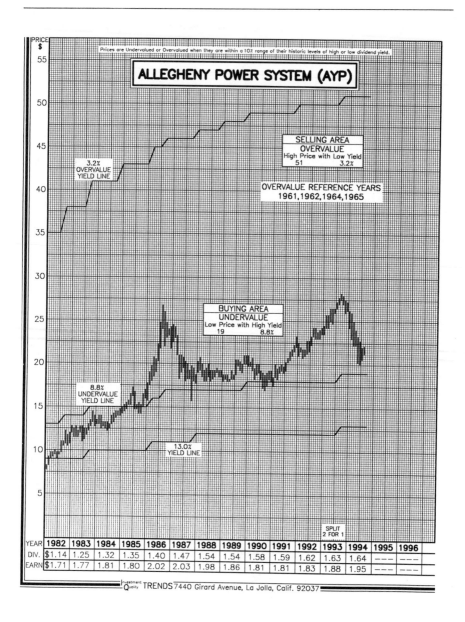

YEAR	1982	1983	1984	1985	1986	1987	1988	1989	1990	1991	1992	1993	1994	1995	1996
DIV.	$1.14	1.25	1.32	1.35	1.40	1.47	1.54	1.54	1.58	1.59	1.62	1.63	1.64	---	---
EARN	$1.71	1.77	1.81	1.80	2.02	2.03	1.98	1.86	1.81	1.81	1.83	1.88	1.95	---	---

Investment Quality TRENDS 7440 Girard Avenue, La Jolla, Calif. 92037

- Geographic mix is 45% Pennsylvania, 31% Ohio/West Virginia, 24% Maryland/Virginia.

- Total population of its service area is 3 million.

- Dividends paid since 1935 have been increased 35 times in the past 36 years.

Like most utilities stocks, AYP has established three benchmarks of value. When this stock is priced to yield 8.8%, as it was numerous times from 1986 to the present, it is undervalued and a purchase is recommended. The chart shows only the past 12 years of AYP history, but if it were extended back an additional 20 years, it would reveal an overvalued yield of 3.2% from 1961 through 1965. The chart does show an extraordinary yield of 13% in 1981 and 1982. Still, in view of the current interest rate environment, an 8.8% yield is a reasonable benchmark of good value. Rate increases are essential. Beyond that, Allegheny must keep costs low and construction at a minimum. The service area is growing, and its future is stable. At undervalue, investors can plug into a purchase of AYP and light their way to a brilliant total return.

General Mills, Inc. (NYSE:GIS)

Filling America's breakfast bowls with crunch and its shareholders' pockets with value, General Mills is a worldwide leader in consumer foods and restaurant operations. The company's financial performance ranks in the top 10% of all major U.S. corporations. Some popular brands include Betty Crocker, Bisquick, Colombo, General Mills, Gold Medal and Yoplait. Its three restaurant chains are Red Lobster, The Olive Garden and China Coast.

As a top banana in the ready-to-eat cereal business, General Mills continues to increase its market share among children and adults with famous brands such as Cheerios, Kix, Lucky Charms, Shredded Wheat and Wheaties. Cereal earnings were soggy in 1994 due to a forced suspension of cereal production. The stoppage occurred when it was discovered that millions of bushels of grain had been mistakenly sprayed with Dursban, an unauthorized pesticide.

General Mills is combating competitive challenges by changing its promotional strategy and lowering prices. It has discontinued $175 million worth of cereal coupons—98% of which never are

FIGURE 5.8   The Dividend Connection Chart

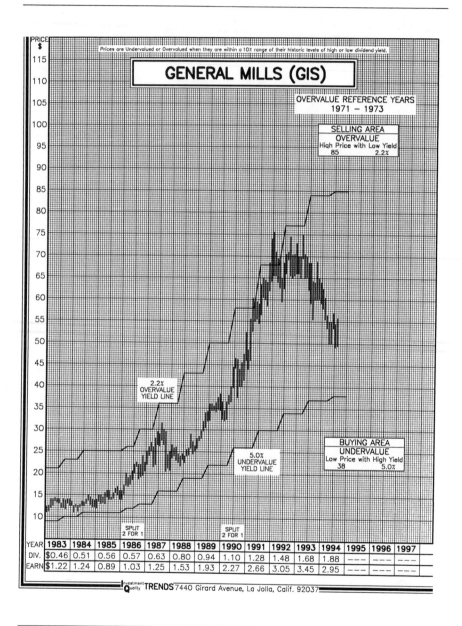

Prices are Undervalued or Overvalued when they are within a 10% range of their historic levels of high or low dividend yield.

GENERAL MILLS (GIS)

OVERVALUE REFERENCE YEARS
1971 – 1973

SELLING AREA
OVERVALUE
High Price with Low Yield
85   2.2%

2.2%
OVERVALUE
YIELD LINE

5.0%
UNDERVALUE
YIELD LINE

BUYING AREA
UNDERVALUE
Low Price with High Yield
38   5.0%

SPLIT
2 FOR 1

SPLIT
2 FOR 1

YEAR	1983	1984	1985	1986	1987	1988	1989	1990	1991	1992	1993	1994	1995	1996	1997
DIV.	$0.46	0.51	0.56	0.57	0.63	0.80	0.94	1.10	1.28	1.48	1.68	1.88	---	---	---
EARN	$1.22	1.24	0.89	1.03	1.25	1.53	1.93	2.27	2.66	3.05	3.45	2.95	---	---	---

Investment
Quality TRENDS 7440 Girard Avenue, La Jolla, Calif. 92037

redeemed—and is increasing value to its customers by reducing prices on its top-selling brands by $110 million.

Other Interesting Qualities

- Sales mix is 65% consumer foods, 35% restaurants.
- General Mills operates roughly 1,000 restaurants in the United States, Canada and Japan.
- Betty Crocker is the market leader in dessert mixes.
- Gold Medal is the world's top-selling consumer packaged flour.
- Dividends paid since 1898 have been increased in each of the past 29 years.

When this stock is priced to yield 5%, as it was in 1984 and 1985, GIS is undervalued and a purchase is recommended. But when the price rises and the yield falls to 2.2%, as it did in 1987 and from 1991 to 1993, GIS is overvalued and a sale should be considered. The stock launched a primary rising trend in 1985 that ended at overvalue in 1987. The price was hit hard during the October crash of that year, but the 34% decline was not as brutal as most consumer goods stocks endured. By the end of 1987, GIS launched a new rising trend that performed magnificently. It gained 275% in four years, while the dividend rose by more than 100%. The share price has grown at an 11% compound annual rate over the past five years, while the dividend has doubled. The total return to shareholders has increased at a 14% annual rate over that period, outpacing the S&P index by 3%. Wait for the price to retreat to undervalue, where General Mills will provide gold medal results for the patient, long-term investor.

Developing Your Successful Stock Strategy

Should I Aim for Income or Growth?

Among all of the questions we read and hear from investors, this is the one most frequently asked: Should I sacrifice the reality of income for the potential of rapid growth, which may or may not coincide with rapid capital gains? In other words, is a bird in the hand worth more than two in the bush?

The answer to that question generally depends on the age and the investment objectives of the person who is asking. A relatively young investor with a long-term investment horizon and sufficient income from a job to maintain a comfortable lifestyle can forego a high current return in favor of a lower-yielding growth stock. If a rapid growth stock lives up to its reputation, it will produce a vastly higher total return over a ten-year period than a slower-growing company with a generous cash dividend that produces an above-average yield.

Some studies have shown that companies which reinvest a large percentage of their net income into new areas of research or expansion can grow more rapidly than companies which pay most of their profits out to shareholders in the form of cash dividends. The question that we as owners and investors must ask is: Are these profits being invested wisely in areas that do promise future growth, or are they being used to raise the salaries of management, which only produce additional income for corporate officers rather than shareholders?

Even if the available capital is being reinvested in areas perceived to grow a business more rapidly, we also must wonder if the capital is being invested wisely. Some corporate investments produce financial disasters rather than the intended growth. One such example was seen in the 1980s, when a number of utilities invested in savings and loans and other businesses with which they were unfamiliar and from which they suffered great losses. In those cases, a bird in the hand was infinitely better than two in the bush.

So there is a potential downside to stingy dividend payouts as well as to excessively generous dividends that may restrict growth. Remember, a company's dividend payout ratio is the percent of its earnings paid out in the form of a cash dividend. The average payout ratio is 50%. If the ratio is far below that figure, the company is retaining earnings for purposes that should be explained to its shareholders. Perhaps a dividend increase is imminent. But perhaps the management is being unduly tightfisted about sharing profits with the owners of the company (the stockholders) and should be taken to task.

If the payout ratio is significantly above that 50% figure, there may be a different problem that bears investigation. Dividends are paid out of earnings. An indicated annual dividend that approximates or exceeds the company's 12-month earnings suggests that the dividend may be in danger. (See Chapter 4.) Although a company with slim profits may dip into cash flow to cover a dividend for a limited period of time, it obviously cannot continue to pay out as much or more than it earns for very long.

Below are examples of miserly dividend payout ratios. They reflect the expectation of rapid corporate growth and future dividend increases.

Stock	Dividend Payout Ratio
Alberto-Culver Company	19%
American International Group, Inc.	7
Archer Daniels Midland Company	6
Disney (Walt) Company	14
Edwards (A.G.), Inc.	20
Great Lakes Chemical Corp.	10
Manor Care, Inc.	9
McDonald's Corp.	16

Stock	Dividend Payout Ratio
McDonnell Douglas Corp.	5%
Medtronic, Inc.	17
Motorola, Inc.	16
Nucor Corp.	14
Pep Boys	15
Tootsie Roll Industries	12
Wal-Mart Stores, Inc.	14

Below are examples of extravagant dividend payout ratios. They suggest slow growth and potential danger to the dividend unless earnings improve.

Stock	Dividend Payout Ratio
Ametek, Inc.	88%
Angelica Corp.	86
Campbell Soup Company	99
Chemed Corp.	109
Du Pont (E.I.) De Nemours & Company	94
Glatfelter (P.H.) Company	99
Hartford Steam Boiler Inspection and Insurance Company	101
Houghton Mifflin Co.	121
International Multifoods Corp.	108
Kimberly-Clark Corp.	82
Lance Inc.	86
Lilly (Eli) & Company	93
Melville Corp.	123
New England Business	94
Olin Corp.	174
Procter & Gamble Company	496
Shell Transport & Trading Company	95
Witco Corp.	93
Zurn Industries, Inc.	102

Because utilities normally have high dividend payout ratios they must be viewed from a different perspective. (See Chapter 7.) Utilities generally are able to maintain and grow their dividends despite high payout ratios. In fact, utilities provide an attractive stock industry group for investors who aim to increase their current income streams and achieve gradual investment growth.

Retired investors who have little or no earned income often seek high-yielding investments that will protect them from inflation and produce some capital gains and income growth. For them, utilities stocks are ideal investments. In recent years, many utilities companies have used their excess cash to increase dividends and pay down debt, thus reducing their debt-to-equity ratios and strengthening their financial bases.

The answer to the question of growth versus income also depends on whether or not the overall market is undervalued, where long-term investment strategies can be implemented, or overvalued, where protection of capital is the primary concern.

When the market is overvalued, investors are advised to follow a defensive strategy. Stocks with high dividend yields that are protected by earnings are investments of choice. Those stocks are more likely to hold their value and less likely to be sold in a general market decline. Investors are more willing to retain securities that pay an above-average return when their holdings are blue chip stocks.

In an extended bear market, the first stocks that are likely to be sold off are those that pay no dividend; next are stocks that pay a small dividend, producing below-average yields. Investors sell their high-yielding blue chips only when it is absolutely necessary to raise cash, and they rarely margin stocks with rich dividends. Consequently, stocks with above-average dividend yields provide comfort and security in dangerous or declining markets.

Normally, when the market is not overvalued, a balanced blend of growth and income is the recommended mix, supplying both a bird in the hand and the opportunity for two in the bush.

The Dividend Connection
FlightSafety International
Florida Progress

On the following pages are two stocks that illustrate the difference. FlightSafety International is a growth profile, and Florida Progress is an income producer.

FlightSafety International, Inc. (NYSE:FSI)

Headquartered at New York's La Guardia airport, FlightSafety is the world's leading pilot training organization. It also offers training services to shiphandlers and power plant operators. FlightSafety also manufactures simulators and other advanced training equipment. Its major clients are private corporations, commercial airlines, the military and other government agencies.

Business aviation is the company's top-flight performer, with more than 3,000 corporations training crews with FlightSafety. At least 20 aircraft manufacturers have designated the company as their factory-authorized training organization. To maintain its high-flying status and attract more aircraft businesses, FlightSafety has broadened its operational capacity by adding new equipment to the fleet.

The company's nautical division, MarineSafety International, was awarded a $6 million, five-year contract by the U.S. Navy to install and operate a training center in San Diego. Equipped with two state-of-the-art simulators, this new facility is scheduled to be in operation by 1995. It will be available for commercial use when it is not in use by the navy.

Other Interesting Qualities

- Pilot training provides 85% of revenues; simulator sales, 15%.

- FlightSafety owns United Airlines Services Corp.

FIGURE 6.1   The Dividend Connection Chart

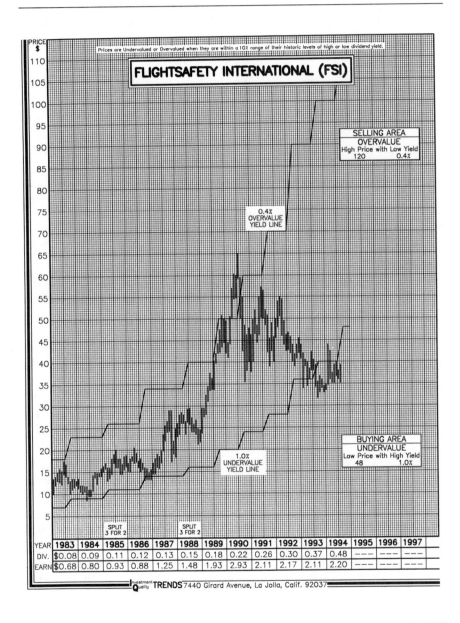

- FlightSafety is the official training organization for all Learjet and Challenger pilots.

- CEO, A.L. Ueltschi, owns 29% of the common stock.

- Dividends paid since 1976 have been increased 11 times in the past 12 years.

FSI's price flies between dividend yield extremes of 1% at undervalue and 0.4% at overvalue. The chart reveals an undervalued price in 1984, 1986 and 1993. The overvalued price was reached in 1983 and 1989. At the height of a military buildup in 1990, FSI topped out at $65 per share. Since then, the price has lost much of its altitude, declining about 50% by 1993.

Although the yield at undervalue appears small, this stock has a compound annual dividend growth rate in excess of 12%. In 1994, the company pursued a stock repurchase program designed to buy back three million common shares. While the move was thought to stimulate investor interest, other industry-related concerns have applied more downward pressure on the stock. Still, there are long-term reasons for optimism. Considering the company's dominance in the corporate sector, growth potential in the airline industry and relative stability in the military arena, FlightSafety is well-positioned for a top gun performance.

Florida Progress Corp. (NYSE:FPC)

The second largest electric utility in Florida lights up the western and central portions of the Sunshine State with 7,000 megawatts of electricity. Headquartered in St. Petersburg, the company provides power to 1.2 million customers in 32 of the state's 67 counties—including Orlando and Walt Disney World. Founded in 1899, the utility operates in one of the nation's fastest-growing service areas. Florida ranks fourth among the most populated states.

Diversified operations are conducted primarily in two business segments. Electric Fuels Corp. is a coal mining and transportation subsidiary that serves Florida Power as well as other electric utilities and industrial companies. Mid-Continent Life Insurance Company is headquartered in Oklahoma City and serves customers in 37 states with policies sold through 7,000 independent agents. It has held the

FIGURE 6.2   The Dividend Connection Chart

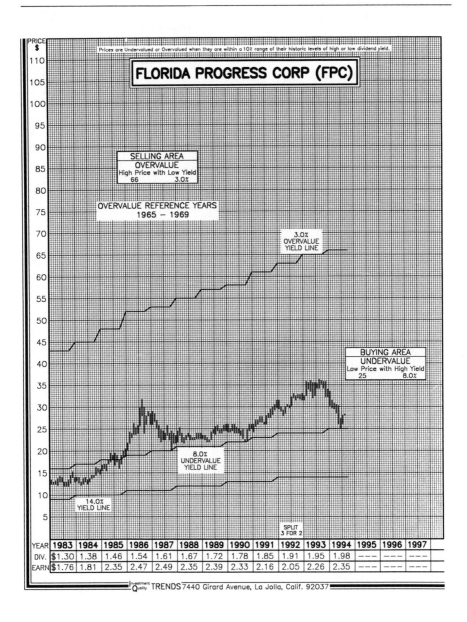

FLORIDA PROGRESS CORP (FPC)

Prices are Undervalued or Overvalued when they are within a 10% range of their historic levels of high or low dividend yield.

SELLING AREA
OVERVALUE
High Price with Low Yield
66   3.0%

OVERVALUE REFERENCE YEARS
1965 – 1969

3.0%
OVERVALUE
YIELD LINE

BUYING AREA
UNDERVALUE
Low Price with High Yield
25   8.0%

8.0%
UNDERVALUE
YIELD LINE

14.0%
YIELD LINE

SPLIT
3 FOR 2

YEAR	1983	1984	1985	1986	1987	1988	1989	1990	1991	1992	1993	1994	1995	1996	1997
DIV.	$1.30	1.38	1.46	1.54	1.61	1.67	1.72	1.78	1.85	1.91	1.95	1.98	---	---	---
EARN	$1.76	1.81	2.35	2.47	2.49	2.35	2.39	2.33	2.16	2.05	2.26	2.35	---	---	---

Investment Quality TRENDS 7440 Girard Avenue, La Jolla, Calif. 92037

highest insurance rating of A+ for 14 consecutive years from the nation's foremost insurance rating agency.

Florida Progress's strategy involves stringent cost efficiency and aggressive adaptation to regulatory changes. In the area of cost cutting, the utility is closing two of its older units while placing newer, more efficient ones on-line. Florida Power is in good shape to glean opportunity from ongoing industry changes. The company's operational efficiency and financial strength portends its ability to prosper where other utilities may falter.

Other Interesting Qualities

- Electric utility contributes 83% of Florida Progress's total revenues.

- Electric revenue mix is 54% residential, 24% commercial, 8% industrial, 14% other.

- Fuel mix is 47% coal, 24% oil, 16% nuclear, 13% purchased.

- Energy costs amount to 34% of revenues.

- Dividends paid since 1937 have been increased in each of the past 41 years.

Similar to most publicly held electric utilities, FPC has established three benchmarks of investment value. When the stock is priced to yield 8%, as it was almost exclusively from 1985 through 1991, FPC is undervalued and a purchase is recommended. If this chart were extended back an additional 20 years, it would reveal an overvalued yield of 3% from 1965 through 1969. In the early 1980s, when interest rates were high, FPC was priced to yield an extraordinary 14%. In view of a low interest rate environment, we do not expect this yield to be revisited in the foreseeable future. Rather, because of sweeping changes in the industry, FPC is more likely to accelerate its growth and return to an overvalued area where the yield is 3%. At undervalue, the stock will generate a bright long-term total return.

Is It Smart To Buy Stocks in a Rising Trend?

Stocks are considered to be in rising trends after they have moved up 10% or more off their undervalued bases. Technically, stocks remain in rising trends until they are within 10% of their overvalued prices or fall back to within 10% of their undervalued prices. To us, the term rising trend is a cyclical indicator, not necessarily a linear price move.

Rising trend stocks do not travel a straight and narrow one-way path. A stock often launches a rising trend, only to return to undervalue in a general market decline. Also, a stock may stay above its undervalued price in a rising trend for some time, moving sideways until the price eventually breaks out and continues up.

All things being equal, stocks that represent the best value and the greatest upside potential are undervalued ones, sporting historically high dividend yields. However, when a stock is near its undervalued price but technically in a rising trend, a buying opportunity still may be at hand.

There are two mitigating factors to consider.

First, is it a bull or a bear market? During a bear market, one rarely should buy a stock in a rising trend. Generally, the downward force of the market will halt and reverse the uptrend. In this case, the stock will return to its undervalued price, disappointing the investor who purchased it prematurely.

The second factor to consider is the upside potential to overvalue versus the downside risk back to undervalue for the stock. When the primary trend is up during a bull market, stocks in newly launched rising trends may be attractive buying opportunities. In this case, the critical question is: How much of the rising trend already has taken place.

If, for example, the broad market is undervalued or in a primary rising trend and the stock in question has risen only 15% or 20% from its undervalued price, a purchase can be considered. Its broad upside potential justifies its limited downside risk—especially if the stock has a strong history of dividend growth. As previously noted, dividend increases will lift the prices at undervalue and overvalue, tightening the safety net under the original purchase. In addition, dividend growth spurs continued price growth and increases investment income, which adds momentum to the uptrend.

The Dividend Connection

Ennis Business Forms

Harcourt General

The following two profiles illustrate stocks in rising trends. One of them, Ennis Business Forms, is newly launched, and the other, Harcourt General, is nearing overvalue. Obviously, the former represents better value.

Ennis Business Forms, Inc. (NYSE:EBF)

Ennis is among the largest producers of business forms in the nation. Founded in Ennis, Texas, in 1909, the company operates 13 manufacturing facilities in 11 strategically located states. About 85% of the business forms are customized and constructed on the basis of each client's individual needs. The company also owns Connolly Tool & Machine Company, acquired in 1980 and located in Dallas, Texas. Connolly designs tools, dies and specialty machinery. Like Ennis's business forms, all the products are highly specialized; but, unlike Ennis, Connolly serves customers primarily in the Southwest.

The most competitive force facing Ennis is the emerging dominance of desktop publishers and laser printers that create low-cost business forms. The segment most affected is small businesses, which account for a large share of Ennis's revenues. Still, the company is effectively counterbalancing the challenge with competitive rate reductions and highly specialized microprinting for small businesses. Another potentially damaging factor is the industry trend toward electronic data interchange, which diminishes the need for hard copy forms. This development is playing a part in the large business divisions, but so far the impact on sales has been slight.

Other Interesting Qualities

- Business forms account for almost 90% of sales.

FIGURE 6.3   The Dividend Connection Chart

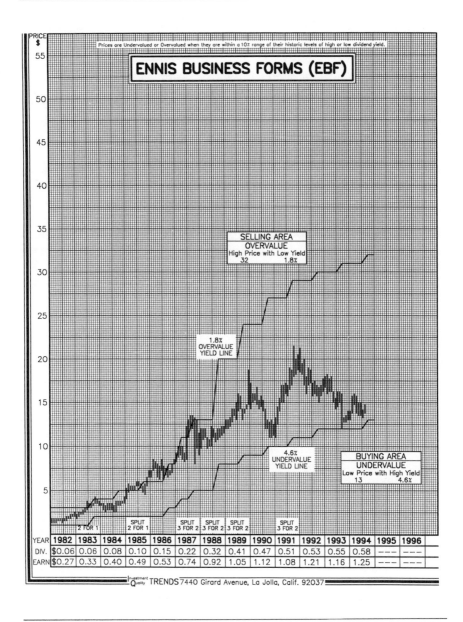

ENNIS BUSINESS FORMS (EBF)

Prices are Undervalued or Overvalued when they are within a 10% range of their historic levels of high or low dividend yield.

SELLING AREA
OVERVALUE
High Price with Low Yield
32   1.8%

1.8%
OVERVALUE
YIELD LINE

4.6%
UNDERVALUE
YIELD LINE

BUYING AREA
UNDERVALUE
Low Price with High Yield
13   4.6%

YEAR	1982	1983	1984	1985	1986	1987	1988	1989	1990	1991	1992	1993	1994	1995	1996
DIV.	$0.06	0.06	0.08	0.10	0.15	0.22	0.32	0.41	0.47	0.51	0.53	0.55	0.58	---	---
EARN	$0.27	0.33	0.40	0.49	0.53	0.74	0.92	1.05	1.12	1.08	1.21	1.16	1.25	---	---

Investment Quality TRENDS 7440 Girard Avenue, La Jolla, Calif. 92037

- Sales are conducted through some 30,000 independent dealers nationwide.

- Debt is only 1% of total capitalization.

- An employee trust fund owns 9% of common stock; directors own 3%.

- Dividends paid since 1973 have been increased every year since then.

EBF fluctuates between yield extremes of 4.6% at undervalue and 1.8% at overvalue. Ennis was undervalued in 1981 and 1982. From mid-1983 through October 1987, the stock was in an overvalued range. After losing almost one-half of its value in 1987, EBF quickly bounced back, but it has not yet reached the heights of overvalue. A relatively young stock in the blue chip ranks, Ennis has had only 20 years to establish its dividend yield profile. Still, the growth rate has been impressive and bodes well for the future. At undervalue, Ennis Business Forms should cut through the red tape and produce black ink for its shareholders.

Harcourt General, Inc. (NYSE:H)

In business, there are times when the child outgrows its parents. Such is the case with Harcourt General. Formed by a merger of Harcourt Brace Jovanovich and General Cinema in 1991, the marriage produced four offspring whose interests lie in international publishing, specialty retailing, insurance operations and professional services.

The publishing segment accounts for roughly 40% of earnings. It is the world's leading publisher of educational, scientific, technical, medical, legal and trade field books. The *Harbrace College Handbook*, first published in 1941, now in its 12th edition, is the best selling college textbook of all time.

The company's specialty retailing segment includes a distinctive collection of stores. Neiman Marcus, the world-renowned high fashion clothier, serves customers through an elite chain of 27 stores in 24 cities. Bergdorf Goodman, with perhaps the world's preeminent retail location at 5th Avenue and 58th Street in New York City, offers customers apparel and accessories from leading international designers. Contempo Casuals provides trendy fashions and accessories for

FIGURE 6.4   The Dividend Connection Chart

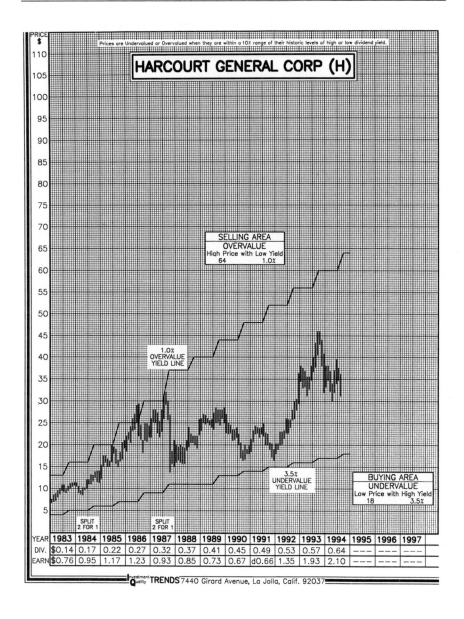

YEAR	1983	1984	1985	1986	1987	1988	1989	1990	1991	1992	1993	1994	1995	1996	1997
DIV.	$0.14	0.17	0.22	0.27	0.32	0.37	0.41	0.45	0.49	0.53	0.57	0.64	---	---	---
EARN	$0.76	0.95	1.17	1.23	0.93	0.85	0.73	0.67	d0.66	1.35	1.93	2.10	---	---	---

Investment Quality TRENDS 7440 Girard Avenue, La Jolla, Calif. 92037

young women through a chain of 290 stores in shopping malls throughout 35 states and Puerto Rico.

Harcourt's insurance divisions are engaged in underwriting individual health, life, accident and credit insurance policies. The company also sells annuity products. The professional services operations are performed by Drake Beam Morin. Professional services are facilitated at 67 domestic and 84 international offices in 26 nations.

Other Interesting Qualities

• Revenue mix is 55% retailing, 26% publishing, 15% insurance, 4% professional services.

• Insiders own 30% of the common stock.

• Dividends paid since 1953 have been increased in each of the past 25 years.

When this stock is priced to yield 3.5%, it is undervalued and a purchase is recommended. However, when the price rises and the yield falls to 1%, it is overvalued and a sale should be considered.

Harcourt entered a rising trend in early 1988, but the recession that began in 1990 reversed the trend. The stock launched another ambitious rising trend in early 1992 that produced extraordinary growth for nearly two years until an overextended bull market pulled in its horns and caused the stock to retreat. Although the chart reflects a technical rising trend, it clearly shows far more downside risk than upside potential. In this case, an investor will be wise to wait for the stock to retreat to undervalue, where Harcourt will produce outstanding growth and solid capital gains.

When Should I Find Stocks in a Declining Trend Attractive?

The stock market obeys the law of gravity. What goes up eventually must come down. Once an overvalued goal has been reached, the downside risk rarely justifies holding the stock for additional upside gain. At overvalue, a sale should be considered to preserve profits and capital.

Stocks should be judged on the basis of risk versus reward. What is the upside potential? What is the downside risk? Investing is a matter of percentages, not points. Stocks listed in the declining trends category already have retreated at least 10% from their overvalued peaks. Sometimes a newly launched decline will reverse and the stock will rise again to overvalue, giving the owner a second chance to sell, but second chances are not guaranteed. Therefore, at the early stage of a declining trend, when the downside risk is large and the upside potential is small, a sale is advisable.

As a declining trend stock moves down, the risk-reward equation changes. In the later stages of a decline, the downside risk may be acceptable and the stock need not be sold. By the time the market has erased 50% from a stock price, most of the damage has been done. At that point, the stockholder may decide to ride out the rest of the decline, if there is more to come. One knows by then where the stock is going and is less likely to sell in despair at the bottom. If cash is available and the company continues to merit confidence, the investor may plan to buy additional shares when the price of the stock returns to undervalued levels, thereby mitigating the loss.

Some investors will choose to hold a stock no matter what, assuming that even if the price declines it eventually will rebound and the losses will be recouped. These loyalists view the sale of a stock that has rewarded them well as a betrayal. Also, there may be tax consequences to consider. If the stock has been held for a long time and there are huge profits to report, the capital gains tax may make a sale undesirable. An owner may decide to hold the stock for income and dividend growth and let his or her heirs grapple with the treatment of capital gains. But from a value standpoint, these considerations should not interfere with the sound judgment of an enlightened investor.

If a stock is in the final stages of a declining trend, a purchase may be considered. The stock will appear in the undervalued category when it is within 10% of its undervalued price. Therefore, when a declining trend stock approaches undervalue and is perhaps 15% to 25% above the undervalued price, an aggressive investor may opt to take a position. As the stock approaches undervalue, dollar cost averaging can be engaged.

Still, the patient investor will simply observe the decline and wait for the stock to settle at an undervalued price where there is a minimum of risk and a maximum potential for long-term investment growth.

In summary, stocks in early declining trends should be sold. As the declines progress, the stocks should be avoided. Stocks in the final stages of a declining trend should be watched in anticipation of an attractive buying opportunity at undervalue.

Figure 6.5 illustrates the risk-reward ratio for selected stocks in the declining trends category. The first table lists stocks with small downside risks versus large upside potentials. These stocks are nearing their undervalued prices and soon may be attractive investment selections. The second table lists declining trend stocks with large downside risks versus small upside potentials. These stocks should be sold to protect profits and should be avoided until their declining trends come to an end.

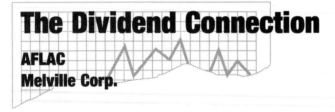

Let's analyze the risk-reward profiles of two declining trend stocks. AFLAC is a stock with large downside risk and small upside potential. Melville Corp. is a stock with small downside risk and large upside potential.

AFLAC Inc. (NYSE:AFL)

A Georgia-based holding company whose principal subsidiary is American Family Life Assurance, AFLAC sells specialty insurance products designed to supplement primary insurance coverage. The company operates primarily in the United States and Japan, but also conducts business in six other foreign countries. In addition, AFLAC owns and operates seven network-affiliated TV stations.

FIGURE 6.5   Stocks in Declining Trends—Risk vs. Reward

	Small Downside Risk	Large Upside Potential
Abbott Laboratories	24%	86%
American Brands, Inc.	22	78
American Business	15	65
American Home Products Corp.	14	70
Church & Dwight Company	18	55
Geico Corp.	24	100
Keystone International, Inc.	14	77
Lance Inc.	12	124
Melville Corp.	21	82
Universal Corp.	21	53

	Large Downside Risk	Small Upside Potential
AFLAC Inc.	82	15
Alltel Corp.	55	12
American Greetings	59	21
Chubb Corp.	64	18
Donaldson Corp.	67	19
Illinois Tool Works Inc.	70	18
Interpublic Group of Companies, Inc.	72	16
Norwest Corp.	65	15
Sherwin-Williams Company	75	16
Tootsie Roll Industries	85	20

Founded 40 years ago, AFLAC has transformed itself from a regional company selling only one product to an international insurer offering a broad range of supplemental policies. Its experience and flexibility has enabled it to grow and adapt to a rapidly changing business environment.

Like the rest of America, AFLAC is braced in anticipation of the long-awaited health care reform. The company is in a unique position to benefit from a universal national health care system. Japan has had such a system for two decades; yet those consumers recognize that their primary health insurance cannot cover all medical expenses. That's why more than 22% of Japan's population relies on AFLAC's supplemental insurance coverage. This type of model could prove

FIGURE 6.6 The Dividend Connection Chart

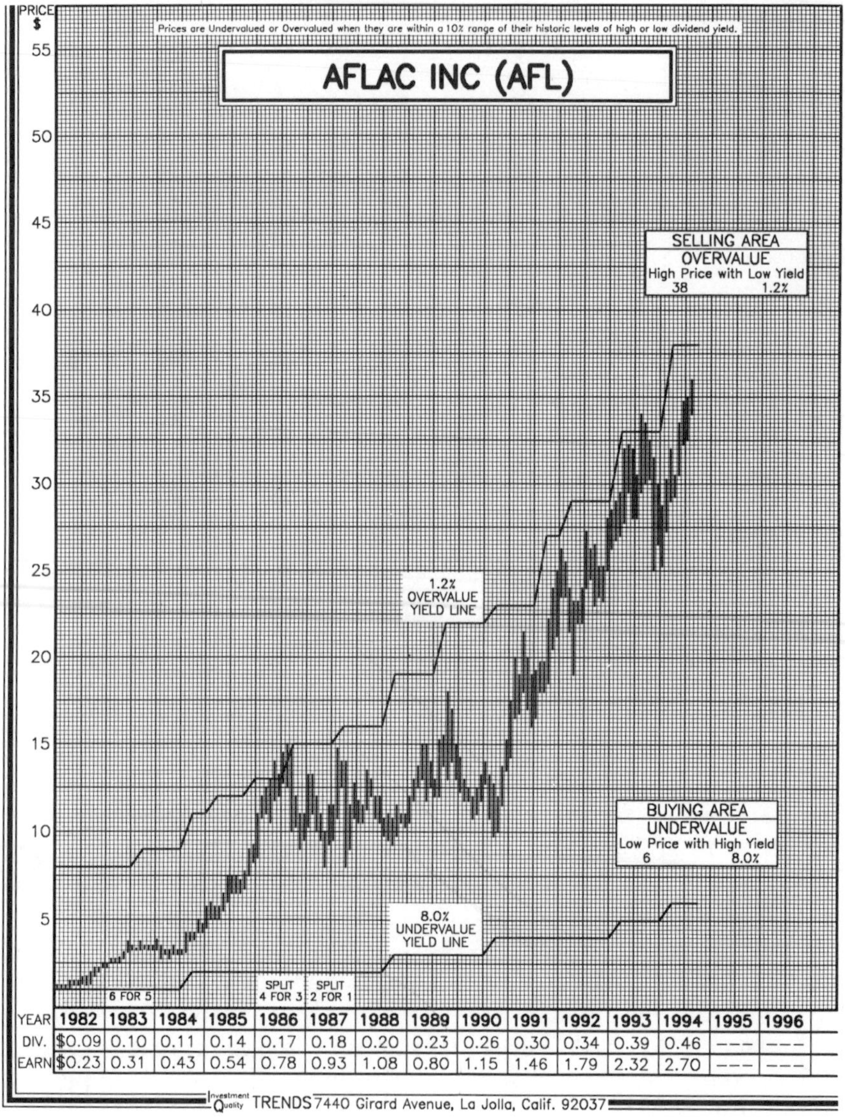

YEAR	1982	1983	1984	1985	1986	1987	1988	1989	1990	1991	1992	1993	1994	1995	1996
DIV.	$0.09	0.10	0.11	0.14	0.17	0.18	0.20	0.23	0.26	0.30	0.34	0.39	0.46	---	---
EARN	$0.23	0.31	0.43	0.54	0.78	0.93	1.08	0.80	1.15	1.46	1.79	2.32	2.70	---	---

Investment Quality TRENDS 7440 Girard Avenue, La Jolla, Calif. 92037

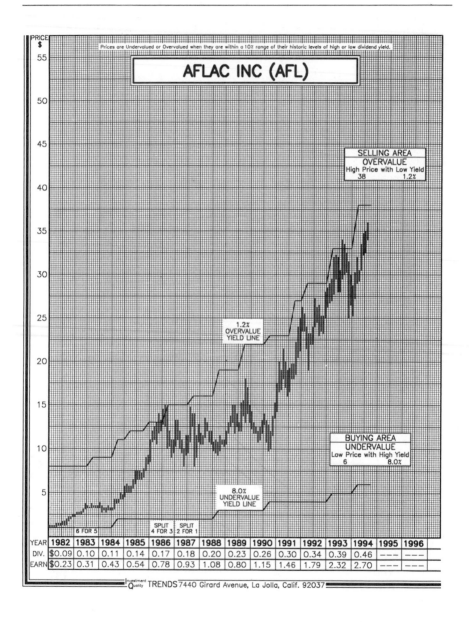

highly profitable for AFLAC's U.S. operations if universal health coverage becomes a reality.

Other Interesting Qualities

- AFLAC is the world's largest underwriter of supplemental cancer insurance.

- Japan operations account for roughly 75% of revenues.

- *Financial World* magazine named AFLAC the number one financially secure insurance company in the United States.

- Dividends paid since 1973 have been increased in each of the past 12 years.

The chart illustrates AFL's tremendous growth over the past 12 years. When this stock is priced to yield 8%, as it was in 1982 and 1984, it is undervalued and a purchase is recommended. However, when the price rises and the yield falls to 1.2%, as it did in 1986, 1991 and 1993, AFL is overvalued and a sale should be considered. Consistent dividend growth has lifted the price at undervalue and overvalue so that from 1991 through 1994 AFLAC remained at or near overvalue.

Besides the irrefutable fact that AFLAC is historically overvalued, other risk factors that support a declining trend include a potential reversal of the exchange rate with the yen and unpredictable health care reform. Still, at undervalue, this well-managed blue chip will provide its shareholders with the coverage necessary for long-term portfolio growth.

Melville Corp. (NYSE:MES)

In the business of satisfying customers through a nationwide network of specialty retail stores, Melville operates in four industry segments. The apparel division includes Marshalls and Wilson's House of Suede and Leather. Drug, health and beauty aids are sold through CVS stores. The footwear division includes Thom McAn, FootAction and Meldisco. Toys and household furniture are sold by This End's Up and Linens 'n Things. Headquartered in Rye, New York, all Melville stores offer a broad range of merchandise appealing to value-conscious consumers.

FIGURE 6.7   The Dividend Connection Chart

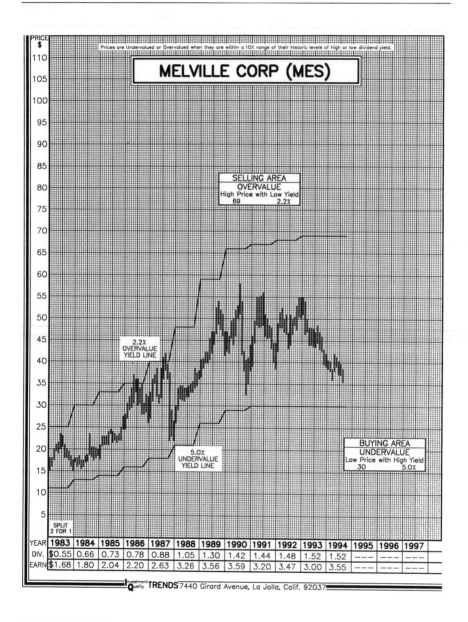

CVS continues to have the right prescription for success as the leading drugstore chain in the Northeast and Mid-Atlantic region of the nation. CVS stores rank first in 20 of the 29 major metropolitan markets they serve. The company also is marketing its pharmacy effectively to insurance companies and health maintenance organizations.

In 1994, Marshalls opened 40 new stores and remodeled about 50 existing stores. Although Marshalls has been adversely affected by a weak retail apparel environment, it has made good progress toward improving its customer appeal. The chain's physical growth plus an aggressive marketing strategy should put earnings back on track in the future.

A large part of the Melville strategy has been to divest its underperforming units. To that end, three of its major subsidiaries were sold—Chess King, Accessory Lady and Print Plus. In addition, 250 Thom McAn stores were closed or redesigned into FootAction stores. Footwear sales have been light in the loafers but are expected to step up as more lackluster units are converted into the trendy sport shoe format.

Other Interesting Qualities

- Sales mix is 35% drugstores, 33% apparel, 18% footwear, 14% toys and household.

- Melville owns and operates 7,300 stores and leased departments.

- Dividends paid since 1916 have been increased in each of the past 30 years.

The chart illustrates the volatile nature of Melville and the retail industry. When this stock is priced to yield 5%, MES is undervalued and represents a good buying opportunity. But when the price rises and the yield falls to 2.2%, MES is overvalued and a sale should be considered. Although MES lost nearly one half of its market value in 1990, it did not come within 10% of undervalue. Therefore, the stock continues to be technically in a long-term declining trend from its high price in 1989. Based on the strength of its drugstore chain and the strategic altering of its apparel segment, Melville is expected to perform well throughout the rest of this century—and beyond.

Is Market Timing Important?

An investment approach that is geared to value will be more success-ful over time than one that attempts to buy only at market bottoms and sell at market tops.

Certainly, market timing is important, and a recognition of values can improve timing strategies. But the perfect timing tool—one that works at all times—has yet to be discovered and probably does not exist. If it did, the entire procedure of auction market buying and selling by which the stock market operates would fail. At critical junctures, there would be no buyers to whom sellers could sell, or no sellers from whom buyers could buy.

Rather than search for the Holy Grail in the stock market, inves-tors should focus on quality and value to point the way to long-term financial security. Investors who buy good quality, dividend-paying stocks at undervalued prices need not worry about market timing.

But good quality, dividend-paying stocks at overvalued prices should be sold. Our research shows that on October 19, 1987, the prices of non-dividend-paying stocks fell 32%, while dividend-pay-ing stocks fell 22%, and undervalued blue chip stocks fell only 2%.

Therefore, while the timing of individual stock value is important, timing the overall stock market is less relevant to a sound investment strategy.

The Dividend Connection

Anheuser-Busch
Brown-Forman (Class B)

The following two stocks illustrate the fact that some stocks will rise in a down market, while others will decline even though the broad market is rising. Anheuser-Busch performed well in a down market, while Brown-Forman fell to undervalued levels in an up market.

Anheuser-Busch Companies, Inc. (NYSE:BUD)

Behind the foam of Budweiser beer is the substance of 137 years of growth and experience by Anheuser-Busch, the nation's largest brewer. Founded in 1852, the company has led the industry in sales, capacity, income and profitability for 32 consecutive years. Beer accounts for 77% of the company's annual sales and 92% of its profits, with the popular Budweiser brand accounting for three-fourths of the total. Other brands include: Bud Light, Busch, Michelob and Natural Light. True to its claim, Anheuser-Busch is the "King of Beers."

The company also is the nation's second largest producer of fresh baked goods through its subsidiary, Campbell Taggart, and a leading supplier of snack foods with its company-owned Eagle brand. Anheuser's amusement park operations around the country are second in size only to the Disney parks.

Other Interesting Qualities

- One out of every four beers consumed is a Bud.
- Carlsberg beer and Elephant Malt Liquor are distributed in the United States by Anheuser-Busch.
- Dividends, paid each year since 1932, average 25% of earnings.

For BUD, a 4.4% dividend yield signals an undervalued buying opportunity. The stock is overvalued when the yield falls to 1%, as it did in 1970, 1971 and 1972—prior to a six-year bear market. Since 1983, annual dividend increases have lifted the payout by 500%. The price also has gained 500%. An investment in BUD in the early 1980s yielded a cash return of 22% on the original capital by 1994. Such are the long-term benefits of investing in blue chip stocks with rising dividend trends.

Following an anticipated stock market correction, the rising trend in BUD should continue to carry the price skyward. The stock is an attractive long-term holding, but new purchases are best delayed until the market offers a more timely buying opportunity. As a core holding in a portfolio of blue chips, "this Bud's for you."

FIGURE 6.8   The Dividend Connection Chart

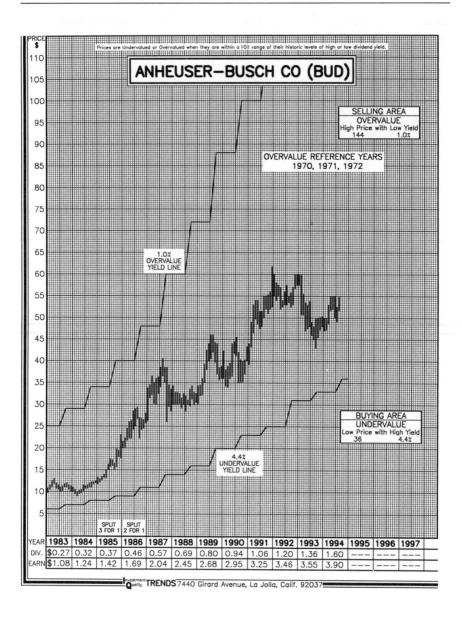

Brown-Forman Corp. (Class B) (NYSE:BFB)

The toast of the distilled spirits industry, Brown-Forman was founded in 1870 and now ranks among the top producers and importers of alcoholic beverages in the United States. The corporate wet bar includes major brand names like Bolla, Canadian Mist, Early Times, Fetzer, Jack Daniels, Korbel and Southern Comfort. Through its Lenox group of companies, BFB also produces fine china, crystal, silver and luggage.

To take advantage of international growth opportunities, BF has brewed a new unified beverage organization that began operation in 1994. Brown-Forman Beverage Worldwide replaces and expands upon two former divisions—domestic and international. The new organization consists of a potent mix of four sales and marketing divisions.

Although there is some criticism of the alcoholic beverage industry in our culture, Brown-Forman sales continue to grow at an intoxicating rate. Despite softness in the distilled spirits business in general and in the whiskey category in particular, Jack Daniels tanked up an increase in U.S. volume in 1994. The brand also gained market share for the ninth consecutive year. Jack Daniels continues to be the top-selling premium distilled spirit in the United States, outperforming its nearest competitor by a staggering 13%.

Other Interesting Qualities

- Revenue mix is 79% spirits, 21% durable goods.

- BFB is a *Fortune* 500 company.

- Insiders own roughly 64% of Class A and 29% of Class B shares.

- Dividends paid since 1960 have been increased ten times in the past 12 years.

The chart clearly illustrates the concept on which our approach is based. When BFB is priced to yield 3.7%, it is undervalued and a buying opportunity is at hand. However, when the price rises and the yield falls to 2%, BFB is overvalued and a sale should be considered. Over the past decade, frequent and generous dividend increases have lifted the prices at undervalue and overvalue. Still, the yield profile has remained constant. When the stock was overvalued in

FIGURE 6.9   The Dividend Connection Chart

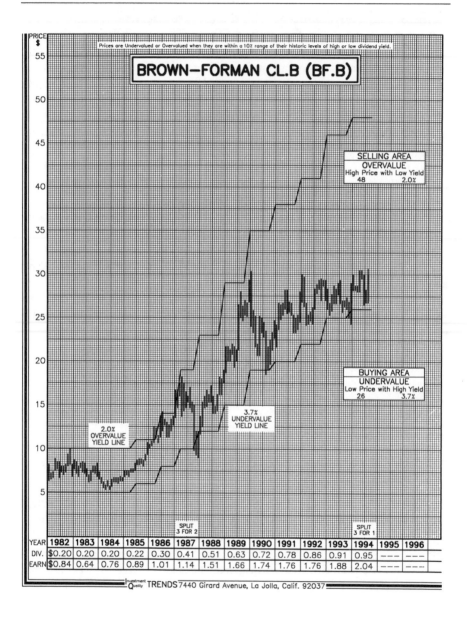

early 1987, a dividend increase added head room to the price of the stock. But before long, the stock took a dive leaving shareholders with an undervalued hangover later that year.

While the yield at undervalue appears modest, this growth stock has increased its dividend at a compound annual rate of 16% over the past ten years. At undervalue, investors can belly up to BFB and nail down a high-proof total return.

Do Institutional Investors Influence Stock Prices?

To deny the importance of institutions on the trends of stock prices is to close our eyes to the market's most influential group of investors. Like it or not, institutions, including banks, insurance companies, mutual funds, pension funds and retirement accounts dominate approximately 90% of all stock trading done in the market on any given day. Money moves the market, and institutions have enough money to move the market significantly.

It is very difficult for professional money managers to make independent determinations about the stock market. Institutional investors tend to associate with, listen to and eventually behave like other institutional investors. They cannot help but be influenced by the opinions of their peers, all of whom speak with great authority but have wide-ranging intellectual capacities. The result is a distilled average of the best and worst advice. And although they would deny it, institutional investors do have conflicts of interest. They want stock prices to rise because they are being paid to invest, not to sit on cash. Therefore, their rose-colored classes often blind them to the signs of danger. They hope that their decisions are right, but they don't mind being wrong if they have acted in concert with their peers.

Institutional interest in a stock is a mixed blessing. Professional investors can bid prices up to overvalue when they favor a particular company or industry group. They also can pull the rug out from under a stock when the news is bad and they all try to sell at the same time. How often have we seen a stock rise on the recommendation of an influential broker, or fall when a popular money manager says to sell? Still, institutional investors are more likely to be buying when a stock is undervalued. They are more apt to bail out when a stock is overvalued.

Institutions dominate stock market trading, and in most cases they are majority shareholders. Therefore, it is far safer for minority shareholders if a large number of institutions own the stock of a company than if there are few owners with large holdings.

We list as one of our six criteria for blue chip quality that at least 80 institutions should hold the stock. We are not as concerned with specific numbers as we are with a wide demonstration of institutional support. We want to own stocks that attract a broad and diverse institutional following. The number 80 is somewhat arbitrary—high enough to indicate significant institutional interest, but not so high that it lacks room to expand.

There is safety in numbers. If institutional investors suddenly panic over some piece of news and drive down the price of a stock, knowledgeable investors can purchase those shares at undervalued levels. When the trend is reversed, the same institutional investors who hastened to sell will be just as anxious to repurchase their shares, and prices will rise.

The companies listed in Figure 6.10 each have 500 or more institutional stock owners. These are the most widely held blue chip companies in America. You will notice that in many cases, institutions hold 50% or more of the total number of shares outstanding. Of course, institutional interest is not the only factor which investors should take into account, but it is a point to consider.

The Dividend Connection

Air Products and Chemicals
AMP Inc.

This section profiles two stocks with 80 percent or more institutional ownership—Air Products and Chemicals and AMP Inc.

FIGURE 6.10   Institutional Blockbusters

Stock	# Inst. Holding	(Shares in millions) Inst. Shares	Total Shares	% Inst. Ownership
General Electric Company	1437	484	857	56%
Philip Morris Companies	1248	473	877	54
AT&T	1154	464	1362	34
Merck & Company	1149	602	1254	48
Exxon Corp.	1132	505	1242	41
Bristol-Myers Squibb Company	1107	242	511	47
Pepsico	1092	468	799	59
Johnson & Johnson	1047	375	643	58
GTE Corp.	980	404	953	42
Motorola, Inc.	974	424	557	76
Pfizer Inc.	966	204	321	64
Coca-Cola Company	957	711	1297	55
American Home Products Corp.	935	194	310	63
Schlumberger	912	144	244	59
Abbott Laboratories	910	423	820	52
American International Group, Inc.	900	172	318	54
Minnesota Mining and Manufacturing Company	899	303	428	71
Royal Dutch Petroleum Company	896	164	536	31
Procter & Gamble Company	889	326	683	48
Wal-Mart Stores, Inc.	879	675	2299	29
McDonald's Corp.	870	234	354	66
Schering-Plough Corp.	864	131	194	68
Disney (Walt) Company	857	249	537	46
Du Pont (E.I.) De Nemours & Company	836	284	679	42
Morgan (J.P.) Company	835	130	193	67
Hewlett-Packard Company	833	146	253	58
Southwestern Bell Corp.	818	231	600	39
WMX Technologies, Inc.	759	255	483	53
Emerson Electric Company	757	147	224	66
Bell Atlantic Corp.	749	147	436	34
Union Pacific Corp.	746	135	205	66
Boeing Company	732	159	340	47
Gillette Company	731	159	221	72
Penney (J.C.) Company	722	187	236	79
Warner-Lambert Company	714	98	134	73
Dun & Bradstreet Corp.	713	128	170	75
Lilly (Eli) & Company	691	199	293	68
Kmart Corp.	690	274	409	67
May Department Stores	655	180	248	73
Weyerhaeuser Company	650	118	205	58
Monsanto Company	646	77	116	66

FIGURE 6.10   Institutional Blockbusters (Continued)

Stock	# Inst. Holding	Inst. Shares	Total Shares	% Inst. Ownership
Anheuser-Busch Companies, Inc.	637	157	266	59%
Raytheon Company	637	102	135	76
Banc One Corp.	636	201	381	53
Ameritech Corp.	635	190	547	35
General Mills, Inc.	634	98	159	62
Sara Lee Corp.	630	224	478	47
General Re Corp.	601	72	84	86
Norfolk Southern Corp.	600	84	138	61
AMP Inc.	594	86	105	82
CPC International, Inc.	593	94	150	63
Kimberly-Clark Corp.	587	111	161	69
Gannett Company	586	104	147	71
Pitney Bowes Inc.	569	123	158	78
Texas Utilities Company	557	118	226	52
Archer Daniels Midland Company	553	168	327	51
Automatic Data Processing, Inc.	551	102	142	72
American Brands, Inc.	535	112	202	55
American Cyanamid	531	61	90	68
Heinz (H.J.) Company	524	136	252	54
Chubb Corp.	519	62	88	70
Southern Company	509	196	751	26
Norwest Corp.	503	216	315	69
PPG Industries Inc.	501	55	106	52
American General Corp.	500	153	214	71
Air Products and Chemicals, Inc.	500	91	114	80

Air Products & Chemicals, Inc. (NYSE:APD)

A leading supplier of industrial gases and equipment to the chemical, steel, electronics, oil and food industries, Air Products and Chemicals also designs and manufactures the facilities and equipment used to control and discharge these products. Based in Allentown, Pennsylvania, Air Products is a *Fortune* 500 company that ranks 150th in terms of sales and 60th in terms of profits.

The company is the third largest supplier of industrial gases in the world. Its principal products include nitrogen, oxygen, hydrogen and helium. Many of these gases are delivered and distributed through cylinders, trucks, pipelines and on-site plants. The chemicals

FIGURE 6.11   The Dividend Connection Chart

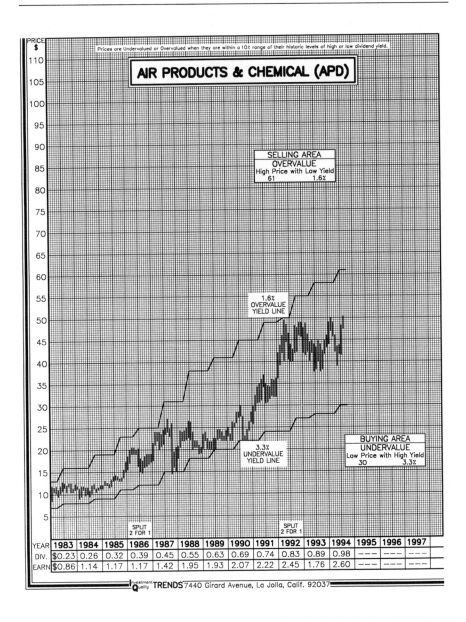

division holds leadership positions in 90% of its markets, which include adhesives, agricultural, furniture, automotive, paints, textiles and building products.

The company's environmental and energy systems are designed to dispose of solid waste, reduce air pollution and generate electric power. This division's major markets are waste-to-energy plants, cogeneration facilities and landfill sites. The political shift toward utility deregulation and environmental sensitivity increases this segment's usefulness.

The equipment and technology unit designs and manufactures products for air separation, natural gas processing and hydrogen purification. These applications are used in steel, oil and gas, chemicals and power generation markets. Although profit margins are tightening, Air Products remains profitable in all four business segments.

Other Interesting Qualities

- Foreign operations account for 25% of sales.

- Institutions hold 80% of the common stock.

- Dividends paid since 1954 have been increased in each of the past 12 years.

When this stock is priced to yield 3.3%, APD is undervalued and a purchase is recommended. However, when the price rises and the yield falls to 1.6%, APD is overvalued and a sale should be considered. Frequent and generous dividend increases have supported consistent price growth, but the yield extremes have remained accurate and inviolate.

Air Products is among the widest institutionally held stocks on the New York Stock Exchange, with 500 separate institutions holding 80% of the common stock. Clearly, institutional interest plays a major role in the price trends of this stock. Since institutions move the market, individual investors are wise to recognize the institutional allure of Air Products & Chemicals.

AMP Inc. (NYSE:AMP)

As the leading producer of electrical devices, AMP is plugged into one of the fastest-growing, most highly competitive businesses in the world. More than 90% of its revenue is generated from the sale of connection devices. Headquartered in Harrisburg, Pennsylvania, the company operates 175 facilities in 33 nations. The undisputed heavyweight in its industry, AMP is four times the size of its closest competitor. The company holds nearly 3,000 product patents in the United States and some 10,000 patents in 37 other countries.

Expansion is at the heart of AMP's strategy. In the United States, a large automotive connector facility in Greensboro, North Carolina, opened in 1994, and construction began on an engineering facility in the Harrisburg area. In Europe, expansion has AMP-lified in Spain, and the company's first plant in Budapest, Hungary, began operations in 1994. Newest projects include a second plant in Korea and marketing subsidiaries in Turkey, Poland and the Czech Republic.

Because of its broadly international nature, AMP was extremely pleased with the passage of the North American Free Trade Agreement. NAFTA will increase its exports to Canada and Mexico. The passage of NAFTA also bodes well for future movement toward mutually beneficial free trade throughout the company's global markets.

Other Interesting Qualities

- Sales mix is 35% communications, 30% transportation, 10% consumer goods, 25% other.

- Geographic mix is 41% United States, 35% Europe, 20% Asia/Pacific, 4% non-U.S. Americas.

- Institutions hold 82% of the common stock.

- Dividends paid since 1951 have been increased in each of the past 41 years.

When this stock is priced to yield 3%, AMP is undervalued and a purchase is recommended. When the price rises and the yield falls to 1.3%, AMP is overvalued and a sale should be considered. This chart illustrates the importance of following the dividend yield approach to investing in the stock market. By observing the extremes of AMP's

FIGURE 6.12   The Dividend Connection Chart

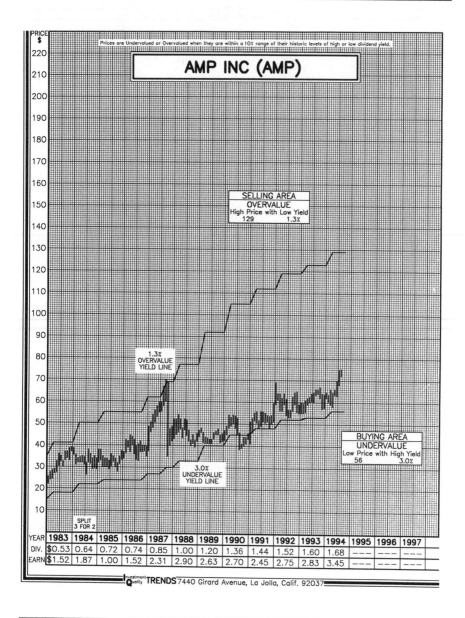

Prices are Undervalued or Overvalued when they are within a 10% range of their historic levels of high or low dividend yield.

AMP INC (AMP)

SELLING AREA
OVERVALUE
High Price with Low Yield
129   1.3%

1.3%
OVERVALUE
YIELD LINE

BUYING AREA
UNDERVALUE
Low Price with High Yield
56   3.0%

3.0%
UNDERVALUE
YIELD LINE

SPLIT
3 FOR 2

YEAR	1983	1984	1985	1986	1987	1988	1989	1990	1991	1992	1993	1994	1995	1996	1997
DIV.	$0.53	0.64	0.72	0.74	0.85	1.00	1.20	1.36	1.44	1.52	1.60	1.68	---	---	---
EARN	$1.52	1.87	1.00	1.52	2.31	2.90	2.63	2.70	2.45	2.75	2.83	3.45	---	---	---

Investment-Quality TRENDS 7440 Girard Avenue, La Jolla, Calif. 92037

yield profile over the past 12 years, an investor would have known when to buy, hold and sell, all the while enjoying an AMPle total return. This blue chip growth stock has boosted its dividend at an average annual rate of 14% over the past decade. At undervalue, AMP will represent a good buying opportunity as it connects its shareholders to excellent value in the market.

As a Small Investor, Do I Stand a Chance?

Emphatically, *yes*. In fact, a small investor has a better opportunity to be positioned for profits in the stock market than a large institutional investor who must get committee approval before making a purchase or sale. The institutional investor then must stand in line behind the individual investor to execute a large order.

Every investor in the stock market—including the largest portfolio manager—makes one of three decisions: to buy, to hold or to sell. The investor who recognizes good value can establish a buy and hold position when a stock is undervalued before the large institutions climb aboard.

Eventually, the pros (people who invest other people's money) will recognize good value, and the stock will rise. As Charles Dow once wrote: "Value has little to do with day-to-day fluctuations in stock prices, but it is the determining factor in the long run."

The stocks profiled in this section, AT&T and Du Pont, have major institutional support, but they also are widely held by individual investors.

AT&T Corp. (NYSE:T)

Today's AT&T is far different from the AT&T of ten years ago. The current company came into being on January 1, 1984, as a result of a court-ordered breakup of the Bell System's telecommunications business. The division consists of seven "baby bells" and AT&T. Now the world's leader of communications services and products, AT&T provides network equipment and computer services to businesses, consumers, telecommunications companies and government agencies. Formerly named American Telephone and Telegraph Company, the new AT&T has become one of the most recognized brand names in the world with operations in more than 200 countries.

After taking it on the chin following the Ma Bell split, AT&T learned from its mistakes and developed an awareness of its strengths. The company's main strength is its ability to build and manage large communications networks. This is the core of AT&T's business. But its network does not stand alone. It is enhanced by a unique business that combines communications and computing with network products and systems.

Other Interesting Qualities

- Revenue mix is 61% phone service, 25% products, 11% rentals, 3% financial services.

- Foreign sales account for 25% of revenues.

- Dividends paid since 1881 average 42% of earnings.

The chart of AT&T reflects an unusual set of circumstances that occurred as a result of the Bell breakup. When this stock is priced to yield 6%, as it was in 1986 and 1988, it is undervalued and a purchase is recommended. When the price rises and the yield falls to 2.5%, as it did in late 1989 and 1993, it is overvalued and a sale should be considered.

News of the Ma Bell division sent the price reeling downward to penetrate the yield at undervalue in 1984. But soon after the initial impact of the news wore off, the stock resurfaced to its established yield at undervalue. Conversely, when the telecommunications industry was all the rage in 1993, AT&T pierced the veil at overvalue but dipped back to revalidate its previously overvalued yield. Aberrations do occur, and parameters of overvalue and undervalue

FIGURE 6.13   The Dividend Connection Chart

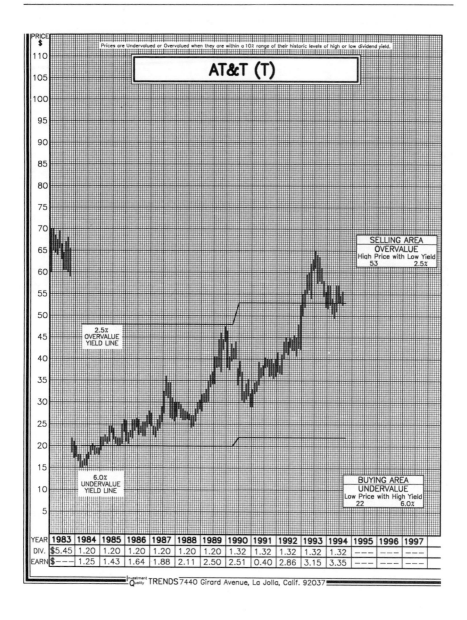

YEAR	1983	1984	1985	1986	1987	1988	1989	1990	1991	1992	1993	1994	1995	1996	1997
DIV.	$5.45	1.20	1.20	1.20	1.20	1.20	1.20	1.32	1.32	1.32	1.32	1.32	---	---	---
EARN	$---	1.25	1.43	1.64	1.88	2.11	2.50	2.51	0.40	2.86	3.15	3.35	---	---	---

Investment Quality TRENDS 7440 Girard Avenue, La Jolla, Calif. 92037

occasionally are violated. Still, they are exceptions, and historical benchmarks of value remain as significant indicators. AT&T is one of the most widely owned stocks on the New York Stock Exchange, with nearly 2½ million shareholders, many of whom are institutional investors. At undervalue, AT&T is a true voice for the small investor who wishes to dial direct for long-term financial growth.

Du Pont (E.I.) DeNemours & Company (NYSE:DD)

The largest chemical company in the United States, Du Pont produces a wide array of industrial and commercial products including: oil, natural gas, gasoline, coal, agricultural chemicals, nylon, film, resins, adhesives, electronic products, automotive paints, acrylics, fibers, x-ray products, diagnostic equipment and pharmaceuticals. Industrial products account for 63% of the company's profits. These goods are produced at 35 plants in the United States and Canada, one in Europe, three in Asia and five in Latin America. Petroleum operations, which account for 18% of profits, are conducted through Conoco, acquired in 1981. The company produces crude oil in the United States, Canada, Europe, Asia and the Middle East.

The petroleum segment is undertaking three major initiatives for the exploration and development of oil and natural gas reserves in the Soviet Union. Two of the initiatives cover oil- and gas-producing areas with potential reserves of 3 to 4 billion barrels. The third initiative involves a gas field in the Barents Sea that is believed to have reserves of more than 100 trillion cubic feet of natural gas.

The issue of rising oil prices is a double-edged sword for Du Pont. On the one hand, higher crude oil prices benefit Conoco, especially in its European market, where Du Pont has been able to pass on increased costs at the gasoline pump. On the other hand, the company's chemical operations are hurt by rising crude oil prices due to a softened effect on consumer spending and increased raw material costs, especially in the fibers division. Taking all things into consideration, a rise in oil prices will not have a favorable impact on the industry. However, Du Pont is better positioned than most to handle the potential hardship.

Other Interesting Qualities

• Foreign sales account for 44% of total sales.

FIGURE 6.14   The Dividend Connection Chart

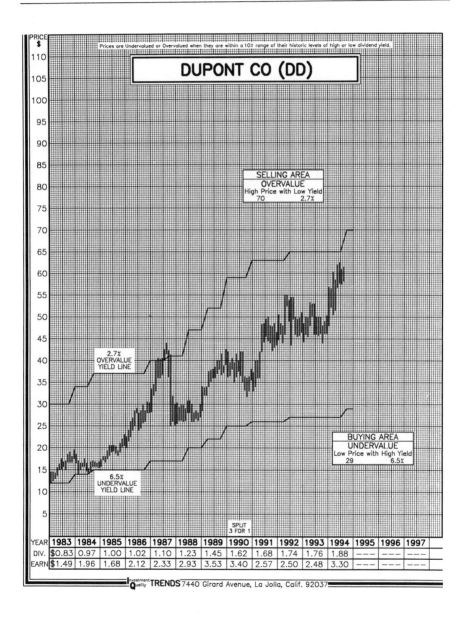

DUPONT CO (DD)

Prices are Undervalued or Overvalued when they are within a 10% range of their historic levels of high or low dividend yield.

SELLING AREA
OVERVALUE
High Price with Low Yield
70   2.7%

2.7%
OVERVALUE
YIELD LINE

BUYING AREA
UNDERVALUE
Low Price with High Yield
29   6.5%

6.5%
UNDERVALUE
YIELD LINE

SPLIT
3 FOR 1

YEAR	1983	1984	1985	1986	1987	1988	1989	1990	1991	1992	1993	1994	1995	1996	1997
DIV.	$0.83	0.97	1.00	1.02	1.10	1.23	1.45	1.62	1.68	1.74	1.76	1.88	---	---	---
EARN	$1.49	1.96	1.68	2.12	2.33	2.93	3.53	3.40	2.57	2.50	2.48	3.30	---	---	---

Investment
Quality TRENDS 7440 Girard Avenue, La Jolla, Calif. 92037

- Du Pont is the world's largest producer of titanium dioxide, used in making paint.

- The company has increased its dividends six times in the past five years.

- Dividends, paid each year since 1904, average 53% of earnings.

When the market reached its peak in 1987, the stock was priced to yield 2.7%. However, when the price fell and the yield rose to 5.2% in mid-1990, Du Pont reached undervalue and a buying opportunity presented itself.

One of the 30 Dow Jones industrial stocks, Du Pont is a powerful corporation. It is well managed and broadly diversified. The company has an important global presence and is increasing its worldwide contribution daily. Its products are valuable and necessary under any political or economic conditions. At undervalue, we recommend Du Pont as an investment choice.

Choosing the Best Stocks for Your Portfolio

Which Companies Are Relatively Debt-Free?

Since we have determined that companies with little or no long-term debt generally represent better quality than those with large debt loads, let's take a look at the companies that have kept their balance sheets relatively clean. We will see why this is an important indicator of good investment quality.

In good times, when the economy is robust, aggressively managed companies turn to the debt market to finance acquisitions or expansion programs. With borrowed capital, they hope to grow earnings more rapidly than would otherwise be possible. In hard economic times, when revenues decline and profit margins contract, the demands of debt pull heavily on corporate purse strings, restricting growth, inhibiting dividends and sometimes leading to bankruptcy. During a recession, companies with little or no long-term debt have a distinct advantage over companies with burdensome obligations in the money market. Debt-free and low-debt companies have the flexibility to reduce their expenses, streamline their operations and purchase assets from companies in need of cash. They also have the capital to support and even increase their dividends.

In addition to selling its products and services, a publicly owned company ordinarily raises capital in two ways—through the sale of common stock (equity) and through the sale of bonds (debt). In normal times, an equal mix of the two is considered a relatively safe and prudent capital structure. However, when the economy is in a recession, companies with a lower percentage of debt are better able to resist the problems of slower sales and lower earnings. Conservative investors should look for companies that carry no more than 20% debt as a percentage of their total capitalization.

Utilities stocks are an exception to the rule. They typically service higher percentages of debt than do industrial stocks. An electric utility with a 50% debt ratio is relatively safe. Still, our basic axiom is: The lower the debt, the safer the investment.

Obviously, a company's debt-to-equity ratio is an important piece of information for investors. When the economy is in the grip of a recession, stockholders should pay special attention to the financial condition of their companies. Figure 7.1 lists 135 blue chip companies with solid finances, where debt is no more than 20% of their total capitalization.

The Dividend Connection

Dun & Bradstreet
Luby's Cafeterias

Dun & Bradstreet and Luby's Cafeterias show the connection between no debt and fine quality. Freedom from debt has enabled these companies to increase their dividends regularly and still finance their growth from sales, earnings and profits.

FIGURE 7.1   Blue Chips with Little or No Debt

Company	Debt-Equity Ratio	Company	Debt-Equity Ratio
Abbott Laboratories	3%	General Re Corp.	6%
AFLAC, Inc.	10	Genuine Parts Company	1
American Cyanamid	15	Gerber Products Company	20
American Home Products Corp.	20	Glatfelter (P.H.) Company	0
AMP Inc.	2	Graco Inc.	14
Aon Corp.	20	Grainger (W.W.), Inc.	1
Automatic Data Processing, Inc.	19	Great Lakes Chemical Corp.	6
Bandag, Inc.	1	Harland (John H.) Company	5
Bard (C.R.), Inc.	16	Hartford Steam Boiler Inspection and	
Block (H.R.), Inc.	1	Insurance Company	15
Bob Evans Farms	0	Hershey Foods Corp.	11
Boeing Company	17	Hewlett-Packard Company	5
Bristol-Myers Squibb Company	2	Hillenbrand Industries, Inc.	20
Brown-Forman Corp. (Class B)	16	Hormel (Geo. A.) & Company	1
Capital Holding	20	Houghton Mifflin Company	13
Carter Wallace, Inc.	4	Hubbell Inc.	1
Central Fidelity	0	Hunt Manufacturing Company	5
Chubb Corp.	20	Illinois Tool Works Inc.	16
Church & Dwight Company	5	International Flavors & Fragrances, Inc.	0
Coca-Cola Company	20	Jefferson-Pilot Corp.	0
Comerica	0	Johnson & Johnson	20
Cooper Tire & Rubber Company	9	Jostens, Inc.	13
Crawford & Company	1	Kellogg Company	15
Crompton & Knowles Corp.	10	Kelly Services	0
Cross (A.T.) Company (Class B)	0	Keystone International, Inc.	5
Deluxe Corp.	12	Kimball International	1
Diebold, Inc.	0	La-Z-Boy Chair	17
Donaldson Company	11	Lance Inc.	0
Dover Corp.	1	Lawson Products	0
Dreyfus Corp.	0	Leggett & Platt, Inc.	16
Dun & Bradstreet Corp.	0	Lilly (Eli) & Company	13
E-Systems Inc.	5	The Limited Inc.	20
Edwards (A.G.), Inc.	0	Lincoln National Corp.	13
EG&G, Inc.	4	Lincoln Telecom	18
Emerson Electric Company	11	Loctite Corp.	4
Ennis Business Forms, Inc.	1	Longs Drug Stores Corp.	3
Exxon Corp.	20	Lubrizol Corp.	4
Family Dollar Stores, Inc.	0	Luby's Cafeterias, Inc.	0
Federal Signal Corp.	10	Marion Merrell Dow, Inc.	7
FlightSafety International, Inc.	6	Martin Marietta Corp.	20
Flowers Industries	15	Medtronic, Inc.	1
Gap, Inc.	7	Melville Corp.	15
Geico Corp.	14	Mercantile Stores Company	20
General Electric Company	12	Merck & Company	9

FIGURE 7.1   Blue Chips with Little or No Debt (Continued)

Company	Debt-Equity Ratio	Company	Debt-Equity Ratio
Millipore Corp.	19%	Shell Transport & Trading Company	12%
Minnesota Mining and Manufacturing		Sherwin-Williams Company	6
Company	9	SmithKline Beecham	5
Morrison Restaurants	6	Smucker (J.M.) Company	0
Motorola, Inc.	17	Snap-on-Tools Corp.	12
National Service Industries, Inc.	4	Standard Register	6
New England Business	0	Stanhome Inc.	1
Newell Company	17	Stride Rite Corp.	1
New York Times Company	17	Tambrands Inc.	1
Old Kent Financial	0	Tootsie Roll Industries	4
Pall Corp.	6	Upjohn Company	20
Pfizer Inc.	11	UST Inc.	0
Pioneer Hi Bred	8	Valspar Corp.	14
Premier Industrial Corp.	2	Vulcan Materials Company	13
Quaker Chemical	15	Walgreen Company	1
Raytheon Company	1	Wallace Computer Services, Inc.	7
Roadway Services	0	Washington Post Company	5
Royal Dutch Petroleum Company	13	Weis Markets, Inc.	0
Rubbermaid, Inc.	2	Winn-Dixie Stores, Inc.	8
St. Paul Companies	20	Woolworth Corp.	15
Sara Lee Corp.	20	Worthington Industries	12
Schering-Plough Corp.	12	Wrigley (Wm.) Jr. Company	0
Schlumberger	10	Zero Corp.	0
Shared Medical	1	Zurn Industries, Inc.	7

Dun & Bradstreet Corp. (NYSE:DNB)

In this age of information, Dun & Bradstreet is a monument of financial stability. Founded in 1841 by Lewis Tappan, the Mercantile Agency, later renamed Dun & Bradstreet, provided credit services to a rapidly expanding American frontier. The world has changed since then, and so has Dun & Bradstreet. Now a global leader in the gathering and circulation of information, it continues to capitalize on its fine reputation by helping businesses minimize risk and uncertainty. As the forefather of the modern information industry, the company provides credit reports to more than 9 million U.S. businesses. Its major subsidiaries include A.C. Nielsen, the world's leading TV audience research group; Moody's Investors Service, a major publisher of financial information and bond ratings; and Reuben H.

FIGURE 7.2   The Dividend Connection Chart

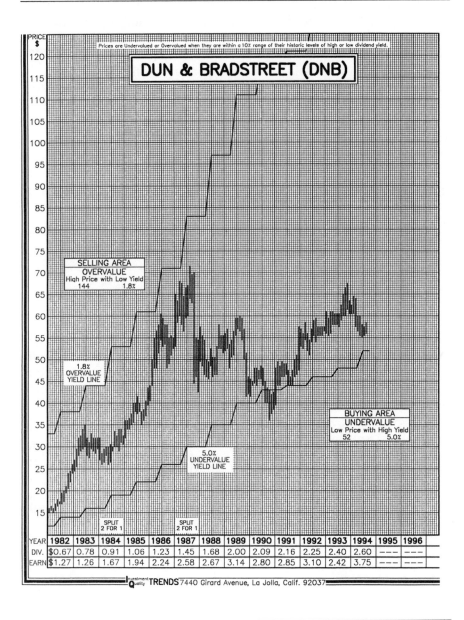

YEAR	1982	1983	1984	1985	1986	1987	1988	1989	1990	1991	1992	1993	1994	1995	1996
DIV.	$0.67	0.78	0.91	1.06	1.23	1.45	1.68	2.00	2.09	2.16	2.25	2.40	2.60	---	---
EARN	$1.27	1.26	1.67	1.94	2.24	2.58	2.67	3.14	2.80	2.85	3.10	2.42	3.75	---	---

Investment Quality **TRENDS** 7440 Girard Avenue, La Jolla, Calif. 92037

Donnelley, which publishes more than 400 yellow pages telephone directories in 17 states and the District of Columbia.

It's hard to find fault with a company that is debt-free, has better than a 26% return on equity, and has more than doubled its earnings per share over the past decade. Yet, Dun & Bradstreet seems to be suffering from an identity crisis. The company plunged into the computer software business a few years ago, only to find that its strategy was inextricably bound to the dying mainframe industry. Another example of corporate schizophrenia is its quick purchase of 70 regional telephone directory yellow pages, only to sell 25 of them in just two years. Its core 154-year-old credit reporting business continues to be a cash cow and reigns as the world's leading supplier of risk management information.

Other Interesting Qualities

- Revenue mix is 38% marketing information, 36% risk management, 26% all other businesses.

- There is no long-term debt.

- Institutions own 76% of the common stock.

- Dividends paid since 1934, have been increased in each of the past 43 years.

When this stock is priced to yield 5%, as it was in 1982 and 1990, it is undervalued and a buying opportunity is at hand. However, when the price rises and the yield falls to 1.8%, as it did in 1986 and 1987, a sale should be considered to protect profits and preserve capital. If an investor had bought at the bottom in 1982 and sold at the top five years later, the capital gain would have been nearly 400%, while dividend increases boosted the payout by 120%. DNB is in a good position to enhance its core businesses. Even its once embarrassing software unit is showing signs of improvement. Together, the sum of its parts add up to a promising future as Dun & Bradstreet embraces today's challenges with tomorrow's answers.

Luby's Cafeterias, Inc. (NYSE:LUB)

At all of its 173 cafeterias throughout ten southern states, Luby's butchers, bakers and salad makers ply their culinary craft to create fresh and wholesome food. The first cafeteria was opened in San Antonio in 1947. Now, more than 125 restaurants freckle the state of Texas.

As the nation's taste turns from the health-oriented light foods of the 1980s to the traditional rib-sticking foods of the 1990s, Luby's is capitalizing on what it always has done best—meat and potatoes. Another trend Luby's has taken advantage of is the increasing number of Americans who rely on quality food-to-go. In 1994, take-out food accounted for almost 20% of revenues. Triggered by increasing competition, Luby's advertising emphasizes quality and value—essential ingredients in a well managed, blue chip company.

Luby's is now working on restaurant design and presentation. The decor has been upgraded in many of its units, and the menu boards have been redesigned to make meal selection easier. The proof is in the pudding, with healthy improvement in store sales.

Other Interesting Qualities

- Luby's has posted record sales and earnings for 25 consecutive years.

- Luby's has no long-term debt.

- Dividends paid since 1965 have been increased every year since then.

When this stock is priced to yield 3.3%, as it was in 1991 and 1992, it is undervalued and a purchase is recommended. However, when the price rises and the yield falls to 1.3%, as it did in 1986 and 1987, LUB is overvalued and a sale should be considered. If an investor had purchased shares at undervalue in 1980 and held them until 1987, the total return (capital gains plus dividends) would have been nearly 1,000%. While the price of the stock approached overvalue several times during that period, frequent dividend increases boosted the prices at undervalue and overvalue and justified holding the stock.

In October 1991, a multifatality shooting at a Killeen, Texas, cafeteria sent the stock reeling downward. The price of LUB penetrated the yield at undervalue in December of that year. The stock

FIGURE 7.3   The Dividend Connection Chart

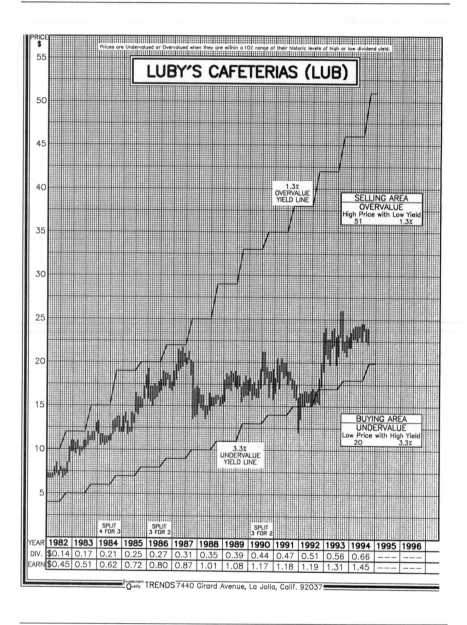

PRICE $

Prices are Undervalued or Overvalued when they are within a 10% range of their historic levels of high or low dividend yield.

LUBY'S CAFETERIAS (LUB)

1.3%
OVERVALUE
YIELD LINE

SELLING AREA
OVERVALUE
High Price with Low Yield
51   1.3%

BUYING AREA
UNDERVALUE
Low Price with High Yield
20   3.3%

3.3%
UNDERVALUE
YIELD LINE

SPLIT 4 FOR 3   SPLIT 3 FOR 2   SPLIT 3 FOR 2

YEAR	1982	1983	1984	1985	1986	1987	1988	1989	1990	1991	1992	1993	1994	1995	1996
DIV.	$0.14	0.17	0.21	0.25	0.27	0.31	0.35	0.39	0.44	0.47	0.51	0.56	0.66	---	---
EARN	$0.45	0.51	0.62	0.72	0.80	0.87	1.01	1.08	1.17	1.18	1.19	1.31	1.45	---	---

Investment Quality TRENDS 7440 Girard Avenue, La Jolla, Calif. 92037

rebounded to its established undervalued level by February 1992, and it launched a rising trend later that year. This high-quality growth stock has a clean balance sheet with zero debt. At an undervalued price, Luby's is a ripe investment opportunity, seasoned to perfection.

Should I Buy Foreign Stocks?

The grass always looks greener on the other side of the fence, but on closer inspection it usually is not. So it is with stocks on the other side of the border, or the other side of the ocean. Many investors feel limited by investing exclusively in U.S. stocks, especially when the market is fundamentally overvalued. Moreover, when interest rates are low, available capital burns a hole in the pockets of investors. As they search for alternatives, some folks look overseas, where stocks may offer better investment opportunities. But do they? On balance, we think not.

Analyzing U.S. stocks and markets is no easy task, even though much information is freely available from the companies themselves as well as from a prolific group of financial publications. How much more difficult the task becomes when information is not readily available; when earnings and dividends are vulnerable to unforeseen changes and fluctuating currency translations.

How many of us can evaluate the investment potential of a company when a report is written in a foreign language, or when unfamiliar customs and diverse rules and regulations enter into the picture? When one factors in the 15% tax on foreign investments that U.S. citizens are obliged to pay, not even interest rates or dividend yields are what they appear to be.

Investors are often told that these problems can be resolved by buying a mutual fund of foreign stocks. Again, we are skeptical. Mutual fund managers face the same problems with the same uncertain answers. Their sources of information are unaccountable and often represent conflicts of interest. Their conclusions may be based on outdated figures, doctored data, or rose-colored rhetoric. Long-term corporate and stock market performance trends usually are unavailable.

One relatively safe way to take advantage of foreign investment opportunities is through U.S. companies with international subsidiaries, foreign outlets and overseas markets for their products and services. Companies that derive a large percentage of their total sales from foreign markets are best prepared to prosper in those countries. They employ financial experts to trade in foreign currencies as a way of protecting their dollar-denominated profits. They hire indigenous managers who know the language, the customs, the rules and the tricks of the foreign trade. These companies offer investors world-wide growth of sales and international marketing representation. Still, they must play by the rules laid down by U.S. agencies and by the Securities and Exchange Commission, and they are compelled to abide by regulations that assure reasonably accurate information. Remember, as the owner of a U.S. company you are protected by all the laws that govern this nation.

The tables in Figure 7.4 identify the percentage of total sales derived in foreign countries for the top 50 U.S.-based international blue chips.

The Dividend Connection

Boeing Company
International Flavors & Fragrances

The stocks profiled on the following pages, Boeing Company and International Flavors & Fragrances, are two U.S.-based multinational blue chips that derive most of their sales from foreign markets.

Boeing Company (NYSE:BA)

Based in Seattle, Washington, Boeing is the largest aerospace firm in the United States, as measured by total sales, and the world's leading manufacturer of commercial jet transports. For the past five years, it has been the nation's largest exporter. The company is a major U.S.

FIGURE 7.4   Percentage of Total Sales Derived from Foreign Markets

---

50% or more of sales		At least 40% of sales (continued)	
Interntional Flavors & Fragrances, Inc.	74%	Heinz (H.J.) Company	42%
Coca-Cola Company	64	Motorola, Inc.	42
Boeing Company	61	Wrigley (Wm.) Jr. Company	42
CPC International, Inc.	60	Kellogg Company	41
Gillette Company	60	Schering-Plough Corp.	41
Loctite Corp.	58	Woolworth Corp.	41
Hewlett-Packard Company	56	American Cyanamid	40
Philip Morris Companies	55	Avery Dennison Corp.	40
Lubrizol Corp.	53	Lilly (Eli) & Company	40
Pall Corp.	53	Upjohn Company	40
Pfizer Inc.	51		
Johnson & Johnson	50	**At least 30% of sales**	
Minnesota Mining and Manufacturing Company	50	Nalco Chemical Company	39%
		Abbott Laboratories	38
		Bandag, Inc.	37
At least 40% of sales		McDonald's Corp.	37
Warner-Lambert Company	48%	PPG Industries Inc.	36
Bausch & Lomb Inc.	46	General Electric Company	35
Merck & Company	46	Quaker Oats Company	35
Procter & Gamble Company	46	Honeywell Inc.	34
Rohm & Haas Company	45	Sara Lee Corp.	34
Stanhome Inc.	45	Emerson Electric Company	33
Whirlpool Corp.	44	McDonnell Douglas Corp.	33
Becton, Dickinson & Company	43	Thomas & Betts Corp.	32
Bristol-Myers Squibb Company	43	American Home Products Corp.	31
Du Pont (E.I.) De Nemours & Company	43	Ralston Purina Company	31
Medtronic, Inc.	43	TRW Inc.	31

---

government contractor, with capabilities in missiles and space, electronic systems, military aircraft, helicopters and information systems.

Sales have declined in recent years from the record pace of the early 1990s, reflecting fewer deliveries of commercial aircraft and a lower altitude in defense spending. Still, the company remains soundly profitable. Net earnings also have trended down due to reduced sales and large research and development expenses to support new programs. However, operating margins before research and development have been maintained. Although worldwide demand for commercial aircraft remains weak, Boeing maintains its market

FIGURE 7.5   The Dividend Connection Chart

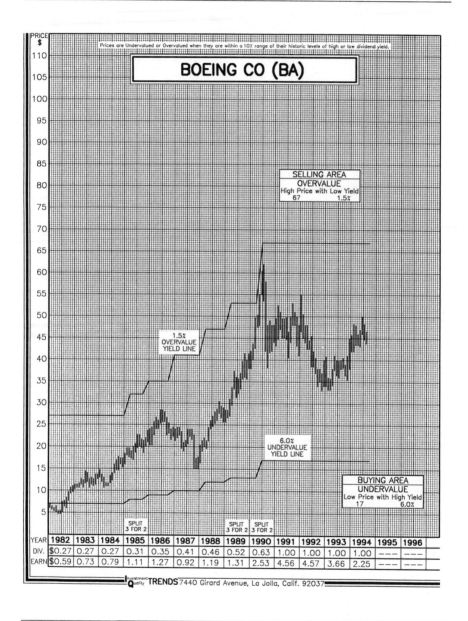

YEAR	1982	1983	1984	1985	1986	1987	1988	1989	1990	1991	1992	1993	1994	1995	1996
DIV.	$0.27	0.27	0.27	0.31	0.35	0.41	0.46	0.52	0.63	1.00	1.00	1.00	1.00	---	---
EARN	$0.59	0.73	0.79	1.11	1.27	0.92	1.19	1.31	2.53	4.56	4.57	3.66	2.25	---	---

leadership. Customer orders for Boeing jetliners valued at nearly $17 billion, represent more than 70% of the worldwide jetliner market.

In defense and space, Boeing continues to record strong profits and improved margins despite sales declines. The company has consolidated and streamlined its defense and space operations over the past several years in response to declines in U.S. defense spending. These changes put Boeing in a good position to remain competitive.

Other Interesting Qualities

- Foreign business accounts for roughly 50% of revenue.

- Foreign business accounts for 61% of sales.

- Boeing is included in the Dow Jones Industrial Average.

- Dividends paid since 1942 have been increased seven times in the past 12 years.

The chart of Boeing illustrates the historic parameters of undervalue and overvalue for the stock. From undervalue in 1982 to overvalue in 1990, the price of the stock rose 1,000%. Then a period of price consolidation began and the rising trend was reversed. What goes up must come down, and for Boeing the limited upside potential may not be piloted again before the price of the stock nosedives back to undervalue, where the dividend yield is 6%.

International Flavors & Fragrances, Inc. (NYSE:IFF)

A company deeply rooted in the strongest desires of human nature— sex and food, International Flavors & Fragrances creates the tastes and scents for a wide variety of consumer products. Fragrance products are sold to the makers of perfumes, cosmetics, hair products, personal care products, soaps, detergents, and household products. Flavors are sold to makers of dairy, meat and other processed foods; beverages; snacks; confectionery and baked goods; pharmaceutical and oral care products; tobacco and animal foods.

Sales outside the United States amount to more than 70% of total sales. Fragrance sales are strongest in Europe and Latin America, while flavor sales achieve their best results in the United States, the Far East and Latin America. Intense competition among international

FIGURE 7.6   The Dividend Connection Chart

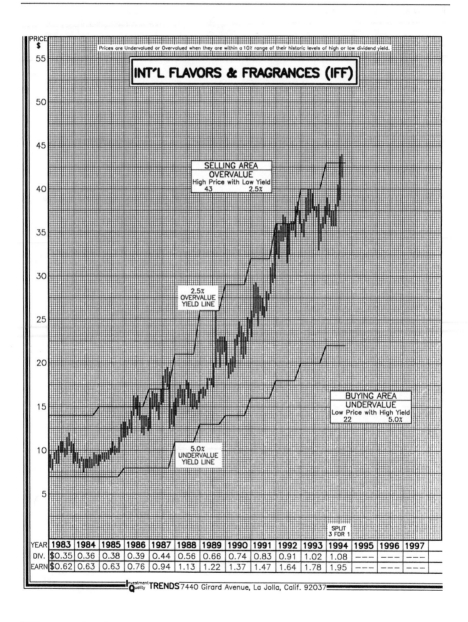

YEAR	1983	1984	1985	1986	1987	1988	1989	1990	1991	1992	1993	1994	1995	1996	1997
DIV.	$0.35	0.36	0.38	0.39	0.44	0.56	0.66	0.74	0.83	0.91	1.02	1.08	---	---	---
EARN	$0.62	0.63	0.63	0.76	0.94	1.13	1.22	1.37	1.47	1.64	1.78	1.95	---	---	---

Investment Quality TRENDS 7440 Girard Avenue, La Jolla, Calif. 92037

soap and detergent companies to expand their markets has resulted in a number of new product introductions in which IFF has participated.

The largest influence on flavor sales is the trend toward healthier diets and lifestyles. The company's flavors are designed to replenish the taste deficits resulting from the removal of sodium, fat, calories and sugar. Product reformulation is increasing to meet market demands for more healthful products, especially in the United States and Europe.

Other Interesting Qualities

- Research and development expenditures amounted to $82 million in 1994.

- The company has no long-term debt.

- Cash and equivalent reserves were $311 million in 1994.

- Dividends paid every year since 1956 have been increased in each of the past 33 years.

The chart of IFF illustrates the parameters of high and low dividend yield for the stock. A 5% yield identifies an attractive, undervalued buying area. The 2.5% yield is the overvalued measure that signals a sell consideration. International Flavors & Fragrances is an ideal way for shareholders to invest in international markets while enjoying the security of a domestic stock. Even though sales and earnings continue to rise, we advise investors to purchase IFF at undervalue, where its industry leadership and financial strength will produce flavorful profits and fragrant growth.

Why Should I Invest Only in Blue Chip Stocks?

We have explained why blue chip stocks are attractive investment vehicles. Their strong management, excellent financial performance, long histories of profitability and records of continuous dividend growth prove their worth to any investor.

Perhaps the biggest reason to invest only in blue chip stocks rests in their ability to endure any economic trauma—to the nation, the stock market or the individual company. Fledgling companies without the financial strength or time-tested experience to cope with such turmoil often slash dividends or fall by the wayside.

The movement toward health care legislation in 1993 is an excellent example of political, economic and industrywide pressure that bowed but did not break the branches of blue chip drug stocks. President Clinton's initial announcement of health care reform lit a firestorm of fear among pharmaceutical stock owners. The potential of price controls sent drug and hospital supply stocks into a severe depression. In a relatively short time, the average drug stock lost 30% of its value; some stocks declined by as much as 60% from their high prices.

Quality did not prevent prices from falling, but it did give investors in search of good quality the incentive to move in and purchase good value. Despite the fear and anxiety on Wall Street, none of the companies went out of business; none omitted its dividend; none suffered serious earnings repercussions. Under a similar scenario, however, many of the newer biotech companies did not survive.

The banking industry is another good example of why investors who want safe havens should invest exclusively in blue chip stocks. In 1982, Wall Street's confidence in bank stocks started to erode. A severe economic recession, inflation and high interest rates fueled fears that many unsecured loans to developing countries would be in default and the entire banking system could collapse. Investors were worried that dividends would not be maintained. But as stock prices fell, dividend yields rose to 10%, 11%, even 12% in some cases. Amazingly, dividends were not cut, the banking system did not collapse, and most investors who took the risk of buying bank stocks in 1982 saw their stocks double in one year's time. Not only were dividends maintained, but in most cases they were increased.

But in the case of savings and loan companies, none of which were blue chip stocks, the story was entirely different. Many of those companies were forced out of business or into government receivership. S&Ls that had been paying dividends, canceled them.

The Dividend Connection

Bankers Trust
Eli Lilly

The following banking and pharmaceutical stocks illustrate the point that an exclusively blue chip stock portfolio minimizes the risk of unfortunate surprises. Investors in prime quality blue chip stocks such as Bankers Trust and Eli Lilly have the comfort of safety along with the power of a cash return.

Bankers Trust New York Corp. (NYSE:BT)

A registered bank holding company incorporated in 1965, Bankers Trust operates a number of financial businesses specializing in investment analysis and risk management. The core banking business accounts for 61% of corporate assets. Founded in 1903, the bank originates loans and other forms of credit, accepts deposits, arranges financing and provides other financial services. Headquartered in Manhattan, Bankers Trust is among the largest commercial banks in New York City and the United States.

The banking and securities businesses are intensely competitive, and Bankers Trust successfully meets its challenges. Its business is inextricably bound to and influenced by prevailing economic conditions and governmental policies, both foreign and domestic. The actions of the Federal Reserve Board also affect the availability of funds for lending and investing. The rise in interest rates in 1994 restricted Bankers Trust's operations, but its global geographic diversification mitigated any extreme impact.

Other Interesting Qualities

- Bankers Trust is the eighth largest commercial bank in the nation.
- Over the past 15 years, shareholders have achieved an average annual return of 19%.

FIGURE 7.7   The Dividend Connection Chart

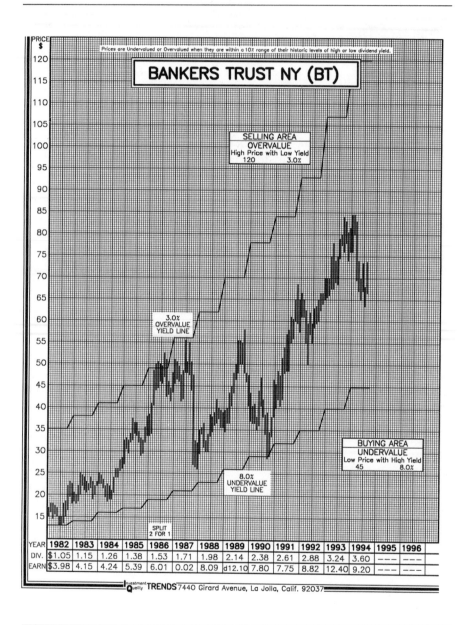

PRICE $

Prices are Undervalued or Overvalued when they are within a 10% range of their historic levels of high or low dividend yield.

BANKERS TRUST NY (BT)

SELLING AREA
OVERVALUE
High Price with Low Yield
120   3.0%

3.0%
OVERVALUE
YIELD LINE

BUYING AREA
UNDERVALUE
Low Price with High Yield
45   8.0%

8.0%
UNDERVALUE
YIELD LINE

SPLIT
2 FOR 1

YEAR	1982	1983	1984	1985	1986	1987	1988	1989	1990	1991	1992	1993	1994	1995	1996
DIV.	$1.05	1.15	1.26	1.38	1.53	1.71	1.98	2.14	2.38	2.61	2.88	3.24	3.60	---	---
EARN	$3.98	4.15	4.24	5.39	6.01	0.02	8.09	d12.10	7.80	7.75	8.82	12.40	9.20	---	---

Investment-Quality **TRENDS** 7440 Girard Avenue, La Jolla, Calif. 92037

- In 1994, *Fortune* magazine ranked Bankers Trust first in innovation among financial institutions.

- Dividends paid since 1904 have been increased in each of the past 15 years.

When this stock is priced in the area of 8%, it is undervalued and a purchase is recommended. However, when the price rises and the yield falls to 3%, BT is overvalued and a sale should be considered. The stock launched a primary rising trend after the 1987 minicrash but was halted far short of its overvalued objective when the banking industry entered its crisis in 1989. Even though Bankers Trust was not directly involved in any savings and loan debacles, it was tarred with the same brush of industry rancor.

The banking disaster of 1990 underscores the importance of holding only blue chip stocks. While its bow was bent, Bankers Trust weathered the storm and produced extraordinary growth soon after many of its competitors went out of business. Considering the strength of its core business plus growth in the highly leveraged derivatives market, we trust that Bankers Trust will continue to derive long-term profitability for its shareholders.

Lilly (Eli) & Company (NYSE:LLY)

As one of the world's leading manufacturers and marketers of pharmaceutical products, Eli Lilly draws from a 120-year history of business and strides toward the next century with innovation and promise. Based in Indianapolis, this research-based global corporation also produces medical devices, diagnostic instruments and animal health care products worldwide. About 30% of sales are generated by anti-infectives. Brand names include Ceclor, Keflex, Kefzol, Lorabid, Nebcin, Tazidime and Vancocin. The second largest drug group is central nervous system agents, including Prozac and Darvon. Important medical devices and diagnostics include intravenous delivery systems, cardiac pacemakers and coronary angioplastic catheters.

The company's top-selling product is the controversial antidepressant, Prozac. After withstanding rigorous scrutiny, Prozac has proven to be a safe and effective drug for a number of central nervous system disorders. Already the world's leading treatment for clinical

FIGURE 7.8   The Dividend Connection Chart

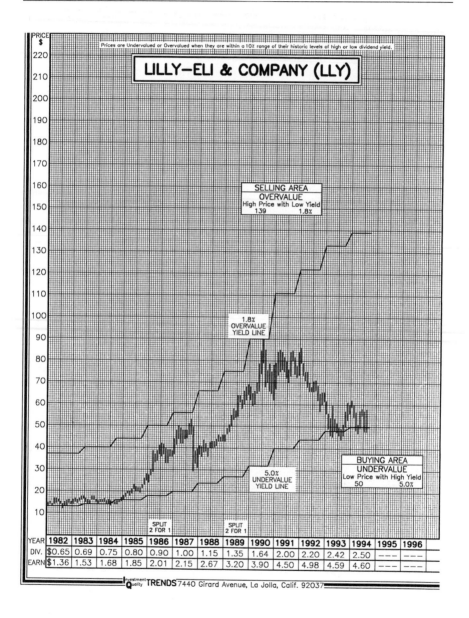

LILLY—ELI & COMPANY (LLY)

Prices are Undervalued or Overvalued when they are within a 10% range of their historic levels of high or low dividend yield.

SELLING AREA
OVERVALUE
High Price with Low Yield
139   1.8%

1.8%
OVERVALUE
YIELD LINE

5.0%
UNDERVALUE
YIELD LINE

BUYING AREA
UNDERVALUE
Low Price with High Yield
50   5.0%

YEAR	1982	1983	1984	1985	1986	1987	1988	1989	1990	1991	1992	1993	1994	1995	1996
DIV.	$0.65	0.69	0.75	0.80	0.90	1.00	1.15	1.35	1.64	2.00	2.20	2.42	2.50	---	---
EARN	$1.36	1.53	1.68	1.85	2.01	2.15	2.67	3.20	3.90	4.50	4.98	4.59	4.60	---	---

Investment
Quality TRENDS 7440 Girard Avenue, La Jolla, Calif. 92037

depression, Prozac now has received FDA approval for use in treating both obsessive-compulsive disorder and bulimia, a chronic eating disorder.

In recent years, Lilly has targeted economically developing countries. In 1994, the company purchased an affiliate in India and opened sales offices in China. Together, these two Asian giants will account for nearly one-half of the world's population in the next century.

Other Interesting Qualities

- Foreign sales account for roughly 43% of revenues.

- It takes an average of three years for a new drug to receive FDA approval.

- The Lilly Foundation owns 16% of the common stock.

- Dividends paid since 1885 have been increased in each of the past 27 years.

The chart of LLY clearly illustrates the concept on which our investment philosophy is based. When Lilly is priced to yield 5%, the stock is undervalued and offers an attractive buying opportunity. However, when the price rises and the yield falls to 1.8%, LLY is overvalued and a sale should be considered. From a high price of $91 per share in 1990, LLY lost roughly 45% of its value by 1994. The company has an extraordinary record of dividend growth, with a 262% increase in the dividend payout over the past decade. Rumors abound concerning a possible merger with the U.K.-based pharmaceutical company, Glaxo. Whether or not an acquisition actually occurs, Lilly stands poised to inject new life into a depressed stock as it administers investment growth to its shareholders.

What Happens When a Blue Chip Cuts Its Dividends?

Besides betraying shareholders' confidence, a dividend reduction undermines both the quality and the value of the stock. Many investors depend on their cash dividends as an important source of income. A reduced dividend may diminish the quality of life for the shareholder. It also sends a loud and clear message that the company is not making profitable progress. Just as a dividend increase suggests fine management and ongoing corporate strength, a dividend decrease shows corporate weakness, the tangible result of poor management.

Wall Street is driven by perception. The negative implication of a dividend reduction sends shock waves throughout the investment community. It casts a pall of doubt about the quality of the company in the minds of potential investors and damages the stock's future investment appeal.

But what does it do to the value of the stock itself?

A dividend reduction significantly reduces the stock's intrinsic value. When a dividend is cut, the yields at undervalue and overvalue remain the same, but the defining prices become lower. Just as a dividend increase lifts the prices at undervalue and overvalue, a dividend decrease reduces them.

Take, for example, a stock that has established its profile of value between yield extremes of 4% at undervalue and 2% at overvalue. If the annual dividend is $2 per share, the price at undervalue is $50 per share (where the dividend yield is 4%) and the price at overvalue is $100 per share (where the dividend yield is 2%). If the annual dividend is cut in half and settles at $1 per share, the price at undervalue slides to $25 per share while the price at overvalue becomes $50 per share. Often, when a stock is undervalued and the dividend is cut in half, the undervalued price becomes the overvalued price and an extended decline down to the new undervalued price may lie ahead. Sometimes, however, Wall Street anticipates a dividend reduction and the price of the stock falls precipitously before the disappointing news is announced.

The Dividend Connection

A.T. Cross
International Business Machines

Dividend stability is important to a value-oriented investor. As long as a dividend is maintained, the prices at undervalue and overvalue remain valid and signal the appropriate buying and selling price parameters. The two stocks profiled here, A.T. Cross Company and International Business Machines, were forced to reduce their dividend payouts in response to economic pressures.

Cross (A.T.) Company (Class A) (AMEX:ATXA)

Crossing the t's and dotting the i's of the world's upscale writing needs is A.T. Cross, a major international manufacturer of fine writing instruments and a marketer of quality leather and gift products. One of the best-known and most-respected brand names, Cross is the only maker of writing instruments included on *Fortune* magazine's list of "America's 100 Best Made Products."

During the recession of the early 1990s, when most people were concerned about maintaining the bare essentials, the company's high-priced pens and luxury leather goods experienced weak sales. A better economic climate together with new products and line extensions should boost sales in the United States.

Although the company still has many rivers to cross, it has taken strong actions to meet the challenges of worldwide economics, including top management reorganization, the introduction of new products and changes in advertising. It also has implemented cost-cutting measures such as a hiring freeze, bonus cuts and pruned budgets. These initiatives should begin to steer its corporate ship back on course.

FIGURE 7.9   The Dividend Connection Chart

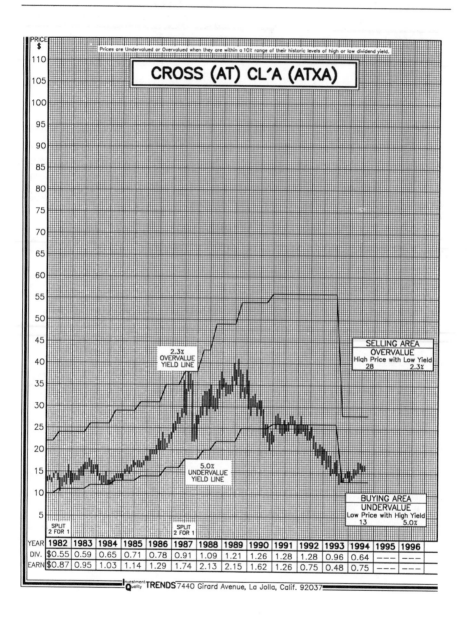

CROSS (AT) CL'A (ATXA)

Prices are Undervalued or Overvalued when they are within a 10% range of their historic levels of high or low dividend yield.

2.3%
OVERVALUE
YIELD LINE

SELLING AREA
OVERVALUE
High Price with Low Yield
28   2.3%

5.0%
UNDERVALUE
YIELD LINE

BUYING AREA
UNDERVALUE
Low Price with High Yield
13   5.0%

SPLIT
2 FOR 1

SPLIT
2 FOR 1

YEAR	1982	1983	1984	1985	1986	1987	1988	1989	1990	1991	1992	1993	1994	1995	1996
DIV.	$0.55	0.59	0.65	0.71	0.78	0.91	1.09	1.21	1.26	1.28	1.28	0.96	0.64	---	---
EARN	$0.87	0.95	1.03	1.14	1.29	1.74	2.13	2.15	1.62	1.26	0.75	0.48	0.75	---	---

Investment
Quality TRENDS 7440 Girard Avenue, La Jolla, Calif. 92037

Other Interesting Qualities

- Revenue mix is 85% writing instruments, 15% leather and gift products.

- Insiders own 24% of the common stock; institutions own 60%.

- There is no long-term debt.

- Dividends paid since 1972 were regularly increased until 1992 when earnings faltered.

A.T. Cross fluctuates between yield extremes of 5% at undervalue and 2.3% at overvalue. The stock was undervalued from 1980 through 1984 and from mid-1990 through mid-1992. During that 12-year cycle, the stock was overvalued only once, at the top of the market in 1987. Cross has two classes of stock, one of which is traded on the American Stock Exchange. The public can purchase Class A shares that enable them to elect one-third of the company's directors. The Cross family owns the Class B stock and elects the remaining majority of directors.

Despite economic vicissitudes, the company managed to increase its dividend for 20 consecutive years, until it was cut in 1993. In turn, Standard & Poor's lowered its quality rank to B (below average), and we were obliged to cross the stock off of our roster of blue chips. We hope that the company's strong cash flow and clean balance sheet will enable it to rise to blue chip status and prove once again that on the battlefield of business, the pen is mightier than the sword.

International Business Machines Corp. (NYSE:IBM)

Who could have predicted that the fickle finger of fate would point so ominously at Big Blue? Still, IBM is fighting back like a champ. Although the battle continues to wage, IBM is emerging as a federation of companies whose businesses still keep pace with advanced information systems, services and technology. Perhaps Blue's biggest strength is the sum of its parts. By offering the largest and most comprehensive range of computer-based choices, IBM stands for value in a world of informational needs.

The two most challenging years in IBM's history were 1992 and 1993. The company's blues lament reached a crescendo in September 1993, when the dividend was cut for the second time in one year. This came on the heels of its biggest earnings losses ever reported by Big

FIGURE 7.10   The Dividend Connection Chart

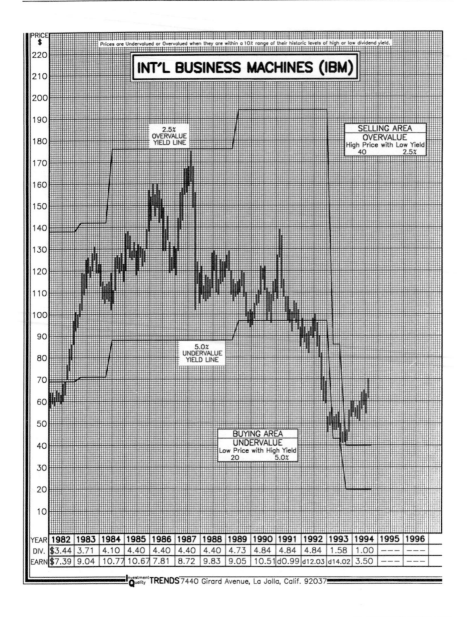

YEAR	1982	1983	1984	1985	1986	1987	1988	1989	1990	1991	1992	1993	1994	1995	1996
DIV.	$3.44	3.71	4.10	4.40	4.40	4.40	4.40	4.73	4.84	4.84	4.84	1.58	1.00	---	---
EARN	$7.39	9.04	10.77	10.67	7.81	8.72	9.83	9.05	10.51	d0.99	d12.03	d14.02	3.50	---	---

Within the chart:

INT'L BUSINESS MACHINES (IBM)

Prices are Undervalued or Overvalued when they are within a 10% range of their historic levels of high or low dividend yield.

2.5%
OVERVALUE
YIELD LINE

SELLING AREA
OVERVALUE
High Price with Low Yield
40   2.5%

5.0%
UNDERVALUE
YIELD LINE

BUYING AREA
UNDERVALUE
Low Price with High Yield
20   5.0%

Investment Quality TRENDS 7440 Girard Avenue, La Jolla, Calif. 92037

Blue. The net loss was caused largely by a $7.2 billion restructuring charge to pay for job cuts and forced retirements. Still, a large part of the loss reflected a significant deterioration in the company's core mainframe business.

Now, IBM's largest division, the mainframe computer, appears to be going the way of the dinosaur, so Blue's ability to form alliances with smaller, cutting-edge companies becomes extremely important. On the other hand, personal computer sales are picking up as IBM's prices become more competitive and product demand remains strong.

Other Interesting Qualities

- Revenue mix is 52% sales, 17% software, 12% maintenance, 12% service, 7% financing and rental.

- Foreign business accounts for about 50% of revenues.

- IBM holds 30,000 patents worldwide.

- The company conducts business in more than 140 nations.

- Dividends have been paid continuously since 1916.

When IBM slashed its dividend twice in 1993, shock waves reverberated throughout Wall Street. Many investors felt a sense of betrayal, as the company had rejected any notion of a dividend decrease just weeks before the surprise announcement. With the Big Blue cat out of the bag, some pressure was lifted from the stock. The yield at undervalue remains at 5%, as it was in 1982, 1989 and 1990. The stock is overvalued when the yield falls to 2.5%, last seen at the top of the market in 1987.

Will IBM ever regain the financial stature it once enjoyed? No one knows. But at a time when applied computer technology is spreading like wildfire throughout the world, IBM has a fighting chance. At its undervalued price, Big Blue still merits serious investment consideration.

How Do I Evaluate Growth Stocks?

Many investors erroneously believe that blue chip stocks represent ponderously capitalized, slow growth companies. This is not necessarily true. Blue chip quality and growth rates are determined not by size, but by long-term financial performance. Many highly capital-ized companies as well as low cap companies have outstanding records of growth.

Small, young companies are often considered to be growth com-panies on the basis of industry perception or potential (unrealized) growth. These investors don't realize that more than 80 percent of new companies fail in the first five years. Initial public offerings (IPOs) sometimes take off like skyrockets, providing their initial shareholders with spectacular returns, but these high flyers often fizzle out shortly after takeoff.

Growth that has been proven in a dependable, consistent pattern over time is what the enlightened investor wants. To these prudent players of the stock market, dividends are the hallmark of true growth. Dividends don't lie. When a dividend grows, it implies growth of sales, earnings and profits as well as new products and services. Remember, too, that well established blue chip companies have the capital to invest in research and development, enabling them to grow from the inside out. They also have the financial strength to acquire other companies, enabling them to grow from the outside in.

In general, growth stocks attract investors at lower yields than do stocks in industries undergoing slower growth. Some stocks may be undervalued when the dividend yields are 2% or 3%. Others are undervalued when their yields are 5% or 6%. Again, each stock establishes its own profile of value and must be studied individually within the context of its industry group. Investors are willing to accept a lower yield at undervalue from a high-tech stock with the expectation that earnings and dividend growth will compensate in the long run.

Furthermore, size is not necessarily synonymous with growth. AMP Inc. has 105 million common shares outstanding and sports a 16% compound annual growth rate; while Diebold, with 30 million shares has grown at the same average annual rate of 16%. Although AMP is more than three times the size of Diebold, both companies have experienced the same rate of growth.

Financial performance denotes both quality and growth. A com-pany's capitalization denotes only its size. The stocks listed in Figure 7.11 are fine examples of good quality accompanied by average annual growth rates of 10% or more.

FIGURE 7.11   Blue Chip Growth Stocks

Stock	Average Annual Growth Rate	Number of Shares (in mill.)	Yield At Undervalue	Overvalue
American Business Products, Inc.	14%	11	4.7%	2.4%
AMP Inc.	16	105	3.0	1.3
Automatic Data Processing, Inc.	15	140	1.9	0.7
Bristol-Myers Squibb Company	18	513	4.0	1.2
Brown-Forman Corp. (Class B)	16	23	3.7	2.0
Bruno's Inc.	16	78	3.0	0.8
Carter-Wallace, Inc.	14	46	6.5	1.3
Diebold, Inc.	16	30	4.0	1.0
EG&G, Inc.	10	57	2.2	1.0
Flowers Industries	18	37	5.0	2.1
Hewlett-Packard Company	18	253	1.5	0.3
Pall Corp.	16	116	1.8	0.9
Wallace Computer Services, Inc.	12	22	4.0	1.5

The Dividend Connection

Hewlett-Packard
Pall Corp.

Some high-tech stocks with well-established rates of growth, such as Hewlett-Packard and Pall Corp. have profiles of value that reflect very low yields at both undervalue and overvalue. Still, from every point of view, they are solid growth stocks.

Hewlett-Packard Company (NYSE:HWP)

With profound changes impacting the computer industry daily, Hewlett-Packard continues to increase its byte in a rapidly expanding, megalithic business. Founded in 1939 as a partnership between Bill Hewlett and Dave Packard, this Palo Alto-based corporation now

FIGURE 7.12   The Dividend Connect Chart

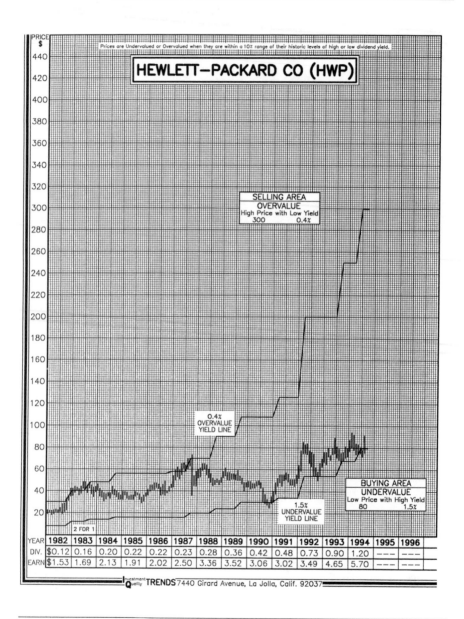

Prices are Undervalued or Overvalued when they are within a 10% range of their historic levels of high or low dividend yield.

HEWLETT–PACKARD CO (HWP)

SELLING AREA
OVERVALUE
High Price with Low Yield
300   0.4%

0.4%
OVERVALUE
YIELD LINE

BUYING AREA
UNDERVALUE
Low Price with High Yield
80   1.5%

1.5%
UNDERVALUE
YIELD LINE

2 FOR 1

YEAR	1982	1983	1984	1985	1986	1987	1988	1989	1990	1991	1992	1993	1994	1995	1996
DIV.	$0.12	0.16	0.20	0.22	0.22	0.23	0.28	0.36	0.42	0.48	0.73	0.90	1.20	---	---
EARN	$1.53	1.69	2.13	1.91	2.02	2.50	3.36	3.52	3.06	3.02	3.49	4.65	5.70	---	---

Investment
Quality TRENDS 7440 Girard Avenue, La Jolla, Calif. 92037

operates in more than 100 nations. The company consists of three major divisions: computer systems, computer products and measurement systems.

Hewlett-Packard is the world's leading manufacturer of electronic test and measuring instruments for engineers and scientists. In the early 1960s, it extended its electronics technology into medicine and analytical chemistry. It introduced its first computer in 1966 to gather and analyze the data produced by Hewlett-Packard electronic instruments. In 1972, it introduced the world's first scientific handheld calculator, quickly making the slide rule obsolete. Hewlett-Packard now is the world's second largest computer manufacturer. With a broad range of products, including mid-range computers, workstations, personal computers, laser printers, plotters and disc drives, the company continues to increase its market share.

Hewlett-Packard's future success is contingent upon the evolution of wireless communications transmission. Just as a toaster plugs into an electrical socket, Hewlett-Packard's "information appliances" connect customers to global information. By taking advantage of its long-standing experience in the field of communications, the company gleans the best from the past and a vision for the future as both coexist in the present.

Other Interesting Qualities

- Foreign sales account for 66% of the total.

- Insiders own 27% of the common stock.

- Dividends paid since 1965 have been increased 15 times in the past 17 years.

When HWP is priced to yield 1.5%, it is historically undervalued and represents an attractive buying opportunity. However, when the price rises and the yield falls to 0.3%, HWP is overvalued and a sale should be considered. Despite the relatively low yield at undervalue, this growth stock rewards its long-standing shareholders generously. An investor who purchased HWP in 1982, when the dividend was $.12 and the price was $20 per share, would have collected a 6% annual cash return on the original investment in 1994. The price of the stock rose by 250%. Thanks to rapid and generous dividend increases, the overvalued price in 1987 became the undervalued price in 1993. Although competition in the industry is formidable, we expect Hewlett-Packard to hold its own in innovation and sales. At undervalue, an investment should compute impressive growth of income and megachips of capital gain.

Pall Corp. (NYSE:PLL)

As the world's preeminent supplier of filtration products, Pall succeeds in a highly specialized technology known as fluid clarification. Simply put, Pall is in the business of separating microscopic contaminants from solid, liquid and gas substances. With today's emphasis on the cleanliness of hospitals and the purity of food products, on protection of the environment and on the importance of minimizing contaminants before disposal, Pall's seemingly narrow business niche takes on much greater significance.

What do a microelectronics academic in Japan, an open-heart surgeon in America and an automobile manufacturer in Germany have in common? They all are important customers of Pall products. Pall's largest infusion of sales comes from its health care division, which accounts for 51% of revenues. Although it is the youngest company segment, it also holds the greatest promise for future growth. In the important debate to lower health care costs, Pall plays a vital role because postoperative infections and intravenous safety significantly impact the total U.S. medical bill.

Pall Aeropower serves the manufacturers of military and commercial aircraft, motor vehicles and ships as well as numerous industrial customers using fluid-powered equipment. The fluid processing division serves customers who must remove contaminants from liquids and gases used to produce their products. These unique disposable metal and ceramic filters remove minute particles that can wreak havoc on sensitive products.

Other Interesting Qualities

- Disposable fluid filters account for about 80% of sales.
- Foreign sales account for 56% of revenues.
- Dividends paid since 1974 have been increased every year.

FIGURE 7.13   The Dividend Connection Chart

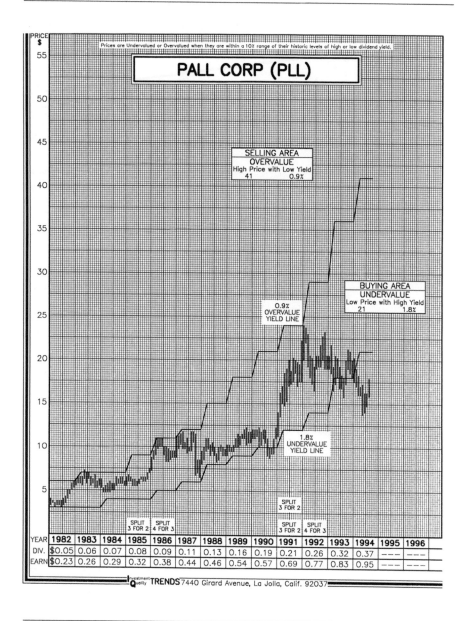

YEAR	1982	1983	1984	1985	1986	1987	1988	1989	1990	1991	1992	1993	1994	1995	1996
DIV.	$0.05	0.06	0.07	0.08	0.09	0.11	0.13	0.16	0.19	0.21	0.26	0.32	0.37	---	---
EARN	$0.23	0.26	0.29	0.32	0.38	0.44	0.46	0.54	0.57	0.69	0.77	0.83	0.95	---	---

Investment Quality TRENDS 7440 Girard Avenue, La Jolla, Calif. 92037

The chart shows the profile of value for Pall. When this stock is priced to yield 1.8%, PLL is undervalued and a purchase is advisable. However, when the price rises and the yield falls to 0.9%, Pall is overvalued and a sale should be considered. In the 1980s, Pall traded within a relatively narrow price range. Then, in 1990, the stock launched a primary rising trend from undervalue, gaining 200% in just over one year. During that time, the dividend was increased by 42%. Ironically, the health care division, which was largely responsible for the stock's growth from 1990 to 1992, can be blamed for PLL's deterioration since then.

Although the undervalued yield does not appear especially attractive, dividends have grown at a compound annual rate of 18% over the past ten years. With an extraordinary record of dividend growth, Pall should provide a "Pall-pable" total return for its shareholders.

Uncovering Hidden Value in Stock Industry Groups

Are Utilities Plugged into Investment Growth?

For safety, growth and income, utilities stocks merit investment attention. Not only are their dividend yields typically far better than interest rates in the money market, but they also offer investors the advantages of capital gains plus dividend growth.

Blue chip utilities with good growth characteristics offer conservative investors the best of all possible worlds. From 1993 through 1994, the dividend yields from utilities stocks were in the 7% to 9% range, which was substantially higher than most rates of return in the money market. And, unlike money market returns, which are fixed, dividends can grow, stock prices can rise, and long-term total returns can better the performance of most other investment vehicles.

Our research has shown that when good times are averaged with bad times and high markets with low markets, the total return from a diversified selection of common stocks averages about 10% per year. Our studies also show that about one-half of that total return comes from the cash dividend. When an investor can capture an initial return of 7% or more, the chance of beating that long-term total return of 10% is considerably improved. If, in addition to the 7%, 8% or 9% annual cash return, an investor can look forward to above-average dividend growth, supporting some capital gains, the 10% average total return can be bettered.

Over the past two decades, electric utilities have struggled under the weight of a wide variety of financial, environmental and regulatory problems. Many companies have been reorganized as utility holding companies, mainly for the purpose of diversifying into non-regulated businesses. Some companies encountered serious operational and financial challenges as they learned by their mistakes and experienced more than their share of growing pains. Companies that were able to stay afloat financially through those decades, boost their earnings and hoist their dividends merit our respect and our investment allegiance.

The utilities industry has embarked upon a sea of change. Consumers, legislators and regulatory agencies are encouraging competition, and there is a hint of deregulation in the air. As a result, investors wonder if the plug has been pulled on investment value in electric utilities.

We think not. The spirit of competition is awakening marketing and management skills that were dormant when these companies operated as virtual monopolies in their service areas. Competition will open up new opportunities for growth.

Of course, there will be losers as well as winners in the new power play. However, the experienced managements of blue chip utilities are the likely winners. Through a process of natural selection, the fittest will survive and the losers will be acquired by the winners. The industry will become stronger and less fragmented.

Blue chip utilities with well-protected dividends are plugged into investment growth. The utilities listed in Figure 8.1 have increased their dividends in each of the past ten years. Those dividend increases boosted the cash returns on investment capital, supported rising price trends and produced outstanding total returns. These well-managed companies should achieve even greater levels of success in the years ahead.

FIGURE 8.1   Best Records of Dividend Growth and Capital Gains Over the Past Decade

Utilities Stock	Recent Price	Annual Dividend	Dividend Yield	10-Year Dividend Growth	Capital Gains
Allegheny Power System, Inc.	21	1.64	7.8%	26%	50%
Atlantic Energy, Inc.	17	1.54	9.1	31	42
Baltimore Gas & Electric Company	21	1.52	7.2	52	40
Carolina Power & Light Company	23	1.70	7.4	36	92
Central & South West Corp.	20	1.70	8.5	89	54
CIPSCO Inc.	26	2.00	7.7	33	86
Consolidated Edison Company of New York	26	2.00	7.7	82	136
Dominion Resources, Inc.	36	2.54	7.1	59	157
Duke Power Company	35	1.88	5.4	59	192
Florida Progress Corp.	25	1.98	7.9	52	92
Hawaiian Electric Industries	31	2.32	7.5	55	107
IPALCO Enterprises, Inc.	28	2.12	7.6	51	115
KU Engergy Corp.	25	1.64	6.6	43	150
LG&E Energy Corp.	36	2.08	5.8	34	140
Northern States Power Company	41	2.64	6.4	76	141
Pennsylvania Power & Light Company	20	1.67	8.3	39	100
San Diego Gas & Electric Company	18	1.52	8.4	54	100
SCANA Corp.	43	2.82	6.6	41	153
Wisconsin Energy Corp.	23	1.41	6.1	100	156
Wisconsin Public Service Corp.	28	1.78	6.4	55	133

The Dividend Connection

Consolidated Edison
Wisconsin Energy

Consolidated Edison Company of New York and Wisconsin Energy Corp. are excellent examples of blue chip utilities with above-average rates of annual dividend growth and long-term capital gains.

Consolidated Edison Company of New York (NYSE:ED)

From the mighty Twin Towers of south Manhattan to the modest public housing projects of the Bronx borough, Consolidated Edison provides electricity, natural gas and steam throughout New York City and Westchester County. Its territory extends across a 660-square-mile region with a population of more than 8 million. A diversified power producer, Con Ed uses a balanced mix of fuel sources, including nuclear, coal, oil and natural gas. Even so, its capacity needs are so great that the company also depends on about 10% of additional purchased power. One of the nation's most financially sound utilities, Con Ed successfully meets the needs of an extraordinarily challenging service area.

Although complete deregulation is some distance down the road, the company acts as if it were already a reality. If competition intensifies, Con Ed will be prepared; if not, the utility will be better off as it operates more efficiently. In 1994, the Public Service Commission awarded the company a $55 million rate increase as the final phase of a three-year rate agreement approved in 1992. As part of the agreement, Con Ed projects what its sales will be. Then, depending on weather conditions, rate payers are either reimbursed or charged extra. This type of progressive, performance-based rate making has become common among major utilities that face increased competition.

Other Interesting Qualities

- Revenue mix is 83% electricity, 12% natural gas, 5% steam.
- Electric revenues are 31% residential, 49% commercial, 12% industrial, 8% other.
- Fuel mix is 33% natural gas, 27% nuclear, 20% oil, 11% coal, 9% other.
- Fuel costs amount to 26% of revenues; labor, 16%.
- Dividends paid since 1885 have been increased in each of the past 19 years.

The chart illustrates the profile of value for ED. If the chart were extended further back, it would reveal an overvalued yield of 3.4% from 1964 through 1965, when virtually all electric utilities were

FIGURE 8.2   The Dividend Connection Chart

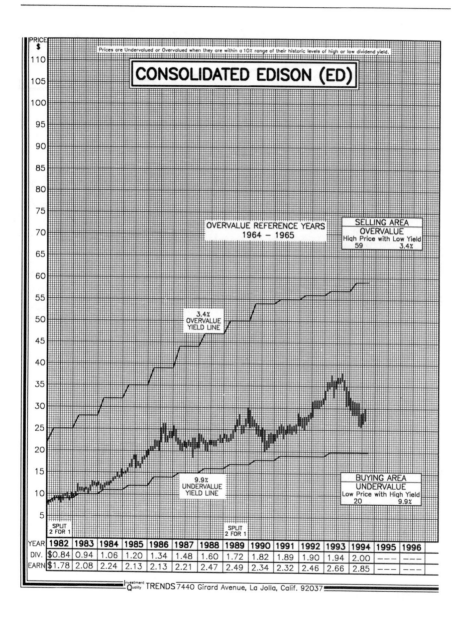

Consolidated Edison (ED)

YEAR	1982	1983	1984	1985	1986	1987	1988	1989	1990	1991	1992	1993	1994	1995	1996
DIV.	$0.84	0.94	1.06	1.20	1.34	1.48	1.60	1.72	1.82	1.89	1.90	1.94	2.00	---	---
EARN	$1.78	2.08	2.24	2.13	2.13	2.21	2.47	2.49	2.34	2.32	2.46	2.66	2.85	---	---

Investment Quality TRENDS 7440 Girard Avenue, La Jolla, Calif. 92037

similarly overvalued. In April 1974, the company disappointed share-holders and shocked Wall Street by omitting its dividend, which at that time had enjoyed steady growth for 90 years. The action sent the stock reeling downward to an adjusted price of $2 per share with the looming threat of bankruptcy. Just two quarters later, the company reinstated the dividend and the stock staged a stunning comeback. This underscores the fundamental importance of the dividend. Without it, Con Edison was on the verge of a corporate blackout. Since the dividend was reinstated, the stock has performed brilliantly.

Wisconsin Energy Corp. (NYSE:WEC)

Milking its revenues from America's Dairy state, Wisconsin Energy Corp. is a diversified holding company with both utility and nonutility operations. Its principal subsidiaries are Wisconsin Electric Power and Wisconsin Natural Gas. The electric company generates and distributes its energy in a territory of 12,600 square miles in eastern Wisconsin and the upper peninsula of Michigan. The operating area includes Milwaukee, with a population of 2 million. Wisconsin Natural Gas purchases gas from various areas and distributes it through the company's pipelines to more than 1 million customers in Milwaukee, Appleton and the Prairie du Chien area.

New rules affecting Wisconsin Electric Power's market have increased exponentially over the past decade. The government motive is to encourage production efficiency, reduce environmental impact and stimulate alternative energy technology. The instrument to achieve this goal is managed competition throughout the utility industry. Through cost cutting and restructuring, Wisconsin Electric Power is combating competition from the inside out. Through bulk energy projects and higher electricity sales, the company is advancing from the outside in.

Other Interesting Qualities

- Revenue mix is 82% electricity, 17% gas, 1% steam.
- Earnings are 35% residential, 29% industrial, 28% commercial, 8% other.
- Fuel mix is 67% coal, 31% nuclear, 2% hydro.

FIGURE 8.3   The Dividend Connection Chart

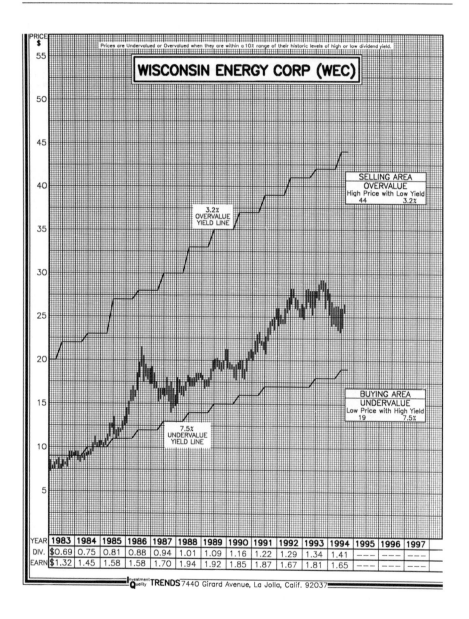

- Fuel costs amount to 31% of revenues.

- Dividends paid since 1939 have been increased in each of the past 25 years.

Similar to most utilities, WEC established an overvalued extreme in the mid-1960s, when it was priced to yield 3.2%. The rising interest rates of the 1970s prompted falling prices in utilities, producing an undervalued yield of 7.5% seen throughout the early 1980s. The ten-year period from 1983 to 1993 saw excellent growth in WEC. Consistently rising dividends supported a substantial capital gain, losing little steam even in 1987. If an investor had purchased shares of WEC at undervalue in 1983 and held them through the top of the utility bull market in 1993, the capital gain would have been roughly 300%, while the dividend grew by nearly 100%.

When the plug was pulled on utilities in September 1993, WEC lost 26% of its per share value in six months. The stock then rallied to regain nearly 50% of that decline. At undervalue, WEC should deliver continued dividend growth and generate ample capital gains.

How Should I Select Utilities Stocks?

We are often asked: What is the best way to fashion a portfolio of utilities stocks? After all, the companies are similar in nature. Most are virtual monopolies in their service areas. All are regulated by the various state and federal regulatory commissions. Rates of return are fixed.

The differences rest in their locations, fuel sources, current dividend yields and records of dividend growth. Steady dividend growth indicates good earnings growth as well as dependable corporate management.

The three most important things to remember in buying utilities stocks are: diversification, diversification and diversification. We refer to three very specific kinds of diversification.

Geographic diversification is a good place to begin. We suggest compiling a list of utilities located in various regions of the nation. Utilities are a rate-regulated industry, vulnerable to the political whims of public utilities commissions (PUC). The members of these commissions are political appointees who can and do change with each new administration when their terms expire. A commission can be friendly and quick to move on rate requests, or it can be slow and unresponsive, causing considerable financial pain to a company under its jurisdiction. The problem to investors is that one may purchase a company in an area with a lenient PUC only to find a changed regulatory climate down the road. Geographic diversification will protect the entire portfolio from the ravages of a hostile or unfriendly regulatory commission. Such diversification also mitigates the risk of natural disasters that plague the earnings and operations of an otherwise well-managed company.

Fuel diversification is another important consideration based on the main sources of energy used by the company. Each fuel has its own problems and benefits. Oil is relatively inexpensive—especially in the areas where it is found—but it is vulnerable to changes in supply and consequently to volatile price swings. Coal is plentiful in the United States, but more costly than either oil or nuclear. Also, acid rain legislation requires major capital expenditures to meet new clean air standards. Companies that haven't conformed to those standards are facing costs that could depress earnings growth. Nuclear power plants are the most cost efficient of all, but they carry the risk of a possible malfunction and the fallout of investor confidence. They are the least "politically correct" fuel source. A diversified selection of utilities stocks reduces the risk of portfolio damage if any one fuel source is hit with bad news.

Yield diversification also should be considered, based on current levels of dividend yield. A high yield may indicate temporary difficulties within the company or a relatively slow rate of dividend growth. But if the dividend is maintained despite the problems, the high yield provides strong support under the price of the stock, and the result can be a splendid long-term total return. High dividend yields can be balanced with lower yields, which suggest fewer problems and more rapid rates of earnings and dividend growth.

Selective diversification is the key to safety and success in this attractive industry group. We follow about 50 blue chip utilities in our universe of 350 select blue chip stocks. The optimum number of stocks in any portfolio is 20 to 25. Utilities portfolios can be launched with as few as two stocks, but four stocks offer greater safety and diversification. More are even better. The number of selections can be broadened when additional capital is available.

Investors who do not require dividend income to maintain their standard of living are advised to participate in the various dividend reinvestment programs that are offered by virtually all of the major utilities companies. When dividends are reinvested, the portfolio grows more rapidly and the total return is larger. Dividend reinvestment plans allow stockholders to purchase additional shares without paying brokerage commission fees. Cash dividends can be accumulated and then invested in other utilities stocks for greater diversification.

To keep a balanced portfolio, it is wise to put the same dollar amount into each new selection. The number of shares is unimportant. If a similar sum of capital has been invested in each selection, the shareholder can easily determine which stocks are the better percentage performers, and laggards will not seriously retard the progress of the entire portfolio.

As long-term holdings, utilities are especially suitable for dividend reinvestment programs, IRA or Keogh accounts and for retirement portfolios. But don't feel guilty if you decide to spend and enjoy your dividends. There is more to life than the accumulation of capital; and if dividends can give you the freedom to buy something you otherwise could not afford, treat yourself. The growth of your portfolio will be a little slower, but the real and tangible purpose of the investment will be served. Hopefully, capital gains will allow you to keep up with inflation and enlarge your net worth.

Figure 8.4 lists the 15 stocks in the Dow Jones Utilities Average and illustrates their diversification in terms of location, fuel source and dividend yield.

FIGURE 8.4   Dow Jones Utilities Stocks

Stocks	Location	Primary Fuel Source	Recent Price	Annual Dividend	Dividend Yield	Ticker Symbol
American Electric Power Company	East	Coal	28	2.40	8.6%	AEP
Arkla Inc.	Central	Natural Gas	7	.28	4.0	ALG
Centerior Energy Corp.	Central	Coal/Nuclear	10	.80	8.0	CX
Commonwealth Edison Company	Central	Nuclear	23	1.60	7.0	CWE
Consolidated Edison Company of New York	East	Oil/Nuclr/Gas	26	2.00	7.7	ED
Consolidated Natural Gas	Central	Natural Gas	38	1.94	5.1	CNG
Detroit Edison Company	Central	Coal	25	2.06	8.2	DTE
Houston Industries Inc.	South	Coal/Gas	33	3.00	9.1	HOU
Niagara Mohawk Power Corp.	East	Coal/Oil/Hyd	15	1.12	7.4	NMK
Pacific Gas & Electric Company	West	Gas/Oil/Nuclr	24	1.96	8.2	PCG
Panhandle Eastern Corp.	South	Natural Gas	20	.84	4.2	PEL
Peoples Energy Corp.	North	Natural Gas	24	1.80	7.5	PGL
Peco Energy	East	Nuclr/Coal	26	1.52	5.7	PE
Public Service Enterprise Group	East	Nuclr/Coal	25	2.16	8.6	PEG
SCEcorp	West	Oil/Gas/Nuclr	13	1.00	7.7	SCE

The Dividend Connection

American Electric Power
Detroit Edison

Let's take a closer look at two of the stocks in the Dow Jones Utilities Average. American Electric Power Company and Detroit Edison Company both use coal as a primary fuel source.

American Electric Power Company (NYSE:AEP)

To 7 million people in Michigan, Indiana, Ohio, Kentucky, Virginia, West Virginia and Tennessee, American Electric Power provides electric energy throughout a 45,500-mile service area. Eight major subsidiaries form an integrated network of coal-fired, nuclear and hydroelectric generating units and transmission/distribution facilities. Since 1906, AEP has been a leader in developing technology for the efficient conversion of fossil fuel to electricity. It has been a leading player in the trend toward energy conservation with the use of efficiency devices such as heat pumps and electric storage heating.

Under a new law, virtually any group can develop a wholesale distributor system. The objective is to increase competition and therefore lower utility rates. The new policy gives any wholesale purchaser access to all transmission lines. Regulators believe this move will promote a healthier, free enterprise utility market. To combat these competitive forces, AEP is initiating sweeping cost-cutting efforts. It entered into a joint venture with Michigan Power and Indiana Power to combine transmission and distribution efforts, leading to greater economies and wider profit margins.

Other Interesting Qualities

- Revenue mix is 38% residential, 35% industrial, 25% commercial, 2% other.

- Sales to other utilities account for 20% of revenues.

- American Electric Power is included in the Dow Jones Utilities Average.

- Fuel mix is 93% coal, 6% nuclear, 1% hydro and purchased.

- Fuel costs amount to 33% of revenues.

- Dividends paid since 1909 have been increased only twice in the past 12 years.

In the high-flying mid-1960s, the stock was overvalued at a yield of 3%. Later, in the early 1980s, the stock was extremely undervalued, yielding 14.3%. In 1987, 1989 and 1990, AEP found undervalued support at 9.2%. Therefore, the area between the two bottom lines on the chart represents an extraordinary buying range.

The striking problem that the chart illustrates is the lack of dividend growth. Still, the annual cash payout represents an attractive yield relative to the industry, and American Electric Power continues to be one of the most widely held electric utility stocks in the nation.

FIGURE 8.5   The Dividend Connection Chart

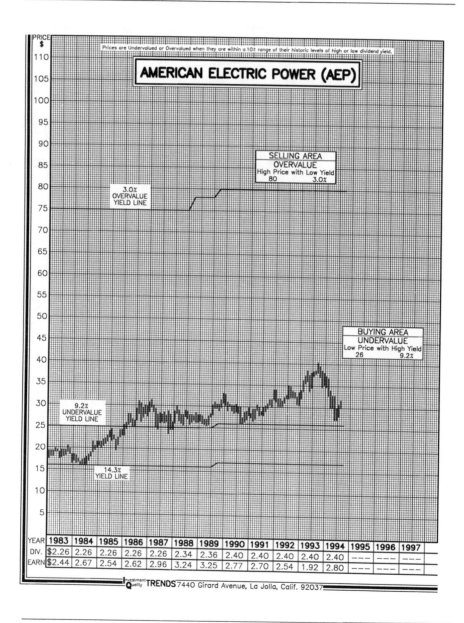

YEAR	1983	1984	1985	1986	1987	1988	1989	1990	1991	1992	1993	1994	1995	1996	1997
DIV.	$2.26	2.26	2.26	2.26	2.26	2.34	2.36	2.40	2.40	2.40	2.40	2.40	---	---	---
EARN	$2.44	2.67	2.54	2.62	2.96	3.24	3.25	2.77	2.70	2.54	1.92	2.80	---	---	---

Investment Quality **TRENDS** 7440 Girard Avenue, La Jolla, Calif. 92037

Detroit Edison Company (NYSE:DTE)

Serving some 2 million customers in a 7,600-square-mile territory, Detroit Edison is Michigan's Cadillac of utilities, based in the automotive capital of the world. This primarily coal-based electric utility generally rides the economic cycles of the auto industry, but steel producers also account for a large percentage of industrial profits. Detroit represents roughly 25% of Edison's total customers and 20% of its revenues. The company also provides steam to downtown Detroit.

Industrywide deregulation is the company's most significant long-term challenge. In 1994, the Michigan Public Service Commission proposed a mandatory retail wheeling program that would require Detroit Edison to deliver the electricity that its large customers purchase from other sources. If the plan becomes a reality, it will not occur before the year 2000. By then, the necessary strategic adjustments should be in place to enable Detroit Edison to stand up to the competition.

Adding salt to the wound, the state's regulatory commission hit the utility with an unfavorable rate decision in 1994 and cut its rates by $78 million. The difficulties of the year, combined with the uncertainties of the future, prompted Detroit Edison's board to maintain the $2.06 dividend with no increase. This was the first time in five years that the dividend had not been increased. However, there is no talk of a dividend reduction and the current dividend appears safe.

Other Interesting Qualities

- Revenue mix is 99% electricity, 1% steam.

- Electricity breakdown is 40% commercial, 32% residential, 20% industrial, 8% other.

- Generating sources are 78% coal, 17% nuclear, 4% purchased, 1% oil and gas.

- Fuel costs amount to 24% of revenues; labor 14%.

- Dividends paid since 1909 have been increased five times in the past 12 years.

The chart indicates an extraordinary yield of 16% present in 1982, 1984 and 1988. This occurred while the U.S. automotive industry was

FIGURE 8.6   The Dividend Connection Chart

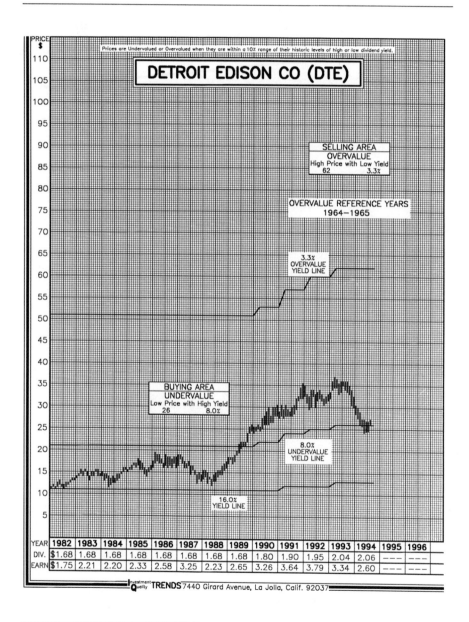

Prices are Undervalued or Overvalued when they are within a 10% range of their historic levels of high or low dividend yield.

DETROIT EDISON CO (DTE)

SELLING AREA
OVERVALUE
High Price with Low Yield
62   3.3%

OVERVALUE REFERENCE YEARS
1964–1965

3.3%
OVERVALUE
YIELD LINE

BUYING AREA
UNDERVALUE
Low Price with High Yield
26   8.0%

8.0%
UNDERVALUE
YIELD LINE

16.0%
YIELD LINE

YEAR	1982	1983	1984	1985	1986	1987	1988	1989	1990	1991	1992	1993	1994	1995	1996
DIV.	$1.68	1.68	1.68	1.68	1.68	1.68	1.68	1.68	1.80	1.90	1.95	2.04	2.06	---	---
EARN	$1.75	2.21	2.20	2.33	2.58	3.25	2.23	2.65	3.26	3.64	3.79	3.34	2.60	---	---

Investment Quality **TRENDS** 7440 Girard Avenue, La Jolla, Calif. 92037

broken down, illustrating the close relationship between Detroit Edison and the Detroit car manufacturers. Undervalue is identified at the 8% yield level. To witness the overvalued yield of 3.3%, one must look back to the mid-1960s, when all utilities were profiting from a favorable interest rate environment. Although the board's decision to end a five-year streak of dividend increases disappointed shareholders, DTE's generous yield and well-protected dividend provide the safety of dual air bags under a low, undervalued sticker price.

How Safe Are the Dividends for Electric Utilities?

Ever since FPL Group slashed its annual dividend by 32% in May 1994 and SCEcorp followed suit in June 1994, there has been growing concern about the safety of all utility dividends. Coming after a 31% decline in the Dow Jones Utilities Average, the news struck many raw nerves among the owners of utilities stocks.

Although the utilities industry is undergoing significant change, the fear of massive dividend reductions is overdone and, in most cases, groundless. Why do investors buy utilities stocks? The answer is dividends. Utilities stock owners are looking mainly for income. They are attracted by a secure dividend that has growth potential and offers a relatively high yield. Unlike bonds, which also produce income, utilities tend to raise their dividends so that income streams can be enlarged over time. And as dividends grow, so do stock prices, resulting in attractive total returns.

The managements of utilities are well aware that the vast majority of their shareholders require cash dividends and do not support a stock repurchase program if it reduces their investment income. We are certain that the owners of FPL Group would rather have had the cash dividend than see their company repurchase 10 million shares over a three-year period of time—a rationalization the company gave for lowering the dividend. In fact, this "financially strong" (according to the press) company had 12-month earnings of $2.33 per share, which was lower than the $2.48 per share dividend it had been paying. Obviously, the payout ratio was an unsustainable 106%. The truth is that the company was not earning its dividend, so a dividend reduction was necessary. This is not the case with the vast majority of blue chip utilities. Admittedly, some of the payout ratios are high.

However, we feel that a payout ratio of 85% or less is safe, and a dividend reduction from such a company is unlikely to occur.

Even if the payout ratio is high, many companies dip into cash flow to meet the promised dividend rather than disappoint their shareholders. Such was the case with Texas Utilities in 1994. With 12-month earnings of $1.26 per share and an annual dividend of $3.08 per share, the dividend would appear to be in grave danger. However, further investigation revealed that the indicated annual dividend would be supported by cash flow, even though the payout would not be covered by earnings that year. So, although an earnings shortfall does not necessarily mean that the dividend will be reduced, it does raise a flag of caution that the dividend may be in jeopardy.

If you are concerned about the safety of your dividends, keep an eye on earnings, and make sure that the payout represents no more than 85% of the profits. It doesn't hurt to call the company and ask about the safety of the dividend. As a stockholder, you are an owner of the company and entitled to a straight answer.

Figure 8.7 lists blue chip utilities stocks that have safe dividends with payout ratios of 85% or less. It also lists stocks that have unprotected payouts that exceed earnings, where the dividend may be in danger. Blue chip utilities that do not appear on either list have payout ratios that are above 85% but less than 100%. The subsequent progress of earnings (up or down) will shift those companies either into the safe or unsafe category of dividend payouts.

The Dividend Connection

Dominion Resources
Texas Utilities

In this section we will profile one utility company with a safe dividend and one with a dividend in jeopardy. Dominion Resources has

FIGURE 8.7   Safe and Unsafe Dividend Payout Ratios

Safe Dividends—Payout Ratio of 85% or Less

Stock	Price	Annual Dividend	Dividend Yield	12-Month Earnings	Payout Ratio
Allegheny Power System, Inc.	22	1.64	7.5%	1.93	85%
Atlantic Energy, Inc.	19	1.54	8.1	1.94	79
Baltimore Gas & Electric Company	23	1.52	6.6	2.03	75
Brooklyn Union Gas Company	26	1.35	5.2	1.75	77
Carolina Power & Light Company	27	1.70	6.3	2.05	83
CIPSCO Inc.	28	2.00	7.1	2.62	76
Consolidated Edison Company of New York	29	2.00	6.9	2.91	69
Delmarva Power & Light Company	19	1.54	8.1	1.85	83
Detroit Edison Company	27	2.06	7.6	3.09	69
Dominion Resources, Inc.	37	2.54	6.9	3.39	75
DPL Inc.	20	1.18	5.9	1.46	81
Duke Power Company	39	1.96	5.0	2.99	66
Houston Industries Inc.	36	3.00	8.3	3.53	85
KU Energy Corp.	27	1.64	6.1	2.09	78
LG&E Energy Corp.	39	2.08	5.3	3.07	68
National Fuel Gas Company	31	1.58	5.1	2.34	68
New England Electric System	33	2.30	7.0	3.17	73
Northern States Power Company	43	2.64	6.1	3.12	85
Pacificorp	18	1.08	6.0	1.58	68
Pennsylvania Power & Light	21	1.67	8.0	2.07	81
SCANA Corp.	45	2.82	6.3	3.76	75
SCEcorp.	13	1.00	7.7	1.39	72
Southern Company	19	1.18	6.2	1.51	78
TECO Energy, Inc.	20	1.01	5.1	1.41	72
Washington Gas Light Company	37	2.22	6.0	2.77	80
Wisconsin Public Service	30	1.82	6.1	2.38	76

Unsafe Dividends—Payout Exceeds Earnings

Stock	Price	Annual Dividend	Dividend Yield	12-Month Earnings	Payout Ratio
American Electric Power Company	31	2.40	7.7%	2.12	113%
Central & South West Corp.	22	1.70	7.7	1.46	116
Hawaiian Electric Industries	32	2.32	7.3	1.72	135
Interstate Power Company	24	2.08	8.7	1.78	117
IPALCO Enterprises, Inc.	31	2.12	6.8	2.01	105
Texas Utilities Company	32	3.08	9.6	1.26	244

a comfortable 75% dividend payout ratio, while Texas Utilities has a shaky 244% payout ratio.

Dominion Resources, Inc. (NYSE:D)

Primarily engaged in the business of producing electricity, Dominion Resources is a holding company with four major subsidiaries. The principal subsidiary is Virginia Power, a regulated electric utility serving nearly 2 million homes and businesses in Virginia and North Carolina. Its 30,000-square-mile territory includes Richmond, Norfolk, Newport News and Virginia Beach. Virginia Power ranks as one of the nation's 15 largest electric power companies in terms of sales, revenues and assets. A diversified and well-balanced power producer, it owns and operates nuclear, coal, natural gas, oil and hydroelectric power plants.

Dominion also is involved in independent power production both domestically and in Latin America, thereby capitalizing on the new world order of electric utility competition. It has ownership and operating interests in 17 independent power and cogeneration facilities in six states, Belize and Argentina. The company is active in the natural gas business and controls large reserves throughout the United States and Canada. The remaining subsidiaries include financial services and real estate. Dominion Capital is the financial group that manages the investments of the parent company and its subsidiaries. Dominion Lands is the real estate subsidiary that owns and operates three residential developments in Williamsburg, Virginia and Charlotte, North Carolina.

Other Interesting Qualities

- Earnings mix is 84% Virginia Power, 16% nonutility.

- Electricity revenue mix is 43% residential, 28% commercial, 11% industrial, 18% other.

- Fuel mix is 31% nuclear, 39% coal, 3% oil, 23% purchased, 4% other.

- Virginia Power's cost of generating electricity is nearly 30% lower than the industry average.

- Dividends paid since 1925 have been increased in each of the past 13 years.

FIGURE 8.8   The Dividend Connection Chart

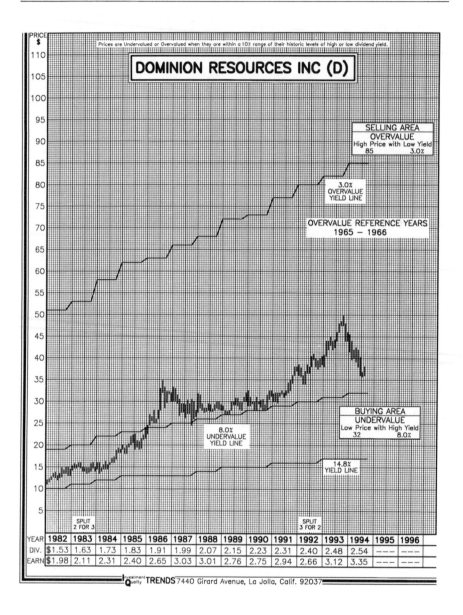

In the early 1980s, Dominion Resources was priced to yield an extraordinary 14.8%. From 1985 through 1990, the undervalued yield of 8% was established and reconfirmed. An overvalued yield of 3% was seen in 1965 and 1966. An excellent history of dividend growth consistently has boosted the price at undervalue and overvalue, providing a strong safety net under the price of the stock. Dominion Resources is easily earning the dividend, and its growth is expected to continue as the company adapts to industry change.

Texas Utilities Company (NYSE:TXU)

Offering a bonanza of diversified energy services to about one-third of the Lone Star State's population, Texas Utilities Company is the parent company of Texas Utilities Electric, the state's largest publicly held utility system. Texas Utilities Company owns 24 generating stations. Nineteen are fueled by gas and oil, four by lignite and one by nuclear fuel. Electricity is provided to 5.6 million customers. The service territory sprawls across 600 miles of its home state, from the western tip of Texas to the Louisiana border, and from the Oklahoma border down into Central Texas, including Dallas—the eighth largest city in the nation—and the Dallas/Fort Worth International Airport.

Texas Utilities Electric was dealt a hard blow in 1994, when the state's public utilities commission refused its request for a 15.3% rate increase and instead recommended only an 8.5% increase. This action motivated a major brokerage company to downgrade the stock, propelling a price decline.

This unfortunate string of events made shareholders and potential investors somewhat insecure regarding the safety of TXU's dividend. After all, the most tangible benefit of a Texas Utilities holding is the reliable dividend with its stainless record of annual growth. In fact, prior to the rate case disappointment, the company was preparing to increase the dividend for the 48th consecutive year. Regrettably, it was not able to extend that record in 1994. Still, a decline in the dividend is unlikely.

Other Interesting Qualities

- Electric revenue mix is 41% residential, 29% commercial, 17% industrial, 13% other.

FIGURE 8.9   The Dividend Connection Chart

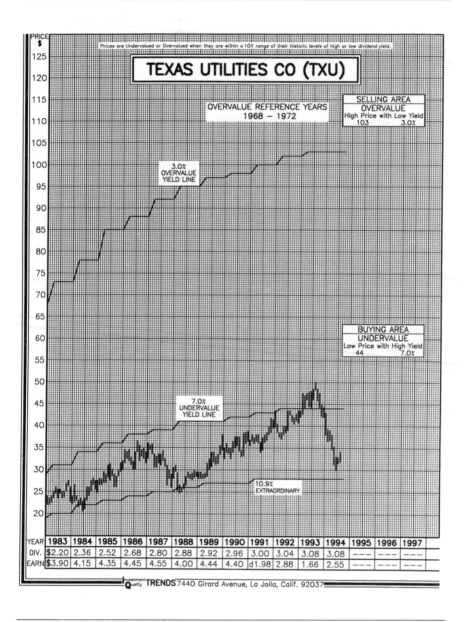

TEXAS UTILITIES CO (TXU)

YEAR	1983	1984	1985	1986	1987	1988	1989	1990	1991	1992	1993	1994	1995	1996	1997
DIV.	$2.20	2.36	2.52	2.68	2.80	2.88	2.92	2.96	3.00	3.04	3.08	3.08	---	---	---
EARN	$3.90	4.15	4.35	4.45	4.55	4.00	4.44	4.40	d1.98	2.88	1.66	2.55	---	---	---

- Fuel mix is 44% lignite, 38% gas, 14% purchased, 4% nuclear.
- Dividends paid since 1917 have been increased in each of the past 47 years.

From 1968 to 1972 when Texas Utilities was considered to be a growth company, it was priced to yield 3%. However, after embarking on ambitious construction projects and incurring mountains of debt, its stock price fell to yield an extraordinary 10.9% in 1984 and 1988. The state experienced an economic depression that applied further pressure on the stock. For the past 20 years, the stock consistently found undervalued support in the 7% yield area.

Although the company's management insisted that it would maintain a $3.08 per share annual dividend with cash flow, earnings do not cover the payout, and the safety of the dividend is in question. In 1994, the yield rose above 10%, reflecting clouds of uncertainty. Finances will continue to be tight in 1995, but by 1996 we expect Texas Utilities Company to dress its wounds and saddle up for a long ride into the sunset of happier financial endings with a resumption of dividend growth.

Are Pharmaceutical Stocks a Drug on the Market?

When President Clinton announced his intention to overhaul the nation's health care system, pharmaceutical stocks became, so to speak, a drug on the market. From 1993 through 1994, these stocks were bitter pills with price performances that were hard to swallow. Some stocks fell more than 60%. The average price declined more than 30%. The fear was government-mandated price controls on drug products. While mandatory controls or restraints are unlikely in a free market economy, the administration hoped to exert pressure on the industry to limit price increases voluntarily. Some companies already have agreed to exercise restraint, and price increases have started to moderate. Pfizer lifted prices about 3% in 1993–1994—in line with growth in the consumer price index. Merck, too, proposed limiting increases to the rate of inflation.

Faced with potential restrictions on their pricing policies, drug companies are creatively preparing for the future. Many producers are branching into the manufacture of generic forms of their proprietary drugs. They are reducing costs by entering into joint marketing

ventures, and they are acquiring discount and mail-order drug distributors, thereby retaining their leadership positions in an increasingly diverse industry. Rest assured, these companies will continue
to grow and lead their industry forward into a profitable future.

Another way in which drug stocks are facing the challenge of
price management is by entering the arena of wholesale drug marketing. Within the past two years, several major drug manufacturers
have purchased wholesale and discount distributors. Merck purchased Medco Containment; Eli Lilly purchased McKesson; and Diversified Pharmaceutical Services has joined forces with SmithKline
Beecham.

One characteristic of drug stocks is their stellar records of growth.
Over the past 12 years, for example, the dividend of Bristol-Myers
Squibb has grown at a compound average annual rate of 17%. A
purchase in 1982, when the cash dividend was $ .52 per share, yielded
4%. Twelve years of dividend growth increased the payout to $2.92,
and the yield on the original invested capital became 22.5%. The
dividend during that time rose 462%, while the price rose 362%.
Frequent dividend increases have lifted the prices at undervalue and
overvalue. So, despite the outstanding capital gains, because of the
persistent dividend growth, Bristol-Myers Squibb has remained an
attractive investment value. Similar examples can be seen in Eli Lilly,
Upjohn, Marion Merrell Dow and Merck.

Current dividend yields for many of these stocks are 5% or more,
reflecting doubt on Wall Street that such impressive growth can
continue in the future.

We believe that it can. Although industry growth may be tempo-
rarily restrained, the long-term outlook commands our enthusiastic
endorsement. Expanding global populations are providing additional markets for health care products, and new drugs continue to flow
through research and development pipelines.

People are living longer, well into the years when prescription
drugs become important facts of life. Adding to future demand, the
baby boomers soon will be 50 years of age, when many diseases
related to aging begin to surface. Drugs are providing the means of
sustaining and extending life, of controlling pain and reducing the
need for costly, prolonged hospital care.

Meanwhile, back at the stock market, some drug companies offer
such spectacular values that they are in danger of being merged with

or acquired by other companies. Such was the case with Syntex Corp. in 1994, when it was purchased by Roche Holding Ltd., of Switzerland for $24 per share. Certainly, a company like Upjohn—with a huge stable of proprietary and ethical drugs, priced at nine times earnings, with earnings in an uptrend and a well-protected dividend that yields about 5%—is an attractive takeover target as well as a worthwhile investment selection.

Although profit margins and growth may be squeezed a bit in the future, there is plenty of juice left in the industry. Margins currently range from 12% to 18%, about three times higher than the average of *Fortune* 500 companies. Still, judging by the stock market's reaction, it looks as though the drug industry is about to have a coronary. Is this the time for value-seeking investors with ailing portfolios to take a dose of drug stocks, or is there more pain to follow?

Whether or not the selling epidemic is over, the values among some drug stocks are compelling. Not every stock in the industry is undervalued, but a number of well-managed, high-quality growth companies are. Figure 8.10 lists 10 blue chip drug companies that offer excellent quality and are at or near their historically established undervalued yields. We feel that undervalued, blue chip drug stocks provide a refillable prescription for long-term investment growth.

FIGURE 8.10   Blue Chip Pharmaceuticals

Stock	Price	Annual Dividend	Dividend Yield	Downside Risk	Upside Potential	Quality Rank
Abbott Laboratories	29	0.76	2.6%	24%	86%	A+
American Home Products Corp.	57	2.92	5.1	14	70	A+
Baxter International Inc.	26	1.05	4.0	–	350	B+
Bristol-Myers Squibb Company	53	2.92	5.5	–	121	A+
Johnson & Johnson	43	1.16	2.7	26	49	A+
Lilly (Eli) Company	50	2.50	5.0	–	178	A
Marion Merrell Dow Inc.	18	1.00	5.6	–	456	A
Merck & Company	29	1.12	3.9	–	221	A+
Pfizer Inc.	63	1.88	3.0	25	130	A–
Schering-Plough Corp.	63	2.04	3.2	30	224	A+
Upjohn Company	29	1.48	5.1	–	324	A

The Dividend Connection

Baxter International
Marion Merrell Dow

Marion Merrell Dow and Baxter International are blue chip pharmaceuticals that are at or near an undervalued buying area.

Baxter International Inc. (NYSE:BAX)

The world's leading supplier of health care products and services to hospitals and alternate treatment settings, Baxter has suffered a year of acute corporate trauma. The company gained international repute in 1954 for its introduction of the first hemodialysis system, which paved the way for an artificial kidney and many forms of dialysis therapy. Today, Baxter is the clear leader in the market with products sold in 85 countries to the tune of $4 billion, annually.

Problems plagued Baxter in 1993. Most alarming was its admission of guilt in cooperating with an Arab boycott of Israel, for which the company agreed to pay $6.5 million in federal antitrust fines. This gross error in judgment resulted in product bans by the U.S. Defense Department, Veterans Affairs Department and the Premier Health Alliance.

The company plans to sell its five diagnostic products divisions. With the income generated from the sale, it will reinvest a total of $2 billion over the next three years to reinforce its core kidney dialysis business and expand its ventricular device unit.

Other Interesting Qualities

- Baxter distributes more than 120,000 products to 100 nations.

- Intravenous solutions and dialysis products account for 70% of sales.

- Dividends paid since 1934 have been increased in each of the past 14 years.

FIGURE 8.11   The Dividend Connection Chart

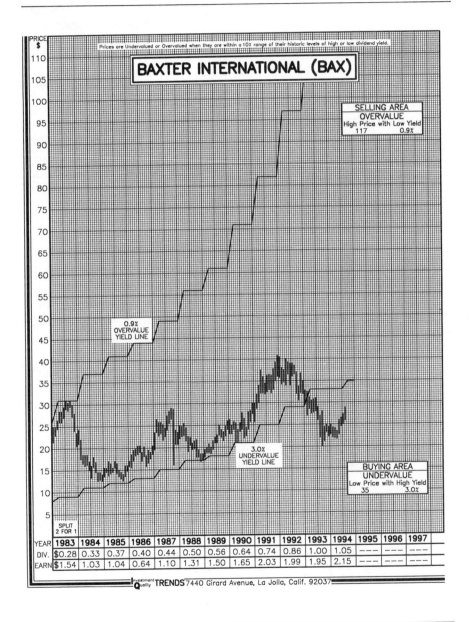

Baxter International (BAX)

YEAR	1983	1984	1985	1986	1987	1988	1989	1990	1991	1992	1993	1994	1995	1996	1997
DIV.	$0.28	0.33	0.37	0.40	0.44	0.50	0.56	0.64	0.74	0.86	1.00	1.05	———	———	———
EARN	$1.54	1.03	1.04	0.64	1.10	1.31	1.50	1.65	2.03	1.99	1.95	2.15	———	———	———

Investment Quality TRENDS 7440 Girard Avenue, La Jolla, Calif. 92037

The chart illustrates Baxter's reversal of fortunes set within the parameters of its dividend yield extremes. When BAX is priced to yield 3%, it is undervalued and a purchase is prescribed. When the price rises and the yield falls to 0.9%, it is overvalued and a sale should be administered. In 1983, the stock lost 50% of its value in six months. That trend was reversed in 1985, when the company announced plans to purchase American Hospital Supply, then the largest health care supplier in the industry. This launched a rising trend that lasted for seven years, until news of the Israeli blacklist scandal came to light.

"Bottom-fishers" began to nibble on these attractive shares in 1994. The company is not yet in the clear, but it deserves a second chance, given its undisputed dominance in such an important industry. Having endured an episode that would have mortally wounded many other companies, Baxter appears to be on the road to recovery.

Marion Merrell Dow Inc. (NYSE:MKC)

This is the dawn of managed health care, and all major pharmaceutical companies are trying to move with the trend. Marion Merrell Dow is no exception and is realigning its business better than most. The Kansas City, Missouri, giant is a worldwide leader of both prescription and over-the-counter drugs. Important brand names include Cardizem, Carafate, Cepacol, Citrucel, Gaviscon, Nicoderm, Os-Cal and Seldane.

Marion Merrell Dow's smoking cessation products more than doubled in 1994 due to the success of its transdermal nicotine patch, Nicoderm. Sales of both the patch and the equivalent chewing gum, Nicorette, are breathing life into this important new health care market.

Until recently, sales reps from pharmaceutical companies promoted new drugs directly to doctors via free samples and personalized brand-name pens. Now, with the advent of managed health care, they must woo well-organized health maintenance organizations and government programs such as Medicare and Medicaid. These large institutions use purchasing committees, which base their drug-buying decisions solely on cost efficiency. Marion Merrell Dow was the first major drug company to adapt to this shift.

FIGURE 8.12   The Dividend Connection Chart

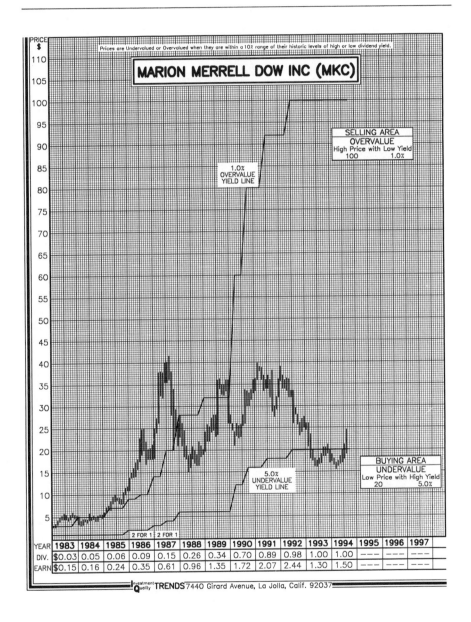

YEAR	1983	1984	1985	1986	1987	1988	1989	1990	1991	1992	1993	1994	1995	1996	1997
DIV.	$0.03	0.05	0.06	0.09	0.15	0.26	0.34	0.70	0.89	0.98	1.00	1.00	---	---	---
EARN	$0.15	0.16	0.24	0.35	0.61	0.96	1.35	1.72	2.07	2.44	1.30	1.50	---	---	---

Investment Quality **TRENDS** 7440 Girard Avenue, La Jolla, Calif. 92037

Other Interesting Qualities

- Foreign sales account for 33% of revenues; R&D costs, 14%.

- Dow Chemical owns 70% of the common stock; institutions hold only 11%.

- Dividends paid since 1957 have been increased in each of the past ten years.

The chart illustrates an unusual profile of value. When MKC is priced to yield 1%, it is overvalued and a sale should be considered. When the price falls and the yield rises to 5%, MKC is undervalued and a purchase is prescribed. From 1992 through mid-1994, virtually all pharmaceutical stocks took it on the chin in the face of feared governmental regulation. During those months, MKC lost roughly 50% of its market value. Thereafter, the stock rebounded along with the industry group. The company has put itself up for sale and a future merger or acquisition will come as no surprise. Meanwhile, the dividend looks safe. The PE ratio is low, and this A quality stock meets all six blue chip criteria. It tops our list for dividend growth with a 2,400% increase over the past 12 years. MKC is in position to deliver a double dose of potent capital gains along with a high-yielding dividend return.

Using the Dow Jones Averages To Spot Value

What Is the Importance of the Dow Jones Industrial Average?

First conceived at the turn of the century, the original Dow Jones Average comprised 14 stocks—12 railroad and 2 industrial companies. As our culture and society have changed, so has the Dow. Now, instead of just one Dow Jones Average, there are three major averages. The first and most prominent is the Dow Jones Industrial Average (DJIA). This average includes 30 of America's largest and most widely held industrial and service companies. The Dow Jones Transportation Average (DJTA) includes 20 airline, motor carrier and railroad companies that reflect the current modes of travel and transport. The Dow Jones Utilities Average (DJUA) includes 15 geographically diversified electric and gas utilities.

While critics claim that it is not an absolute representation of the stock market, the Dow Jones Industrial Average, consisting of 30 giant corporations, has provided a reasonably accurate indication of general stock market trends since 1897. Whatever inaccuracies it may be accorded, the wide acceptance it has enjoyed for so long a period of time by generations of investors underscores its importance and attests to its service as a measure of the market.

Over time, stocks have been deleted from and added to this important average to keep it relevant to the evolution of corporate America and the changing landscape of the U.S. economy. For example, at one time General Foods was one of the Dow 30 stocks. However, when General Foods and Kraft were acquired by Philip Morris, the cigarette company was added to the list. Because one cigarette company was thought to be enough, American Brands was dropped. Two other more recent inclusions that reflect modern trends in the economy are McDonald's and Disney. The only remaining company that appeared on the original list of 14 stocks is General Electric.

The 30 component stocks represent a depth of industry groups, including aerospace (Boeing, United Technologies); aluminum (Alcoa); automotive (General Motors); banking (J.P. Morgan); beverages (Coca-Cola); business machines (IBM); chemicals (Allied Signal, Du Pont, Eastman Kodak, Union Carbide); consumer products (Philip Morris); electrical equipment (General Electric, Westinghouse); entertainment (Walt Disney); equipment (Caterpillar); fast food (McDonald's); household products (Procter & Gamble); insurance (American Express); paper products (International Paper); petroleum (Exxon, Chevron, Texaco); pharmaceutical (Merck); retail (Sears, Roebuck; Woolworth); rubber (Goodyear); steel (Bethlehem Steel); telecommunications (AT&T); tapes and adhesives (Minnesota Mining and Manufacturing.)

Although these stocks account for only about 1½% of the total number of companies on the New York Stock Exchange, they account for about 33% of the total market value. All 30 stocks are listed on the New York Stock Exchange, and all are capitalization companies.

Since these stocks represent the largest companies in America, they accurately reflect economic trends and provide a good sampling of trends among all stock industry groups.

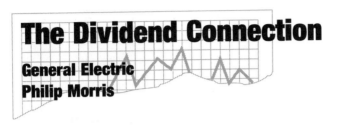

The Dividend Connection
General Electric
Philip Morris

Figures 10.1 and 10.2 show the connection of two Dow component stocks to good quality, good value, little debt and relatively low payout ratios.

General Electric Company (NYSE:GE)

Tracing its roots back to Thomas Edison, who established the Edison Electric Light Company in 1878, General Electric was formed by a merger of Edison and Thomson-Houston Electric Company in 1892. GE is now a diversified technology, manufacturing and services company with worldwide leadership positions in aircraft engines, broadcasting, electrical equipment, capital and information services, lighting, medical systems, plastics and, of course, household appliances. With a corporate portfolio of 12 major businesses, GE reigns as one of the largest and most diversified companies in the world.

GE's longtime strategy has been aimed at rapidly introducing new products that will outperform competitors' older, comparable products. Important new products launched in 1994 included GE's state-of-the-art 30-cubic-foot refrigerator and the world's highest efficiency gas turbine engine. The company adapts to marketplace changes faster than its competitors and has been able to reduce cycle time in design, manufacture and marketing.

The Capital Services arm of GE continues to flex its mighty muscle with an arsenal of 24 business units. During the recession of the early 1990s, when the company's appliance and engine businesses stalled, GE Capital Services was a veritable cash cow. Over the past five years, the unit's assets have more than doubled to $155 billion. For a time, the Capital division was the engine driving its parent's profits.

FIGURE 9.1   The Dividend Connection Chart

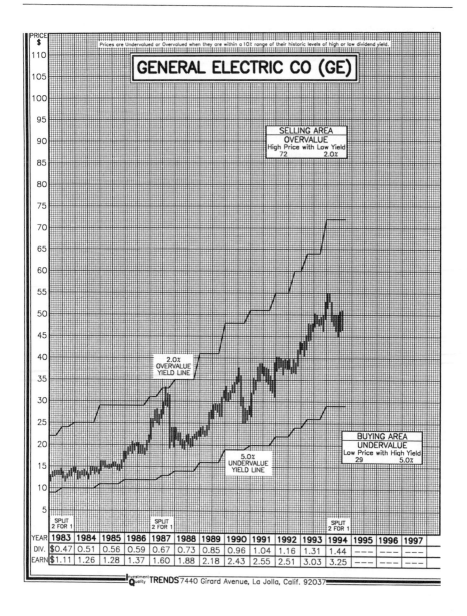

Other Interesting Qualities

- International business accounts for 30% of sales.

- GE is the fifth ranked *Fortune* 500 company based on revenues.

- Debt is only 9% of total capitalization.

- There are 1.7 billion common shares outstanding.

- Dividends paid since 1899 have been increased in each of the past 19 years.

When this stock is priced in the 5% yield area, it is undervalued and a purchase is recommended. However, when the price rises and the yield falls to the 2% range, GE is overvalued and a sale should be considered. In late 1985, GE launched a primary rising trend that found its top at overvalue in late 1987. After the free fall in October of that year, it took almost three years to regain the price it had lost in just one month. This illustrates why it is so critical to sell at overvalue. Still, from its low price in October 1990 to its high price in January 1994, GE gained 120%, while the dividend rose 50%.

General Electric is the only original Dow Jones industrial stock still listed on that exclusive roster. This mature, A+ quality growth stock meets all six blue chip criteria. Forward-looking investors are wise to keep an eye on this stock, where at undervalue GE will "bring good things to light."

Philip Morris Companies (NYSE:MO)

An undisputed industry leader, Philip Morris Companies include several worldwide top-selling consumer products. Its three major businesses are cigarettes, food and beer. Some popular brand names include Marlboro, Merit, Lark, Parliament, Chesterfield, Virginia Slims, Cool Whip, Kraft, Oscar Meyer, Lender's, Post, Kool-Aid, Jell-O, Toblerone, Maxwell House, Sanka, Miller, Molson, Fosters, Dos Equis and Tecate. Through its diversified businesses and abundant product line, Philip Morris continues to succeed as the largest consumer packaged goods company in the world.

Topping its list of blockbuster brands, Marlboro cigarettes are the best-selling consumer packaged product in the world, generating more than $15 billion in 1994 revenues. Marlboro is the market leader

FIGURE 9.2   The Dividend Connection Chart

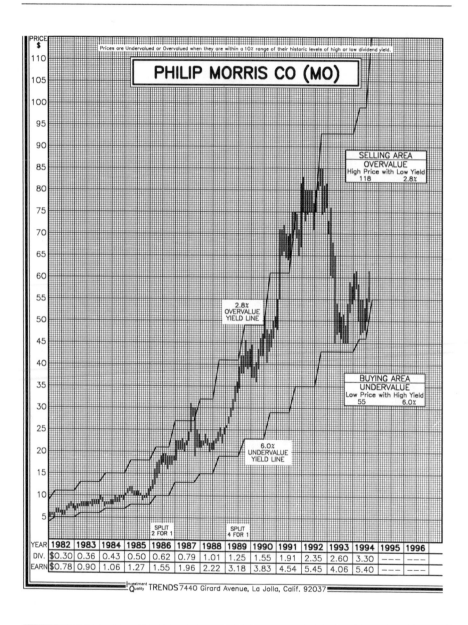

PHILIP MORRIS CO (MO)

Prices are Undervalued or Overvalued when they are within a 10% range of their historic levels of high or low dividend yield.

SELLING AREA
OVERVALUE
High Price with Low Yield
118   2.8%

2.8%
OVERVALUE
YIELD LINE

BUYING AREA
UNDERVALUE
Low Price with High Yield
55   6.0%

6.0%
UNDERVALUE
YIELD LINE

SPLIT 2 FOR 1

SPLIT 4 FOR 1

YEAR	1982	1983	1984	1985	1986	1987	1988	1989	1990	1991	1992	1993	1994	1995	1996
DIV.	$0.30	0.36	0.43	0.50	0.62	0.79	1.01	1.25	1.55	1.91	2.35	2.60	3.30	---	---
EARN	$0.78	0.90	1.06	1.27	1.55	1.96	2.22	3.18	3.83	4.54	5.45	4.06	5.40	---	---

Investment Quality TRENDS 7440 Girard Avenue, La Jolla, Calif. 92037

in the United States, Germany, Hong Kong, Mexico and 16 other important international markets. Overall, Philip Morris is the largest and most profitable cigarette company in the world, with leading positions in the United States and more than 30 other major global markets. While investors have been leery of tobacco companies due to the recent blast of antismoking fervor in this country, Philip Morris has strategically offset the potential damage by investing largely in more friendly international markets.

Other Interesting Qualities

- Philip Morris controls about 45% of the domestic cigarette market.
- The company acquired General Foods in 1985 and Kraft in 1988.
- The company's Miller Light is the world's leading low-calorie beer.
- Philip Morris is one of the 30 Dow Jones Industrial stocks.
- Dividends paid since 1928 have been increased in each of the past 27 years

The chart faithfully illustrates MO's profile of value based on historic extremes of dividend yield. When the stock is priced to yield 6%, it is undervalued and should be purchased. But when the price rises and the yield falls to 2.8%, the stock is overvalued and a sale should be considered. From an undervalued price in 1982 to the all time high price at overvalue in 1992, the stock rose roughly 600%. Meanwhile, the dividend gained more than 400%. In late 1992, times became tough in Marlboro country and MO lost 50% of its per share value in just five months. Although the domestic tobacco business is under fire, sales are smoking abroad. At undervalue this A+ quality growth stock will rise from the ashes and ignite a blazing total return.

Are All Dow Industrial Stocks Blue Chips?

Formerly considered a blue chip indicator, the Dow Jones Industrial Average no longer qualifies as a true measure of prime investment quality. Only 12 of the 30 component companies meet our blue chip criteria. They include AT&T, Boeing, Coca-Cola, Disney, Du Pont, General Electric, McDonald's, Merck, Minnesota Mining and Manufacturing, Philip Morris, Procter & Gamble and Woolworth. These 12 stocks all have Standard & Poor's quality ranks of A+, A or A- and meet all six of our blue chip criteria. The remaining Dow industrial stocks fall short on the basis of their quality rankings, earnings, dividend stability and growth.

A Standard & Poor's ranking of B+ denotes average investment quality. In some cases, that rank represents improvement from a below-average rank of B. In other cases, it represents a decline from an A– grade. Five B+ stocks listed in the Dow Jones Industrial Average are Chevron, Exxon, International Paper, J.P. Morgan and Westinghouse. Not too long ago, these stocks were prime-quality blue chips.

The remaining 13 stocks carry quality ranks of B (below average), B– (even lower) or C (the lowest). These beleaguered blue chips include Alcoa (B–), Allied Signal (B), American Express (B), Bethlehem Steel (C), Caterpillar (B–), Eastman Kodak (B), General Motors (B–), Goodyear (B), IBM (B–), Sears, Roebuck (B), Texaco (B–), and United Technologies (B). Rounding out the list of 30 stocks is Union Carbide, which has no S&P quality rank.

Figure 9.3 lists the 30 Dow Jones industrial stocks and offers additional information about each company. Besides considering quality and value, investors are wise to look at the company's long-term debt as a percentage of total capitalization. Attention also should be paid to the company's dividend payout ratio (the percent of earnings paid out in dividends). A company with a high level of debt is not as prudently managed or as safe as one with relatively little debt. Dow Jones industrial stocks where debt as a percentage of total capital is far greater than 50% include American Express (66%), Caterpillar (72%) and General Motors (63%).

A stock with a high payout ratio may have a dividend that is in danger. In any case, that stock is less likely to boost its dividend than one with a relatively low payout ratio. Dow Jones industrial companies with high dividend payout ratios that undermine dividend safety and potentially retard future growth include Alcoa (100%), Du Pont (100%), Exxon (70%), General Motors (100%), IBM (100%), International Paper (100%), Procter & Gamble (100%), Texaco (88%), Union Carbide (87%), United Technologies (100%), Westinghouse (100%) and Woolworth (100%).

FIGURE 9.3 The Vital Statistics on the Dow Jones Industrial Average

DOW JONES INDUSTRIAL AVERAGE

Status key: O-Overvalue, U-Undervalue, R-Rising, D-Declining

Status	STOCK	Price	Ind Ann Div	Divd Yield	Undervalue Pot. Pts Down	% Down	to Low Price	Undervalue High Yield	Overvalue Pot. Pts Up	% Up	to High Price	Overvalue Low Yield	S&P Qual Rank Value	Per Share Book Value	Div % Pay Out	Shrs In Mills	Earn Last 12 Mos	Price/ Earn Ratio	52 Week High	Low	Debt as % of Capital	Ticker Sym
O	ALCOA	81	1.60	2.0%	49	60%	32	5.0%	—	—	80	2.0%	B-	38	0%	89	Deficit	0	83	64	29%	AA
O	ALLIED SIGNAL	37	0.67	1.8%	27	73%	10	7.0%	—	—	19	3.5%	B+	4	28%	285	2.40	15	41	33	39%	ALD
R	AMER EXPRESS	26	0.90	3.5%	11	42%	15	6.0%	24	92%	50	1.8%	A-	17	29%	495	3.13	8	32	23	65%	AXP
O	AT&T	54	1.32	2.4%	37	69%	17	8.0%	—	—	44	3.0%	A-	10	42%	1358	3.14	17	65	49	33%	T
-	BETHLEHEM STEEL	22	0.00	0.0%	—	—	—	—	—	—	—	—	C	1	0%	107	Deficit	39	24	13	55%	BS
D	BOEING COMPANY	45	1.00	2.2%	28	62%	17	6.0%	22	49%	67	1.5%	A	26	28%	340	3.56	13	50	35	22%	BA
O	CATERPILLAR	108	1.20	1.1%	78	72%	30	4.0%	—	—	67	1.8%	A	12	15%	102	8.27	13	122	75	72%	CAT
R	CHEVRON	43	1.85	4.3%	18	42%	25	7.5%	10	23%	53	3.5%	B	22	105%	652	1.76	24	49	41	23%	CHV
D	COCA COLA	43	0.78	1.8%	27	63%	16	5.0%	22	51%	65	1.2%	A+	3	43%	1293	1.80	24	45	39	25%	KO
D	DISNEY CO-WALT	43	0.30	0.7%	30	71%	12	2.5%	33	79%	75	0.4%	A+	9	20%	537	1.47	29	49	36	29%	DIS
O	DU PONT	60	1.76	2.9%	33	55%	27	6.5%	5	8%	65	2.7%	B+	16	169%	680	1.04	58	62	44	39%	DD
R	EASTMAN KODAK	48	1.60	3.3%	16	33%	32	5.0%	75	156%	123	1.3%	B	7	86%	331	1.85	26	51	40	54%	EK
D	EXXON	58	2.88	5.0%	24	41%	34	8.5%	18	31%	76	3.8%	B+	27	69%	1242	4.19	14	67	56	20%	XON
R	GENERAL ELECTRIC	49	1.44	2.9%	20	41%	29	5.0%	23	47%	72	2.0%	A+	9	47%	1710	3.08	16	55	45	11%	GE
O	GENERAL MOTORS	51	0.80	1.6%	38	75%	13	6.0%	—	—	27	3.0%	B-	1	22%	745	3.57	14	65	42	63%	GM
O	GOODYEAR	36	0.80	2.2%	26	72%	10	8.0%	—	—	33	2.4%	B-	15	23%	151	3.50	10	49	34	41%	GT
O	IBM	62	1.00	1.6%	42	68%	20	5.0%	—	—	40	2.5%	B-	31	0%	583	Deficit	0	65	41	43%	IBM
O	INTERNAT'L PAPER	73	1.68	2.3%	42	58%	31	5.5%	—	—	62	2.7%	B+	50	70%	125	2.40	30	78	57	35%	IP
O	MCDONALDS	27	0.24	0.9%	15	56%	12	2.0%	—	—	24	1.0%	A+	9	16%	708	1.50	18	31	24	37%	MCD
U	MERCK	30	1.20	4.0%	—	—	34	3.5%	70	233%	100	1.2%	A+	9	52%	1257	2.33	13	38	28	10%	MRK
R	MINNESOTA MINING	51	1.76	3.5%	22	43%	29	6.0%	96	188%	147	1.2%	A+	15	61%	424	2.87	18	57	46	11%	MMM
R	MORGAN J P	62	2.72	4.4%	21	34%	41	6.7%	47	76%	109	2.5%	B+	49	31%	193	8.70	7	79	60	0%	JPM
R	PHILIP MORRIS	55	2.76	5.0%	9	16%	46	6.0%	44	80%	99	2.8%	A+	1	65%	877	4.25	13	61	45	56%	MO
R	PROCTER GAMBLE	54	1.40	2.6%	26	48%	28	5.0%	39	72%	93	1.5%	A-	3	189%	684	0.74	73	60	45	40%	PG
R	SEARS ROEBUCK	48	1.60	3.3%	25	52%	23	7.0%	85	177%	133	1.2%	B	29	30%	351	5.28	9	60	42	57%	S
D	TEXACO	62	3.20	5.2%	30	48%	32	10.0%	9	15%	71	4.5%	B	35	92%	259	3.46	18	70	60	39%	TX
O	UNION CARBIDE	27	0.75	2.8%	16	59%	11	7.0%	—	—	21	3.5%	NR	10	68%	151	1.11	24	29	18	40%	UK
O	UNITED TECH	62	1.80	2.9%	38	61%	24	7.5%	—	—	60	3.0%	B	21	47%	127	3.83	16	72	54	36%	UTX
O	WESTINGHOUSE	12	0.20	1.7%	9	75%	3	8.0%	—	—	8	2.5%	B	7	0%	354	Deficit	0	17	11	51%	WX
R	WOOLWORTH-FW	15	0.60	4.0%	7	47%	8	8.0%	9	60%	24	2.5%	A-	9	0%	132	Deficit	0	27	13	19%	Z

What Is the Profile of Value for the Dow Jones Industrial Average?

Just as parameters of value can be established for individual stocks, so, too, good buying and selling areas have been established for the Dow Jones Industrial Average based on its composite dividend. The chart of the Dow Jones Industrial Average is a technical portrait of fundamental value, expressed by the dividend yield extending back over the past 48 years.

The composite dividend for the Dow Jones Industrial Average is determined by adding up the indicated annual dividends for all 30 stocks included in the average and then dividing by a divisor that changes whenever a stock is split to keep the result consistent with the past.

The chart in Figure 9.4 reveals that the Dow Jones Industrial Average has offered historically good value whenever the yield has risen above 6% (the bottom horizontal line on the chart), as it did in 1949 to 1953, in 1974 and from 1978 to 1982. In those years, the market offered excellent buying opportunities. Investors who recognized good value then loaded up on blue chip stocks. The dividend yield for the Dow Jones Industrial Average in 1982 just prior to an accelerated 12-year bull market was 6.9%.

The chart also shows that whenever the price of the Dow reaches a 3% yield (the top horizontal line on the chart) a rising trend has been reversed. This occurred in 1950, 1961, 1966, 1968, 1973, 1987 and 1990. If the chart were extended all the way back to 1929, it would reveal that the dividend yield at the top of the market in that infamous year also was just under 3%.

Strong price support also has been evidenced at the 4% yield level, which halted and reversed declines in 1960, 1962, 1966, 1971 and, notably, on October 19, 1987. A 5% yield halted and reversed a major decline in 1970.

So we see that all four yields have a significant history. But at no time did a 3% yield fail to signal the approach of a serious market decline. And, whenever the Dow Jones Industrial Average was priced to yield 6% or more, the market offered a profitable buying opportunity.

The chart in Figure 9.4 clearly illustrates the dividend connection between the Dow Jones Industrial Average and benchmarks of value as reflected by the yields.

FIGURE 9.4   Dow Jones Industrial Average

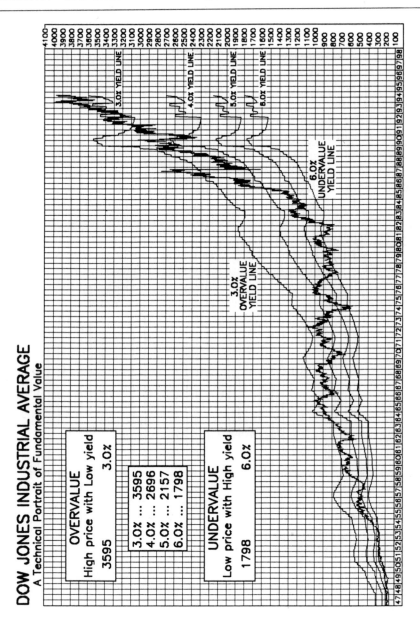

Is There a Profile of Value for the Dow Jones Utilities Average?

The Dow Jones Utilities Average has etched a profile of value between dividend yield extremes of 3% at overvalue and 12% at undervalue.

In the early 1960s, when utilities stocks were thought to be growth stocks, they were priced to yield 3%. Problems in the industry trace back to the late 1960s, when many of these companies launched ambitious and costly nuclear construction programs. As a result, utilities became vulnerable to high interest rates and inflation, and investors changed the way they viewed the stocks.

Problems in the industry were exacerbated by the fuel crisis and the financial turbulence of the 1970s, when utilities became hostage to rising costs and to regulatory agencies that were slow to move on requested rate increases and politically motivated to refuse them. The companies had a hard time making ends meet in addition to continuing their construction programs—which, in some cases, took more than ten years to complete.

Meanwhile, construction and operating costs continued to escalate. Adding insult to injury, after new plants were built, the regulators refused to allow many of the companies to include cost overruns in their rate bases. Accounting changes were needed, and some utilities stocks were required to lower their cash dividends. During this period, from the late 1970s to the early 1980s, the Dow Jones Utilities Average was priced to yield 12%, while many individual stocks produced extraordinary yields, some as high as 14% to 16%. That was a period of very high interest rates during which the companies were obliged to borrow money at virtually any cost. And so, utilities became known as interest rate-sensitive securities. When interest rates were up, the stocks were down; and when interest rates declined, the stocks rose.

Old perceptions die hard. Most major construction projects are completed. The companies are starting to benefit from modern, more efficient facilities that are reducing costs and providing capital for expansion into nonregulated businesses. Capital also is being used to reduce debt and boost dividends. Utilities are no longer so vulnerable to changes in interest rates.

Now there are new challenges. Deregulation and retail wheeling by independent power producers continue to change the landscape of the industry and force the major power producers to become even more creative and cost effective.

We feel that competition will bring out the best in these well-managed companies and that in the future, utilities will be viewed as growth stocks, just as they were in the 1950s, when interest rates were approximately what they are now.

The Dow Jones Utilities Average comprises 15 geographically diversified utilities with long histories of profitable progress and many decades of investor acceptance. They are: American Electric Power, Arkla Inc., Centerior Energy, Commonwealth Edison, Consolidated Edison, Consolidated Natural Gas, Detroit Edison, Houston Industries, Niagara Mohawk Power, Pacific Gas & Electric, Panhandle Eastern, Peoples Energy, Peco Energy, Public Service Enterprise, SCEcorp.

The chart in Figure 9.5 shows that in the early 1960s, when utilities were thought to be growth stocks, the Dow Jones Utilities Average was priced to yield 3%. A bear market that began in 1965 lasted for nine long years, finally ending at a yield of 12% in 1974. From 1977 to mid-1982, the Utilities Average moved sideways as interest rates climbed to their highest level in history.

Does the Dow Jones Transportation Average Have a Profile of Value?

There was a time when one could board the Dow Jones Transportation Average and accurately predict the peaks and valleys of its yield profile. From 1966 through 1983, the Dow Jones Transportation Average fluctuated faithfully between yield extremes of 6% at undervalue and 3% at overvalue.

In the early days, it was primarily a railroad average. But changing times and modes of transportation reduced the dominance of rail freight and made way for motor carriers and airline companies.

Now there are 20 stocks in the Dow Jones Transportation Average—eight airline, one containership, six railroads and five trucking companies.

In 1983, the Dow Jones Transportation Average violated its established yield parameter at overvalue as the price rose up into the wild blue yonder. However, during the past ten years, the Transportation Average has established new benchmarks of value between yield extremes of 1.5% and 2.4%. At the top of the market in 1987, 1989 and 1994 the price of the Transportation Average peaked at a yield of

FIGURE 9.5   Dow Jones Utilities Average

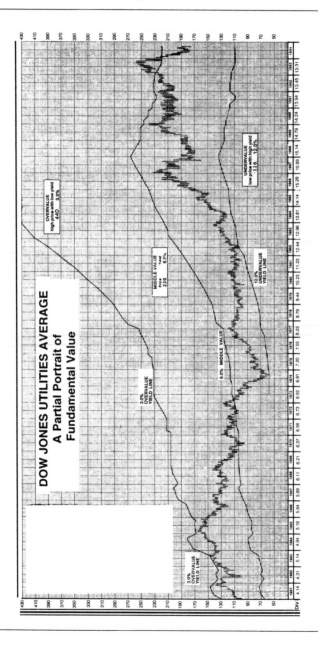

1.5%. Conversely, at the bottom of the declines in 1987 and 1990, when the Dow Jones Industrial Average was priced to yield 4%, the Transportation Average was yielding 2.4%.

During the past decade, erratic earnings and inconsistent dividend growth distorted the fundamental profile of value for the Transportation Average. The dominance of airline companies within the average has disproportionately affected the composite yield.

When the bear market cycle comes to an end and the Dow Jones Industrial Average is priced to yield 6%, we will know if the original 6% yield at undervalue will revalidate itself for the Transportation Average or if the profile established over the past 12 years will serve as a more accurate long-term indicator. Time alone will tell.

Until then, the table in Figure 9.6 tells the tale. Among the 20 transportation stocks, only three can be called blue chip—Norfolk & Southern, Roadway Services and Union Pacific. Those three carry A– quality rankings, but their dividends are not covered by earnings, so the dividends may be in danger and their quality could slip. A further look at investment quality among the transportation stocks shows us that the other 17 stocks are virtual flat tires. Seven pay no dividends, seven have deficit earnings, and the ones that do pay dividends have minuscule yields. Eight of the stocks that do pay dividends are not earning the payout.

What Is the Average Dividend Growth Rate?

Dividends for the Dow Jones Industrial Average have traveled a two-way street over the past 65 years, moving neither continuously up nor down. There have been years of extraordinary growth, when the dividend advanced at double-digit rates. But there also have been years when dividend growth stagnated, or even slid. Still, over the past half century, the up years have been far more numerous than the down years, and the payout has ballooned from $12.75 per share in 1929 to $99.66 in 1993, a gain of 682%.

An ominous statistic appears from 1929 through 1933 (the depression years), when the composite dividend fell from $12.75 per share to $3.40 per share, a loss of 73.3% It was the worst sustained loss of value in stock market history. The worst single year was 1932, when the dividend fell 81.8%; in 1938 it fell 43.3%.

FIGURE 9.6   Profile of Dow Jones Transportation Stocks

Stock	Price	Annual Dividend	Dividend Yield	S&P Quality	12-Month Earnings	Ticker Symbol
AMR Corp.	55	Nil	Nil	C	Deficit	AMR
Airborne Freight	35	.30	0.9%	B	1.83	ABF
Alaska Air	16	Nil	Nil	C	Deficit	ALK
American President Companies	22	.40	1.8	B	2.56	APS
Burlington Northern	53	1.20	2.2	NR	.90	BNI
CSX Corp.	76	1.76	2.3	B	.71	CSX
Carolina Freight	10	Nil	Nil	C	Deficit	CAO
Conrail Inc.	24	Nil	Nil	B–	.28	CNF
Consolidated Freightways	55	1.30	2.4	B–	Deficit	CRR
Delta Air Lines	45	.20	0.4	B–	Deficit	DAL
Federal Express	75	Nil	Nil	B–	2.22	FDX
Norfolk Southern	63	1.92	3.0	A–	1.05	NSC
Roadway Services	63	1.40	2.2	A–	.40	ROAD
Ryder System	25	.60	2.4	B	.30	R
Santa Fe Pacific	21	.10	0.5	B–	.36	SFX
Southwest Airlines	26	.04	0.2	B+	.28	LUV
UAL Corp.	127	Nil	Nil	C	Deficit	UAL
USAir Group	6	Nil	Nil	C	Deficit	U
Union Pacific	57	1.60	2.8	A–	1.38	UNP
Xtra Corp.	48	.56	1.2	B	1.65	XTR

The table in Figure 9.7 records 65 years of dividend history for the Dow Jones Industrial Average. The record shows that the composite dividend rose in 46 years and declined in 18. The longest periods of sustained dividend growth were eight consecutive years from 1944 through 1951 and another eight-year period from 1983 through 1990. There were three times when the dividend declined for two consecutive years: 1942–1943; 1957–1958; and 1970–1971. The worst sustained decline in the payout occurred during four depression years.

Over the past six decades, average annual dividend growth has amounted to 11.2%. However, the five years of extraordinary growth from 1946 through 1950 alone amounted to average annual growth of 19.4%. If we omit those years, the average annual dividend growth rate for the Dow Jones Industrial Average is approximately 7%. For the 18 years in which the dividend fell, the average decline was –14.6%. If we omit the extraordinary depression years, the average decline amounted to –5.6%. As noted, the worst decline was in 1932,

FIGURE 9.7   Sixty-Five Years of Dividend Growth Including Annual Dividend Gains or Losses and Prices at Undervalue and Overvalue for the Dow Jones Industrial Average

Year	Annual Dividend	% Gain/Loss	Price at Undervalue	Price at Overvalue
1993	99.66	−1.1%	1661	3322
1992	100.72	+ 5.8	1679	3357
1991	95.18	−8.2	1586	3173
1990	103.70	+ 0.7	1728	3457
1989	103.00	+29.5	1717	3433
1988	79.53	+11.7	1326	2651
1987	71.20	+ 6.2	1187	2373
1986	67.04	+ 8.1	1117	2235
1985	62.03	+ 2.3	1034	2068
1984	60.63	+ 7.6	1011	2021
1983	56.33	+ 4.0	939	1878
1982	54.14	− 3.7	902	1805
1981	56.22	+ 3.4	937	1874
1980	54.36	+ 6.6	906	1812
1979	50.98	+ 5.1	850	1699
1978	48.52	+ 5.8	809	1617
1977	45.84	+10.7	764	1528
1976	41.40	+10.5	690	1380
1975	37.46	− 0.7	624	1249
1974	37.72	+ 6.8	629	1257
1973	35.33	+ 9.5	589	1178
1972	32.27	+ 4.6	538	1076
1971	30.86	− 2.1	514	1029
1970	31.53	− 7.0	526	1051
1969	33.90	+ 8.2	565	1130
1968	31.34	+ 3.8	522	1045
1967	30.19	− 5.3	503	1006
1966	31.89	+11.5	532	1063
1965	28.61	− 8.4	477	954
1964	31.24	+33.4	521	1041
1963	23.41	+ 0.5	390	780
1962	23.30	+ 2.4	388	777
1961	22.75	+ 6.5	379	758
1960	21.36	+ 3.0	356	712
1959	20.74	+ 3.7	346	691
1958	20.00	− 7.5	333	667
1957	21.61	− 6.0	360	720
1956	22.99	+ 6.5	383	766
1955	21.58	+23.5	360	719
1954	17.47	+ 8.4	291	582
1953	16.11	+ 4.4	269	537

FIGURE 9.7   Sixty-Five Years of Dividend Growth Including Annual Dividend Gains or Losses and Prices at Undervalue and Overvalue for the Dow Jones Industrial Average (Continued)

Year	Annual Dividend	% Gain/Loss	Price at Undervalue	Price at Overvalue
1952	15.43	– 5.6%	257	514
1951	16.34	+ 1.3	272	545
1950	16.13	+26.1	269	538
1949	12.79	+11.2	213	426
1948	11.50	+24.8	192	383
1947	9.21	+22.8	154	307
1946	7.50	+12.1	125	250
1945	6.69	+ 1.8	112	223
1944	6.57	+ 4.3	110	219
1943	6.30	– 1.6	105	210
1942	6.40	–15.6	107	213
1941	7.59	+ 7.5	127	253
1940	7.06	+15.5	118	235
1939	6.11	+22.7	102	204
1938	4.98	–43.3	83	166
1937	8.78	+24.5	146	293
1936	7.05	+54.9	118	235
1935	4.55	+24.3	76	152
1934	3.66	+ 7.6	61	122
1933	3.40	–24.6	57	113
1932	4.62	–81.8	77	154
1931	8.40	–24.5	140	280
1930	11.13	–12.7	186	371
1929	12.75		213	425

when the dividend was reduced by –81.8%. The best year of dividend growth was 1936, when the payout rose 54.9%.

The table also reveals that there is no apparent correlation between bull markets and dividend increases or bear markets and dividend decreases. For example, although the dividend declined –5.3% in 1965 prior to the 1966 recession, it rose 11.5% in the actual year of the recession. And, despite that above-average dividend growth in 1966, the price of the Dow fell –25% in what proved to be the first down leg in the bear market cycle. In 1973 and 1974, years when the Dow Jones Industrial Average declined all the way from overvalue down to undervalue, the dividend actually grew 9.5% and 6.8%. Conversely, in 1982, when an accelerated phase of the bull market began, the dividend fell by –3.7% and scored only modest single-digit gains in the ensuing five years, while the Dow Jones Industrial Average moved up from 800 to 2,700, a gain of 238%. The only time when the dividend and the Dow moved in concert was the primary bear market and dividend debacle from 1929 through 1933.

Since 1989, there have been only minor changes in the composite dividend—two modest gains and two small losses. The dividend contracted in 1993—due largely to two dividend cuts by IBM.

In 1994, the dividend again was on the rise, while the market was in decline. If dividend growth in 1994 matches the average rate of dividend growth in other years following declines, the payout for the year should rise by about 6%. In that case, the dividend at year-end will be $105.64. Based on this projected dividend, the price at under-value, where the yield is 6%, will be 1,761; the price at overvalue, where the yield is 3%, will be 3,521; a 4% yield will appear when the price is 2,641; a 5% yield will be available at a price of 2,111. All four yields are historically significant benchmarks of value for the Dow Jones Industrial Average.

Is There a Connection Between Blue Chips and Major Market Trends?

We have developed an analytical tool that clearly reveals the important relationship between undervalued blue chip stocks and the Dow Jones Industrial Average. This significant market indicator is called the Blue Chip Trend Verifier. (See Figure 9.8.) It measures degrees of risk in the stock market based on cycles of dividend yields. The figures are drawn from the 350 blue chip stocks we regularly follow. Those figures report the number and percentage of stocks in each of our four trend categories—undervalued, overvalued, rising and declining. Most importantly, the Blue Chip Trend Verifier charts the percentages of undervalued stocks recorded twice monthly since we began our analysis in April 1966.

Those many years of history have produced some meaningful technical data. The Blue Chip Trend Verifier has become a significant market indicator for several other respected market analysts. Yet it is not so widely followed that its value and validity have become jeopardized.

Comparing the percentages of undervalued blue chip stocks with the peaks and valleys of the Dow Jones Industrial Average, we find an inextricable connection. Relating the Blue Chip Trend Verifier to a chart of the Dow Jones Industrial Average, we see that whenever the number of undervalued stocks rises above 70%, the market offers great value with large numbers of blue chip stocks at historically undervalued prices. That figure rose to 73% in 1970, when the Dow Jones Industrial Average fell to a dividend yield of 5%. It rose to 82% in 1974 when the yield on the Dow was 6%. We also saw an 80% figure in 1978, 1980 and 1982—all years in which investors who bought a diversified selection of undervalued blue chip stocks later were richly rewarded.

Conversely, when the number of undervalued stocks falls below 20%, the market is at or near a price peak. At the top of the trend in January 1973, prior to a 50% decline in the Dow that carried the price all the way down from overvalue to undervalue, 17% of our blue chip stocks were undervalued. In August 1987, two months before the infamous October 19 crash, that figure was 12%. In 1989, two months before the October minicrash, the figure was 13%. In March 1993, that number dropped to 6%, the lowest such figure in our history. It has been in single digits since 1991.

The message is loud and clear. At those levels, the Blue Chip Trend Verifier speaks of caution; it speaks of danger; it points to a broadening market top that began in 1987 and from which major declines are launched.

There is another point to be made about the percentages of blue chip stocks in our major categories. In terms of value, the Dow Jones Industrial Average peaked in August 1987, when the dividend yield was 2.6% and the price-earnings ratio was 21 to 1. At that time, with the Dow Jones Industrial Average priced at 2,722, 40% of the stocks listed in *I.Q. Trends* were in the overvalued category. Since then, although the Dow has scored higher prices, the percentage of over-valued stocks has declined steadily. When the Dow reached the intraday price peak of 4,000 on January 31, 1994, only 24% of our stocks were listed in the overvalued category. It is an ominous sign that since the price peak in 1987, about 50% of the stocks that were listed in the overvalued category had moved into declining trends despite an advancing Dow Jones Industrial Average.

If it is true that history repeats itself, the Blue Chip Trend Verifier once again will provide an accurate measure of long-term value in the stock market.

FIGURE 9.8　Relationship Between Undervalue Blue Chips and Major Market Trends

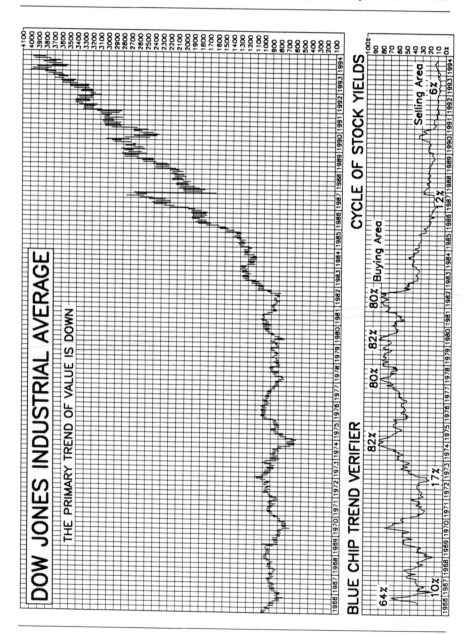

Hedging in the Stock Market

Are Stocks a Good Hedge Against Inflation?

Inflation is the enemy of retired and fixed-income investors. When it rears its ugly head, it causes investors to step aside and wonder how to protect their lifestyles and their investment capital.

Ironically, the specter of inflation is often raised because of good news in the economy. Low unemployment, reduced deficits and a rise in factory output are all possible consequences of inflation. Other indicators are rising prices of fuel and food. Still, the fear of inflation is based on potentials, and the market, as usual, overreacts to perceptions.

In 1994, economic analysts were evenly divided on whether we were heading into a long period of inflation or deflation. Federal Reserve Board Chairman Alan Greenspan tightened credit by forcing short-term interest rates up in an attempt to stop inflationary momentum. However, the situation continues to concern investors who wonder how to protect themselves against the ravages of inflation.

Bonds, even high-yielding bonds, offer investors no protection. They provide a fixed income that locks the investor into rates of return that cannot keep pace with rising levels of inflation. A 9% yield on a bond sounds attractive until one factors in taxes and inflation. Then the presumed 9% return can be whittled down to 6% or less, depending on the tax rate and the inflation rate. In addition to a diminished real return, bond prices always decline when inflation is noted in the economy so the bond holder loses both liquidity and purchasing power.

Stocks with rising dividend trends are the best hedge against inflation. Rising dividends not only provide increased income, allowing the stockholder to keep pace with inflation, but they also support stock prices and increase stock values. Dividend growth is the stockholder's best friend—providing protection against inflation and producing growing streams of income in a deflation.

One major advantage to investing in blue chip stocks is that the companies have verifiable records of dividend payouts. A long record of dividend increases suggests good management and the ability to sail through economic storms with steadily rising sales and earnings.

To maintain their standard of living, investors should aim to cover the prevailing rate of inflation and taxes with the return on their investments. Rates of inflation vary, but typically a 6% to 7% cushion of return is necessary. Therefore, stocks that raise dividends at a compound annual rate of 10% or more provide a more than adequate hedge against most inflationary periods.

The blue chip stocks listed in Figure 10.1 have provided compound annual dividend growth of 10% or more over the past 12 years, offering their shareholders a reliable hedge against inflation.

Do Stock Market Trends Mirror the Economy?

During the early 1990s, the stock market appeared oblivious to the economic stresses of a long and painful recession. Investors were watching the trend of interest rates, not the trend of the economy. In fact, the worse the economic numbers grew, the more encouraged they became that interest rates would continue to decline. And they did.

Every time interest rates fell, the stock market rejoiced. The reason is easy to understand. As interest rates slid to 5%, 4%, 3% and less, savers who were accustomed to getting 8% and 9% returns on their capital in the money market became speculators in the stock market, hoping that the total returns would sustain their shrinking investment income and improve their deteriorating living standards.

As a result, huge sums of money poured into the stock market from the hands of individual investors and the coffers of stock mutual funds. It soon became clear that low interest rates were boosting and supporting stock prices. Each time interest rates were reduced, each

FIGURE 10.1   Blue Chip Stocks with Compound Annual Dividends of 10% or More

Stock	Yield	Stock	Yield
Abbott Laboratories	18%	Dean Foods Company	15%
AFLAC Inc.	13	Deluxe Corp.	16
Air Products & Chemicals, Inc.	14	Diebold, Inc.	12
Alberto-Culver Company	12	Donnelley (R.R.) & Sons	10
Albertson's, Inc.	16	Dreyfus Corp.	22
American Business Products, Inc.	14	Dun & Bradstreet Corp.	13
American General Corp.	11	E-Systems, Inc.	14
American Greetings (Class A)	12	Echlin Inc.	10
American Home Products Corp.	10	Edwards (A.G.), Inc.	14
American International Group, Inc.	14	EG&G Inc.	11
American National Insurance	10	Ennis Business Forms, Inc.	22
American Stores Company	18	Family Dollar Stores, Inc.	14
American Water Works Company	12	Federal Signal Corp.	12
AMP Inc.	12	First of America Bank Corp.	12
Anheuser-Busch Companies, Inc.	18	First Union Corp.	13
Archer Daniels Midland Company	10	First Virginia Banks, Inc.	10
Automatic Data Processing, Inc.	14	Flightsafety International, Inc.	16
Avemco Corp.	12	Flowers Industries	14
Avery Dennison Corp.	14	GAP, Inc.	24
Banc One Corp.	16	Geico Corp.	16
Bandag, Inc.	12	General Electric Company	12
Bankers Trust New York Corp.	12	General Mills, Inc.	13
Bard (C.R.), Inc.	18	General Re Corp.	13
Barnett Banks, Inc.	11	Genuine Parts Company	10
Baxter International Inc.	15	Gerber Products Company	12
Bemis Company	15	Giant Food Inc.	18
Bergen Brunswig Corp. (Class A)	12	Gillette Company	10
Betz Laboratories	12	Glatfelter (P.H.) Company	15
Block (H&R), Inc.	14	Graco Inc.	10
Bob Evans Farms	10	Handleman Company	10
Bristol-Myers Squibb Company	17	Hannaford Bros. Company	16
Brown-Forman Corp. (Class B)	14	Harcourt General, Inc.	14
Browning-Ferris Industries Inc.	12	Harland (John H.) Company	18
Bruno's Inc.	16	Hartford Steam Boiler Inspection and	
Carter-Wallace, Inc.	14	Insurance Company	16
Central Fidelity	12	Heilig-Meyers Company	11
Church & Dwight Company	10	Heinz (H.J.) Company	15
Clorox Company	13	Hershey Foods Corp.	12
Coca-Cola Company	12	Hewlett-Packard Company	20
ConAgra, Inc.	16	Hillenbrand Industries, Inc.	18
Cooper Tire & Rubber Company	17	Hormel (Geo.) & Company	12
Crawford & Company	12	Hubbell Inc.	12
Crompton & Knowles Corp.	17	Hunt Manufacturing Company	12
Dayton Hudson Corp.	10	Illinois Tool Works Inc.	12

FIGURE 10.1   Blue Chip Stocks with Compound Annual Dividends of 10% or More (Continued)

Stock	Yield	Stock	Yield
International Flavors & Fragrances, Inc.	10%	Penney (J.C.) Company	10
Interpublic Group of Companies, Inc.	12	Pep Boys	14%
Jefferson-Pilot Corp.	11	Pepsico, Inc.	12
Johnson & Johnson	14	Pfizer Inc.	14
Jostens, Inc.	10	Philip Morris Companies	22
Kmart Corp.	10	Pitney Bowes Inc.	14
Kellogg Company	12	PPG Industries Inc.	11
Kelly Services	14	Premier Industrial Corp.	15
KeyCorp	10	Quaker Oats Company	14
Keystone International, Inc.	11	Ralston Purina Company	10
Kimball International, Inc.	12	Rite Aid Corp.	14
Kimberly-Clark Corp.	12	Rohm & Haas Company	10
Knight Ridder Inc.	10	RPM Inc.	14
La-Z-Boy Chair	11	Rubbermaid, Inc.	16
Lance Inc.	10	Russell Corp.	10
Lawson Products	12	Ryland Group, Inc.	10
Lee Enterprises, Inc.	10	Safety-Kleen Corp.	14
Leggett & Platt, Inc.	11	Sara Lee Corp.	14
Lilly (Eli) & Company	13	Schering-Plough Corp.	13
The Limited Inc.	22	Seagram Company	12
Loctite Corp.	16	Service Corp. International	18
Loral Corp.	10	Shared Medical Systems	11
Luby's Cafeterias, Inc.	14	Shaw Industries, Inc.	22
Marion Merrell Dow Inc.	28	Sherwin-Williams Company	14
Marshall & Ilsley	10	Smucker (J.M.) Company	16
Masco Corp.	12	Sonoco Products	12
May Department Stores	10	Standard Register	12
McCormick & Company	14	Stanhome Inc.	12
McDonald's Corp.	14	State Street Boston	16
Medtronic, Inc.	13	Stride Rite Corp.	14
Melville Corp.	10	Super Food Services	13
Mercantile Stores	12	Sysco Corp.	18
Merck & Company	18	Tasty Baking	14
Millipore Corp.	10	Teleflex Inc.	14
Morgan (J.P.) & Company	10	Tootsie Roll Industries	12
National Service Industries, Inc.	10	Torchmark Corp.	14
NBD Bancorp, Inc.	12	Universal Foods Corp.	10
Newell Company	16	Upjohn Company	12
Nordstrom Inc.	12	U.S. Bancorp	10
New York Times Company (Class A)	10	UST Inc.	20
Old Kent Financial	12	VF Corp.	14
Owens & Minor, Inc.	13	Valspar Corp.	16
Pall Corp.	18	Wachovia Corp.	14

FIGURE 10.1   Blue Chip Stocks with Compound Annual Dividends of 10% or More (Continued)

Stock	Yield	Stock	Yield
Wal-Mart Stores, Inc.	22%	Weis Markets, Inc.	11%
Walgreen Company	16	WMX Technologies, Inc.	20
Wallace Computer Services, Inc.	12	Worthington Industries	13
Warner-Lambert Company	10	Wrigley (Wm.) Jr. Company	14
Washington Post Company	16	Zero Corp.	10

---

time new data suggested that the economy was in a slump, Wall Street speculated on yet another cut in interest rates and the stock market took heart.

But there is another side to that coin. In 1994, when the economy showed signs of improvement, interest rates appeared to have hit bottom and started to inch up. As rates rise, low-yielding stocks become less attractive, savers return to the money market, and stock prices decline.

Like a hungry monster looming in the background, the national debt needs to be fed. Unless interest rates rise in the money market, Treasury bills, notes and bonds will not attract sufficient capital to service interest obligations.

The stock market anticipates future trends in the economy more than it reflects current economic conditions. Sometimes the market is mistaken. Still, it is more often correct than incorrect. It is sarcastically said that the stock market has accurately predicted 11 of the past 7 recessions. Therefore, the market does not mirror economic trends. It acts not as a thermometer, but as a barometer of things to come.

What Stocks Are Best To Buy in a Recession?

During the 1980s, America rode the crest of economic bounty. Then came four long years of what experienced economists had predicted—recession. While some regions of the nation fared better than others, America at large suffered a long and painful economic drought. Among the hardest hit were heavily populated and productive industrial regions like California and New York, where the bread of corporate America is buttered. Sales, earnings and profits declined.

Dividend growth was slowed, unemployment figures rose, and the burdens of debt became a serious problem.

Although the nation had avoided the pain of recession for eight dynamic years, we dangerously hid our heads in the sand toward the end. Recessionary cycles generally come around every four years. The fact that we skipped a cycle in the mid-1980s boded ill for the recession that was looming just around the corner. The recession of the early 1990s was twice as severe as usual. It would take more than a quick fix to reduce the mountain of accumulated debt and shrink the financial excesses of the 1980s—ask Donald Trump.

Still, every cloud has a silver lining. Warnings of impending recession were not lost entirely on the managements of blue chip companies, many of which aggressively reduced their debt and prepared for lean times.

Responsible companies operate with as little debt as possible. A 50% ratio of debt to equity is considered relatively safe. Of course, it depends on the industry. Utility companies, for example, can operate safely with a greater level of debt than can retail companies. Still, low debt ratios (below 50%) are safer than high ones. In hard times, when sales and earnings falter, companies with little debt to service can continue to grow and are unlikely to disappoint their shareholders by reducing dividends. Many low-debt companies continue to increase dividends, even in a recession.

Among the 350 blue chip companies listed in *I.Q. Trends*, 135 have little or no debt on their balance sheets. Taking debt as a percentage of equity, these companies, which are listed in Chapter 1, all have debt ratios at or below 20%. In this group, 77 companies have single-digit debt ratios; 24 are debt-free.

Royal blue chips with no debt include: Bob Evans Farms, Diebold, Dun & Bradstreet, Family Dollar Stores, H&R Block Company, Hubbel (Class B), International Flavors & Fragrances, Jefferson-Pilot, Lance Inc., Weiss Markets and Zero Corp.

While the vast majority of companies we follow have manageable levels of debt, low-debt companies are the most recession-resistant. These companies are best able to withstand financial pressure and take advantage of investment opportunities when they become available. In a recession, high-debt companies with financial problems may be forced to liquidate valuable assets that low-debt companies can buy at bargain prices.

In a recession it is best to buy companies that produce the necessities of life. When paychecks and profits shrink, consumers can forego luxury items, but they will continue to buy food, drugs and household products. They will continue to turn on the lights, heat their homes and run their automobiles. Therefore, food, drug, utilities and oil companies generally hold up well in a recession. Cyclical products, factory equipment and luxury retail goods become less imperative in hard times.

But attention always should be paid to value, and no stock should be bought unless its price is relatively undervalued.

In summary, during a recession, we suggest shortening the field of recommended stocks to those with strong balance sheets. Then select from that limited pool companies that create products and generate services necessary to everyone's basic needs. Last and most important, select among stocks that represent good value.

What About Gold?

Gold is a speculation, not an investment. A speculation produces no income, but it can produce attractive capital gains if the price rises. If the price declines, it is a degenerating vehicle, reducing the value of the asset and producing no cash return.

We have never been strong advocates of gold. Their stocks offer poor quality, unreliable dividends and are largely unpredictable. Gold futures are far too speculative for our tastes. Metal and coins are difficult to store safely and provide no income.

In spite of these drawbacks, 1993 saw the launch of a major bull market in gold. At that time, the European Economic Community began planning to establish a common currency to facilitate trade across multinational borders. Any international currency probably will be backed by gold. There really is no other way for a new monetary system to be constructed fairly. Also, trade with Russia will be linked either to payments in gold or to a ruble that is convertible into gold. For all these reasons, we see investment opportunity in gold. However, it is critical to decide the best and safest way to act on that opportunity.

Following a high price of $850 an ounce in 1980, gold suffered a five-year decline to $284 an ounce in 1985, a loss of 67%. From 1985 to 1988, the price rose 74% to $500 an ounce, after which another five-year decline took hold, this time reducing the price to $326, down 35%. In 1993, gold resumed an uptrend, bolstering our confidence in a possible purchase of gold stocks.

Unfortunately, there are no gold mining stocks that meet our criteria for blue chip quality. Among this relatively lackluster group of stocks, ASA Ltd. is perhaps the best quality. Other gold stocks worth mentioning include: Freeport McMoran Copper & Gold, Newport Mining, Newmont Gold, Homestake Mining, Placer Dome, American Barrick Reserves, Pegasus Gold, Royal Oak Mines, Angico Eagle Mines and Echo Bay Mines.

Still, ASA remains our favorite, having paid cash dividends continuously since 1959. One offsetting factor to this recommendation is that the company holds shares of gold and diamond mines primarily in South Africa, where political and economic risks are considerable.

We do not generally advocate the purchase of equity mutual funds because we feel that a knowledgeable investor can select a better portfolio of stocks based on individual profiles of value. However, since we are not able to apply our concept to most gold stocks, this may be an area in which gold stock mutual funds are of value. When the price of gold moves upward, all gold stocks generally glitter.

Getting Started!

Does this system really work? In a word, yes. The dividend yield-total return approach to stock selection has borne rich fruit for thousands of readers of *I.Q. Trends* and has placed our service consistently in the top percentile of major market advisory services. Perhaps most notable is the recognition received by market maven Mark Hulbert, who wrote in *Forbes* magazine in November, 1992: "Weiss writes a top-performing newsletter devoted to this strategy . . . *I.Q. Trends* has easily beaten the Wilshire 5000 total return, gaining nearly 155% since the beginning of 1986, vs. the Wilshire's 125%—and did so with 20% less volatility." In the January 31, 1994, issue of *Forbes*, Hulbert wrote: "Her approach deserves respect; she's one of a fairly small group of letter writers who garner honor grades in both up and down markets."

Successful investing in the stock market is not brain surgery. Anyone can be a successful investor. The secret is no secret. It is simply that you confine your selections to blue chip stocks, you buy them when they are undervalued, and you sell them when they become overvalued. This is the well-lit path of the enlightened investor. We wish you lifelong investment success, with many happy dividends along the way.

Index

A

AAR Corp., 85, 87
  dividend connection chart, 88
Abbott, Dr. William C., 13
Abbott Laboratories, 13—15
  dividend connection chart, 14
Acquisitions, 214
Aerospace, 62, 134
AFLAC Inc., 162–65
  dividend connection chart, 164
Agricultural seeds, 69
AIDS research, 13, 15, 69, 94
Air cargo containers and systems, 129
Aircraft industry, 196–98, 219
  engines, 253
  maintenance, 138
Air Products & Chemicals, Inc., 176–78
  dividend connection chart, 177
Aladdin, 90
Alcoholic beverages
  American Brands, Inc., 42–44
  Anheuser-Busch Companies, Inc.,
    169–70
  Brown-Forman Corp., 168, 171–73
  Philip Morris Companies, 255–57
Allegheny Generating Company, 141
Allegheny Power System Inc., 140–43
  benchmarks of value, 143
  dividend connection chart, 142
Allstate Insurance, 35
American Brands, Inc., 42–44
  dividend connection chart, 16
American Business Products, 214–15
American Electric Power, 231–32
  dividend connection chart, 233
American Express, 258
American Family Life Insurance, 162
American Greetings, 78–80
  dividend connection chart, 79
American Home Products, 15–17
  dividend connection chart, 16

AMP Inc., 179–81, 214–15
  dividend connection chart, 180
Amtek, Inc., 25, 27–29
Analytical chemistry, 217
Anheuser-Busch Companies, Inc., 169–70
Animated films, 90
Annuities, 132
Annuity drugs, 22
Anti-infectives, 205
Antiviral therapies, 94
Anvil, 129
Appliances, 35, 253
ASA Ltd., 280
AT&T Corp., 181–84
  dividend connection chart, 183
Automotive products, 20
  batteries, 80–82
  Genuine Parts Company, 20–22
  seating, 80–82
  Teleflex, Inc., 62–64
Avery Dennison Corp., 98–101
  dividend connection chart, 99
Aviation industry, 85–87, 196–99
AxSYM system, 15

B

Bakeries, 50–52
Bankers Trust New York Corp., 203–5
  dividend connection chart, 204
Banking industry, 91, 202, 203–5
Baruch, Bernard, 77
Baxter International Inc., 246–38
  dividend connection chart, 247
Beauty and the Beast, 90
Benson & Hedges, 42, 44
Bergdorf Goodman, 158
Bergen Brunswig, 31, 25, 127–28
Berry Bearing Company, 20
Betty Crocker, 143, 145
Biaxin, 13

Big B Inc., 128
Bioscience, 96
Block (H&R), Inc., 48–50
  dividend connection chart, 49
Blue chip stock(s)
  affordable, 126
  capital allocation and, 131–32
  compound annual dividends of 10% or
    more, 275
  compound annual growth rate of more
    than 10%, 118
  connection to major market trends,
    269–71
  debt-free, 189–90, 278
  defined, 8–9
  dividend reductions and, 207–13
  DJIA as indicator, 257
  downside risks of 70% or more, 86–87
  faded, 24–25, 26, 31–32
  growth stocks, 214
  institutional investors and, 173–74,
    175–76
  limiting investments to, 201–2
  listed, 10–13
  royal blue chips, 18–19, 278
Blue Chip Trend Verifier, 269–71
Boeing Company, 196–99
  dividend connection chart, 198
Bonds, 132, 187
  and utilities compared, 236
Borden, Inc., 29–31
  dividend connection chart, 30
Breast cancer therapy, 105
Bristol-Myers Squibb Company, 105–7, 244
  dividend connection chart, 106
Broadcasting, 253
Brown-Forman Corp., 168, 171–73
  dividend connection chart, 172
Bruno, Angelo, 74
Bruno's Inc., 72–75
  dividend connection chart, 73
Budweiser beer, 169
Business forms, 156–58
Business information services. *See*
  Information services

C

Cable transmissions, 68

Campbell Taggart, 169
Cancer
  supplemental insurance, 165
  therapies, 17, 105
Capital
  gains, 2
  investment, 147
  raising, 187
Capital Services, 253
Cardpro Services Inc., 54
Carlsberg beer, 169
Carolina Power & Light Company, 112–14
  dividend connection chart, 113
Cash flow, 111
Cash payout, 47
Caterpillar, 258
Cereal, 143–45
Check printing, 54–56
Chemicals, 69, 121, 176
  Du Pont, 181, 184–86
Cigarette companies
  American Brands, Inc., 42–44
  Philip Morris Companies, 255–57
Clairol hair coloring, 107
Clarithromycin, 13
Clinton, Bill, 243
Coca-Cola Company, 3–5
  dividend connection chart, 4
Coldwell Banker, 35
Commercial jet transports, 196
Communications networks, 181, 217
Compact disc production, 101
CompuServe Inc., 48
Computer industry
  Hewlett-Packard Company, 215
  International Business Machines Corp.,
    209, 211–13
Computer software, 192
Connection devices, 179
Connolly Tool & Machine Company, 156
Conoco, 184
Consolidated Edison Company of New
  York, 223–26
  dividend connection chart, 225
Consumer goods, 15–17
Consumer paper products, 136–38
Contempo Casuals, 158, 160
Corporate earnings, and blue chip stocks, 9
Corporate investments, 147

Creamette, 29
Cross (A.T.) Company, 209–11
    dividend connection chart, 210
CVS stores, 165, 167
Czechoslovakian retail market, 60

D

Dairy companies, 29–31
Dean Witter, 35
Debt, as percentage of total capitalization, 258
Debt-free companies, 187–90
Debt-to-equity ratio, 188
Declining trend stocks, 160–62, 163
    case studies, 162–68
Defense, 134, 199
Dennison Manufacturing, 100
Department of Energy, 134
Desktop publishers, 156
Detroit Edison Company, 231, 234–36
    dividend connection chart, 235
Diagnostic products
    Baxter International Inc., 246–48
    Eli Lilly & Company, 205–7
    Syntex Corp., 75–77
Dialog Information Services, 68
Diebold, 214–15
Discover Card, 35
Disney (Walt) Company, 87, 90–91
    dividend connection chart, 89
Disposable diapers, 138
Diversification, 139–40
    global, 203
    sample portfolio, 141
    utility stocks and, 228–29
Diversified Pharmaceutical Services, 244
Dividend(s)
    building a stock portfolio and, 124–25
    defined, 47–48
    electrical utilities, safety of, 236–37
    growth, 2, 8,116–17, 155
    importance of, 58
    omissions of, and stock quality, 32
    payout ratio, 147–48, 258
    reasons for payment of, 53
    reductions, and blue chip stocks, 207–13
    reinvestment, 133, 230

signals, 110–11
and stock prices, 97–98
and overvalued stock, 110
and undervalued stock, 71, 110
uninterrupted, 9
yield, 41–42, 97, 103–4
Dollar cost averaging, 133
    undervalued stock and, 161
Dominion Resources, Inc., 237, 239–41
    dividend connection chart, 240
Donnelley (Reuben H.), 190, 192
Dow, Charles, 103, 181
Dow Jones Averages, 251–52
Dow Jones Industrial Average, 251–52, 257–61
    average dividend growth rate, 265–69
    as measure of investment quality, 257–61
    profile of value for, 258, 260–61
    undervalued blue chip stocks and, 269–71
    vital statistics, 259
Dow Jones Transportation Average, 251–52
    profile of stocks, 266
    profile of value, 263–65
Dow Jones Utilities Average, 251–52, 262–63
Drake Beam Morin, 160
Drug retailers
    Bruno's Inc., 72–75
    CVS stores, 167
Drugs. *See* Pharmaceuticals
Dun & Bradstreet Corp., 188, 190–92
    dividend connection chart, 191
Du Pont DeNemours & Company, 181, 184–86
    dividend connection chart, 185
Durr–Fillauer Medical Inc., 31, 128
Dursban, 143

E

Eagle snack foods, 169
Earnings reports, 59
Edison, Thomas, 253
EG&G, Inc., 134–36
    dividend connection chart, 135
Eisner, Michael, 90
Electrical devices, 179–81

Electric companies, 222. *See also* Utilities
    Allegheny Power System Inc., 140–43
    American Electric Power Company,
        231–33
    Carolina Power & Light Company,
        112–14
    Consolidated Edison Company of New
        York, 223–26
    debt and, 188
    Detroit Edison Company, 231, 234–36
    dividends, safety of, 236–37
    Dominion Resources, Inc., 237, 239–41
    Florida Progress Corp., 152–53
    SCEcorp, 114–16
    Texas Utilities Company, 237, 239,
        241–43
    Wisconsin Energy Corp., 223, 226–28
Electric Fuels Corp., 152
Electromechanical products, 25, 28
Electronic data interchange, 156
Electronics, 35, 215
Elephant Malt Liquor, 169
Ennis Business Forms, Inc., 156–58
    dividend connection chart, 157
Entertainment business
    Disney (Walt) Company, 87, 90–91
Environmental systems, 178
Equity, 187
Equity mutual funds, 280
European Economic Community, 279

F

Facilities services and control systems, 80–82
Fasson Films, 100
Fayetteville, N.C., Public Works
    Commission, 112
Federal Reserve Board, 203
Filtration products, 217
Financial performance, 1
Financial stationer, 54
Flavor products, 199, 201
FlightSafety International, 150–52
    dividend connection chart, 151
Florida Progress Corp., 152–54
    dividend connection chart, 153
    value benchmarks, 154
Flower Industries, 50–52
    dividend connection chart, 52

Fluid purification, 94–96, 217–19
Food, packaged
    Eagle brand, 169
    General Mills, Inc., 143–45
    Philip Morris Companies, 255–57
Food retailers
    Bruno's Inc., 72–75
    Flower Industries, 50–52
Footwear, 165, 167
Foreign stocks, 195–96
Fragrance products, 199
Franklin Life Insurance Company, 42
French Broad Electric Membership, 112
Frozen foods, 51
Fuel
    crisis, 262
    diversification, 229
Furniture, 119, 165

G

General Cinema, 158
General Electric Company, 253–55
    dividend connection chart, 254
General Mills, 143–45
    dividend connection chart, 144
General Motors, 258
Genetic antibody therapies, 17
Genetics Institute, 17
Genuine Parts Company, 20–22
    dividend connection chart, 21
Geographic diversification, 228–29, 263
Gilbert, John, 129
Glaxo, 207
Global diversification, 203
Gold, 279–80
Gold Medal, 143, 145
Graham, Benjamin, 40
Greenspan, Alan, 273
Growth/income considerations, 146–49
Growth stocks
    blue chip, 214
    evaluating, 213–15
    selecting, 228–30
    utilities, 221–28

H

Halcion, 71

Halliburton, 129
Hallmark, 78
Handleman Company, 101–3
    dividend connection chart, 102
Harcourt General, Inc., 158–60
    dividend connection chart, 159
Harland (John H.) Company, 54–56
    dividend connection chart, 55
Health care, 5, 13. *See also* Health care
    products; Pharmaceutical companies
        National Medical Enterprises, 33–35
        reform, 163, 202, 243
        Syntex Corp., 75–77
Healthcare Distributors of Indiana Inc., 128
Health care products
        Baxter International Inc., 246–48
        Johnson & Johnson, 56–58
Hedging, 273–80
    market trends, and the economy, 274,
        277
    stocks and inflation, 273–74
Heinz, Henry J., 44
Heinz (H.J.) Company, 44–47
    dividend connection chart, 45
Hewlett, Bill, 215
Hewlett-Packard Company, 215–17
Home furnishings market, 119
Home improvement market, 119
Hulbert, Mark, 281

I

IBM. *See* International Business Machines
    Corp.
Income/growth considerations, 146–49
Indianapolis Power & Light, 92
Indiana Power, 232
Industrial gases, 176–78
Industrial products and services
        Ametek, Inc., 28
        Genuine Parts Company, 20–22
        Teleflex Inc., 62–64
Infant formula, 13
Inflation, stocks as hedge against, 273–74
Information services, 48, 253
        Dun & Bradstreet Corp., 190–92
        Knight-Ridder Inc., 66–69
Information systems, 211
Initial public offerings, 213

Institute of Nuclear Power Operators, 114
Institutional investors, and stock prices, 173–
    74, 175–76, 181
        case studies, 176–81
Insurance companies, 160, 162. *See also* Life
    insurance
        and interest rates, 91
Intelligent Investor, The, 40
Interest rates, and stock yields, 91, 274, 277
International Business Machines Corp., 209,
    211–13
        dividend connection chart, 212
International Flavors & Fragrances, Inc., 199–
    201
        dividend connection chart, 200
International subsidiaries, 195–96, 197
Investment analysis, 203
Investment capital, allocating, 131–32
Investment performance, 2
IPALCO Enterprises, 92–94
        dividend connection chart, 93
IQ Trends, 282
IRAs, 230

J

Jack Daniels, 171
Japan, insurance coverage in, 163, 165
Johnson Controls, Inc., 80–82
        dividend connection chart, 81
Johnson & Johnson, 56–58
        dividend connection chart, 57
Journal of Commerce, 68

K

Katzenberg, Jeffrey, 90
Keogh accounts, 230
Kimberly-Clark Corp., 136–38
Kmart, 37, 59–62, 101
        dividend connection chart, 61
Knight-Ridder Inc., 66–69
        dividend connection chart, 67
Kresge, 60

L

Laser surgery, 136
Latin America, power facilities in, 239

Leather products, 209
Lenox, 171
Liberty Media Corp., 68
Life insurance, 152, 160, 162
 American Brands, Inc., 42–44
Lilly (Eli) & Company, 205–7
Lion King, The, 90
Liquidity, market, 8
Long, Joe, 107
Long, Tom, 107
Longs Drug Stores Corp., 107–9
 dividend connection chart, 108
Luby's Cafeterias, 188, 193–95
 dividend connection chart, 194

M

McKesson, 244
Mainframe computers, 211
Marine products and services
 Teleflex Inc., 62–64
MarineSafety International, 150
Marion Merrell Dow, 244, 246, 248–50
 dividend connection chart, 249
Market timing, 168
Marlboro cigarettes, 255, 257
Marshalls, 165, 167
Masco Corp., 119–21
 dividend connection chart, 120
Measurement systems, 215
Medco Containment Services, 22, 244
Medi-Link, 109
Medical markets. *See also* Health care; Health
 care products; Pharmaceutical companies
 Teleflex Inc., 62
Melville Corp., 165–67
Merck & Company, 22–24, 58, 243, 244
 dividend connection chart, 23
Mergers, 244–45
Michigan Power, 232
Michigan Public Service Commission, 234
Microprinting, 156
Mid-America Capital Resources, Inc., 92
Mid-Continent Life Insurance Company,
 152, 154
Millipore Corp., 94–96
 dividend connection chart, 95
Minute Maid, 3
Mission companies, 114, 116

Monongahela Power Company, 140–41
Moody's Investors Service, 190
Motion Industries, 20

N

NAFTA, 179
Naprosyn, 75, 77
National Medical Enterprises, 32–35
 dividend connection chart, 34
Neiman Marcus, 158
Network television stations, 162
Nicoderm, 248
Nielsen (A.C.), 190
North American Free Trade Agreement, 179
North Carolina Electric Membership
 Corporation, 112
Nuclear construction programs, 262
Nutritional products, 13

O

Odd lot purchases, 125
Office products, 20
Oliver Industrial Ltd., 20
Outstanding shares, 8
Overvalued stock, 2–3, 41
 declining trends, 160–62
 defined, 77
 dividends and, 110
 dollar cost averaging and, 133
 interest rates and stock yields, 91
 reason for selling, 83–84

P–Q

Packard, Dave, 215
Paint chemicals, 186
Pall Corp., 215, 218–20
 dividend connection chart, 218
Paper products, 136–38
Pasta, 29
Petroleum, 184
Pfizer Inc., 5–7, 243
 dividend connection chart, 7
Pharmaceutical distribution
 Bergen Brunswig Corp., 125, 127–28
Pharmaceuticals
 Abbott Laboratories, 13–15

American Home Products, 15–17
blue chip, 245
Bristol-Myers Squibb Company, 105–7
Eli Lilly & Company, 205–7, 244
health care reform and, 202
Johnson & Johnson, 56–58
market and, 243–45
Marion Merrell Dow Inc., 246, 248–50
Merck & Company, 22–24, 243, 244
Millipore Corp., 94–96
Pfizer, Inc., 5–7, 243
Syntex Corp., 75–77
Upjohn Company, 66, 69–71
Philip Morris Companies, 255–57
    dividend connection chart, 256
Phone service, 182
Photo developing, 109
Pilot training, 150–52
Plastic packaging, 80–82
Portfolio, building, 124–25, 138–40
    debt-free companies, 187–90
    declining trend stocks, 160–62
    income/growth considerations, 146–49
    rising trend stocks, 154–55
    sample diversified, 141
Potomac Edison Company, 141
Precision instruments, 25, 28
Preferred stock, dividend-paying, 47
Press-Link, 68
Price-book value ratio, 39–40
Price-earnings ratio, 38–39
Prices (stock), and dividends, 97–98
Procardia XL, 5
Procter & Gamble, 75
Production performance, 1–2
Prozac, 205, 207
Publishing, 158
Quaker Chemical Corporation, 119, 121–23
    dividend connection chart, 120
Quality, determining, 1–2, 8–9, 24–25

R

Recession, stocks to buy during, 277–79
Reinvestment of dividends, 133
REITs, 132
Reorganization, 24
Research and development, 214
Restaurant chains, 143–45, 193–95

Retailers
    clothing, 158, 165, 167
    food and drug, 72–75
    Kmart Corp., 60–62
    Sears, Roebuck & Company, 35–37
Retirement portfolios, and utilities, 230
Risk
    management, 203
    vs. reward, 160–62, 163
Rising trend stocks, 154–55
    case studies, 156–60
Robbins (A.H), 17
Roche Holding Ltd., 75, 245
Royal blue chips, 18–19, 278–79

S

Sapirstein, Jacob, 78
Savings and loan companies, 202
SCEcorp, 114–16
    dividend connection chart, 115
Scientific products and services, 134–36
Sears, Roebuck & Company, 35–37, 258
    dividend connection chart, 36
Security Analysis, 40
Self-adhesive materials, 98–101
Shiley heart valve, 6
Shoes, 165, 167
Smith (Dr. T.C.) Company, 128
SmithKline Beecham, 244
Smoking cessation products, 248
Snack foods, 51, 116
Sony Music, 100
South African investments, 280
Southern California Edison, 114
Southwestern Hospital Supply Group, 128
Specialty chemicals, 69, 121
Speculation, 279
Standard & Poor's quality rank, 8, 24, 258
Stock portfolio, building, 124–25, 138–40
    debt-free companies, 187–90
    declining trend stocks, 160–62
    income/growth considerations, 146–49
    rising trend stocks, 154–55
    sample diversified, 141
Stock prices
    dividends and, 97–98
    institutional investors and, 173–74
Stop loss order, 83

Syntex Corp., 75–77, 245
    dividend connection chart, 76

T

Take-out food, 193
Tappan, Lewis, 190
Taxol, 105
Tax preparation, 48
Telecheck Services Inc., 54
Telecommunications, 182
Teleflex, 59, 62–64
    dividend connection chart, 63
Television stations, 162
Texas Utilities Company, 237, 239, 241–43
    dividend connection chart, 242
Titanium dioxide, 186
TKR Cable, 68
Tobacco sales
    American Brands, Inc., 42–44
    Philip Morris Companies, 255–57
Total return, 103–4
Trends
    major market, and blue chip stocks,
        269–71
    as mirror of economy, 274, 277

U

U.S. Gauge, 28
Uelschi, A. L., 152
Undervalued stock, 2, 41
    defined, 65–66
    dividends and, 110
    dollar cost averaging and, 133
    Dow Jones Industrial Average and,
        269–72
    interest rates and stock yields, 91
    reasons for buying, 71–72
    rising trends, 154–55
United Airlines Services Corp., 150
United Business Company, 48
Universal health coverage, 165
Upjohn Company, 66, 69–71, 245
    dividend connection chart, 70
Utilities. *See also* Dow Jones Utilities
    Average; Electric companies
        Allegheny Power System Inc., 140–43

American Electric Power Company,
    231–32
Carolina Power & Light Company,
    112–14
Consolidated Edison Company of
    New York, 223–26
debt and, 188, 278
diversification and, 228–29
dividend reinvestment programs, 230
Florida Progress Corp., 152–54
growth and, 221–28
interest rates and, 91
IPALCO Enterprises, 92–94
payout ratios, 111, 148–49, 238
SCEcorp, 114–16
selecting, 228–30
Wisconsin Energy Corp., 223, 226–28

V

Value, 1–2, 38–64
    case profiles, 42–47, 48–52, 54–58, 59–64
    dividends and, 41–42, 98, 208
    Dow Jones Averages and, 251–52
    price-book value ratio, 39–40
    price-earnings ratio, 38–39
Value-oriented investors, 59
Virginia Power, 239

W

Wal-Mart, 5, 37, 60, 101
Waste disposal, 178
Weight Watchers, 46
West Penn Power Company, 141
Whitehall Laboratories, 15, 17
Wilson's House of Suede and Leather, 165
Wisconsin Energy Corp., 223, 226–28
    dividend connection chart, 227
Writing instruments, 210
Wyeth-Ayerst, 15

Y–Z

Yield, 97, 103–4
Yield diversification, 229
Zero Corp., 129–31
    dividend connection chart, 130
Zierold Sheet Metal Company, 129